W. Droll

phone Myers J. to see
how it is.

                                    professionally,
Seminaries are schools which train people
for church vocations. They offer degrees in religion.
Some are denominally supported, such as SFTS;
others are independent. Dr. Hubbard, our guest, is president
of Fuller Theo. Sem. in Pasadena, one of the — largest
independent & quality seminaries in the country. Over 50%?
of Student body are Presbyterian. Also Dr. Hubbard took
his Ph.D degree at New College, Edinburgh -- a divinity school
of the Pres. Church in Scotland.

A Genuinely Human Existence

By the same Author:

ANGLICANISM
THE UNFINISHED TASK
CHRISTIAN FAITH TODAY
THE CHRISTIAN SOCIETY

A Genuinely

Human Existence

Towards A Christian Psychology

or the model of Christ

by Stephen Neill

Doubleday & Company, Inc., Garden City, New York, 1959

Preface

This book has grown out of long thought and innumerable conversations. It has had the advantage of being read and discussed by a considerable number of laymen, among them several doctors distinguished in various branches of the profession, including psychiatry. In particular I am grateful to Dr. A. Torrie, formerly Director of Psychiatry at the War Office, London; Dr. G. I. Ingram of St. Thomas's Hospital, London; Dr. R. H. Thomlinson of the Medical Research Centre, Shepherd's Bush; and to Dr. J. A. Waycott, doctor and lawyer both, of Charterhouse School, all of whom have been in close touch with the development of the book from its first inception until now. Each has read the book in one or more of its various forms and has commented with candour—memorable candour—and particularity upon it. None of them would, I think, wish to be committed to anything that I have written; but perhaps without the stimulus of their continued interest I might not have persisted in the labour of writing and rewriting. It is heartening to a theologian to be supported by such enthusiastic encouragement from lay colleagues, whose fields of activity are so different—and yet not wholly different—from his own.

S. N.

CONTENTS

I.	Man on Himself.	11
II.	Genuinely Human Nature.	42
III.	Order against Freedom.	71
IV.	Meet Mr. Hyde.	95
V.	I and Thou.	122
VI.	The Courteous Rebel.	142
VII.	Real People in a Real World.	169
VIII.	The Three Great Enemies.	190
IX.	The Way to Freedom.	214
X.	Perfect Freedom.	234
XI.	Towards a Human Family.	255
XII.	The Eternal Dimension.	278
	Conclusion.	303
	Index.	309

not happiness

I Man on Himself

MAN HAS AN ENQUIRING MIND and has extended his enquiries in almost every imaginable direction. It may seem strange that it was only at a comparatively late stage of his development that he began to turn his enquiries directly on himself, and that on the whole he has been more successful in accumulating reliable knowledge concerning the world around him than concerning man himself and the nature of man.

But when the situation is more exactly considered, this may not seem so surprising after all.

The experience of every child in some measure summarises the experience of the race. The child at first does not distinguish itself from its surroundings. Then comes the discovery of the difference between the self and the not-self, with the gradual discrimination of the not-self into people and things. It is only at a later stage of development that the growing individual looks back at himself, and begins to ask the fundamental questions, "Who am I?" "Where did I come from?" "What am I here for?" The moment such questions are formulated, the difficulties involved in answering them become apparent.

Such questions can be approached in two different ways, each legitimate but each markedly different from the other. There is the approach which concerns itself with man as an individual, with that which makes him different from any other specimen of the species. There is a sense in which the whole significance of human life can be apprehended in each individual. This approach may be called intuitive. It attempts to catch the reality of man in his wholeness, in the actuality of a three-dimensional situation in which he has to move. It has naturally found its principal medium of expression in the arts. The other approach concerns itself with the race, and with the individual only as one specimen of the larger whole. Here the method is intellectual and analytic; its aim is classification and generalisation, the statement of principles which are true of all men everywhere, and the establishment of categories in the light of which human nature can be understood. This form of the study of man by man has generally been pursued as one department of philosophy. It is more akin to science than to the arts.

It seems likely that man's questionings about himself and his place in the universe began at an early and primitive stage of his development. It is certain that such answers as he discovered for himself at that stage found their expression in the form of myths. The interpretation of such myths, whether of those that have come down to us from antiquity or of those which have been collected in recent times from the lips of primitive peoples, is a difficult and delicate task in which even the expert is liable at times to go astray. But there is something of the primitive left in every single one of us, and in none of us is the mythopoeic faculty entirely dead. We shall have occasion later to consider the part that this faculty may play in the inner experience of contemporary man. For the moment we shall limit ourselves to a rapid survey of the study of man by man in historically recorded time.

The study of ancient history suggests that an astonishing advance in the interest of man in man took place almost simultaneously, about three thousand years ago, in two remarkably different areas of ancient civilisation. The first is represented by the beginning of historical writing among the Hebrews; the second by the rise of the Greek epic. Each of these forms of literary expression is marked by a notable interest in the individual in his wholeness, in the individual not as representative of a type but as bearing within his individuality the significance of human life and destiny.

Scholars now seem to be generally agreed that the most ancient stratum of the Old Testament documents, the records of the reigns of Saul and David, must have been written almost contemporaneously with the events which they describe. This kind of history-writing is sharply distinct both from the quasi-mythical, quasi-poetical form in which the Hebrew memories of earlier periods are set forth, and from the tedious annals of the kings of Assyria and Babylonia. The new art appears to have been born as it were full-grown. In brilliance and precision of characterisation it has never been surpassed by any later historical writing. The inmost springs of human motive and character are understood and laid bare. There is neither adulation nor denigration. Men are shown as they were, in their strength and their weakness, their glory and their shame. David is the hero of the story; but no attempt is made to hide the baseness and weakness that offset his more splendid qualities. The treatment of the minor characters is equally successful. In the incomparable narrative of Absalom's rebellion (II Samuel 11–19), the traitor Ahithophel, the counsellor Hushai the Archite, the honest soldier Ittai the Gittite, though drawn in only a few lines, stand out clear and sharp as in a cameo, unmistakable and identifiable to the end of time. In the rather later story of Naboth's vineyard, recorded in only twenty-four verses of the first Book of Kings (chapter 21), the three chief actors, Ahab, Jezebel, and Elijah, are delineated in a three-dimensional depth and richness that inevitably remind the reader of the ampler presentation of a similar theme in the tragedy of *Macbeth*.

Striking testimony has been borne to this special character of the Old Testament narratives by two writers who have an exceptionally wide knowledge of the earliest written records of the human race. They write:

> All this may help to explain the strange poignancy of single individuals in the Old Testament. Nowhere in the literature of Egypt or Babylonia do we meet the loneliness of the Old Testament figures, astonishingly real in their mixture of ugliness and beauty, pride and contrition, achievement and failure.*

Perhaps these learned writers have made too sweeping a generalisation. An exception might be made in favour of Akhnaton, the king of Egypt, whose heroic and unavailing attempt to introduce

*H. and H. A. Frankfort: *Before Philosophy* (London, Penguin Books), p. 245.

13

a pure monotheism into idolatrous Egypt seems to detach him as a recognisable individual from the background of history. Otherwise their judgment must be deemed to be correct. Through the patient labours of scholars in the decipherment of the ancient languages, we now have an astonishingly complete knowledge of the life and history of the Near and Middle East for two thousand years before the period of the early Hebrew history writing. Doubtless those whose records we can read lived as individuals; then as now, men must have been marked by differences of quality and temper, of genius or stupidity. But how many of the kings whose lengthy inscriptions we can read have managed to convey to us anything of their quality as individuals? Tiglath-pileser and Assurbanipal remain figures in a museum. David and Ahab are our contemporaries.

From Israel we turn to the great discoveries recorded in the imaginative literature of Greece.

The Homeric poems belong roughly to the same period as the earliest historians and prophets of Israel. The *Iliad* and the *Odyssey* have never lacked readers. This is due, no doubt, in part to the fact that they are such superlative examples of straightforward storytelling; and what most readers of books want above all is a good story. If three quarters of a million readers have thought it worth while to acquire a copy of Dr. E. V. Rieu's recent translation of the *Odyssey*, that is above all a tribute to the changeless and enduring interest of the tale of Odysseus and his wanderings. But there is much more to it than that. These poems are less simple and unsophisticated than was at one time supposed. They are not so much a direct transcript from the life of the camp and the palace as a reflective description of a kind of civilisation that was already passing away. One aspect of this reflectiveness is an appreciation of the splendour and pathos of human life and of the finer shades of human character. No modern psychological study has surpassed in delicacy such touches as the shrewd thrust and parry of the conversation that takes place between the long-lost Odysseus and his wife Penelope before Odysseus has revealed his identity, or the lament of the women for the dead Hector, especially the words of Helen over the fallen hero who had ever been kind and courteous to her.

14

After an interval of several centuries the Homeric poems were followed by the classical drama of the Athenians. This was a highly artificial and limited literary form. The stories were all well known; there was little opportunity for surprise and originality in the development of the theme. As the form developed, the very limitations led to an increasing concentration on the psychological problems involved in each situation. The characters in these plays are men and women of exceptional stature and position, called to face situations and agonies far beyond the limits of ordinary human experience. It is precisely this that gives them their universal and representative character. That which is obscure in the conflicts and destinies of each of us is displayed, enlarged, and elucidated, in them and in that which befalls them. Oedipus is all mankind, wrestling with a destiny that it can neither control nor understand, but here in the end purified and raised by suffering to a great splendour of nobility. The real tragedies through which we have lived in the twentieth century have rendered us sensitively accessible to the message of ancient tragedy. Once again the Greeks speak to us as our contemporaries.

The Christian faith contributed, even more than the Hebrews and the Greeks, new dimensions to the understanding of man and of his nature. Its central principle was *agape*, that undemanding love that puts itself unquestioningly at the service of the one who is loved. With this went a fuller understanding of suffering as potentially creative in its influence. Furthermore, the Christians were marked by an abounding joy, which was widely different both from the earlier Greek zest for life, and from the cheerfulness and equanimity which became the watchwords of the later Greek philosophy.

It is perhaps surprising that these profound new insights, this fresh understanding of human life and destiny, found so little record in works of art and imagination. Perhaps the early Christians were so much occupied with the business of living, and dying, that they had little time for the detachment and reflection which are the preconditions of artistic production. Be that as it may, it is the fact that from the early Christian world there comes to us only one supreme masterpiece of imaginative psychological interpretation, through which the limits of our understanding of human nature are enlarged—the *Confessions* of Augustine. This work is almost unique (Pascal is perhaps the nearest parallel) in that here we see one of the intellectual giants of the ages at work on the material provided by his own heart and his own inner experience. Scholars have pointed out that at certain points Augustine's account of his development lacks historical precision and is even contradicted by some of his other works. But this is of comparatively small importance. Augustine is not writing as an historian. In subtlety of perception and accuracy in the delineation of the finest shades of feeling he has had few rivals, perhaps no superiors, in the literature of later centuries.

The Middle Ages were dominated by theology; and it is not surprising that the imaginative approach to the problems of human personality is rare until the Middle Ages begin to pass over into the Renaissance. The Renaissance was a time of new discovery. It was marked among other things by a new interest in the individual in his demand for the expression of his native genius, by a new sense of his responsibility for his own destiny, by renewed interest in his capacity both for exaltation and for tragedy. The development of these discoveries can be followed along two diverse but not unrelated lines.

In the field of the plastic arts the most significant innovation is the art of the individual portrait. In the great Byzantine tradition the portrait is symbolic rather than personal. A king must be represented in robes of state and crowned; what particular face appears in the midst of these royal appanages is hardly a matter of primary interest. This Byzantine influence is strong in the west until almost the end of the Middle Ages. Then something new appears. With the Renaissance the individual reclaims his own. This reassertion of right is only gradual. In most Renaissance portraiture there is still an element of statuesque immobility; the individual is still to some extent a representative of a type or of a class Greater plasticity of technique later makes possible more accurate representation than the earlier masters had cared to aim at. The real development, however, is not technical but psychological; when the art of the portrait reaches in Rembrandt the greatest height that it has yet attained, what is offered to us by the artist is the individual in his wholeness, marked by his own secret and

16

incommunicable experiences, and therefore different from every other member of the species. He is not typical of anything except himself; and yet in his real human experience he is significant to every man.

The second development is that of the drama.

It is no accident that one of the latest and most moving of the medieval mystery plays is that of *Everyman*. These plays deal with the race, the type, the abstraction. Everyman is also No man. In little more than half a century European drama leaped to its maturity and, in the single century that elapsed between Shakespeare's *Richard III* and the *Athalie* of Racine, produced a series of masterpieces which after three centuries remains unsurpassed, if not unequalled.

It is naturally to Shakespeare that we turn for the supreme manifestations of that new understanding of man, for which in that period the drama seemed to be the natural expression. There is a great deal in Shakespeare that is second-rate and betrays hurried workmanship, even when the defects cannot be attributed to other hands, or to an older text that Shakespeare has merely adapted. But, when he is working at the fulness of his powers, he has an amazing capacity for seeing human nature in the round, for seeing each character three-dimensionally, as a real being moving in his own path and working out his own unique destiny. Even the minor characters are endowed with this mysterious power of life. Autolycus and Parolles are real people, no less than Othello and Macbeth. Holbein in a few lines drawn on a sheet of paper can depict for us not merely a likeness but a character. Similarly, in the few words that these minor characters speak we come to know them; we can guess how they will react in other situations; we can infer something of the way in which the world has treated them, and of the kind of experiences that have made them what they are.

Theoretically it might be argued that what is most general and least particular should have the greatest significance for the largest number of people. Paradoxically, the exact opposite is the case. In this field at least it is the individual which is the universal. The character who is most completely individualised, who is most unlike any other, who is vitally related to one unique situation which is his

17

own, has greater power than any other to move and to instruct the spectators. Their situation may be as little like his as could be imagined; this makes no difference to his significance for them. None of us is likely to find himself in a situation in the least resembling that of Hamlet. But no reader or spectator who has even a grain of imagination has any difficulty in entering into the drama of a young man faced by an intolerable conflict of loyalties. If Hamlet were a simple character, if, that is, there were any element of generalisation in the portrait, the last word would long ago have been spoken about him. The many and various interpretations of his character that have been worked out suggest that here Shakespeare has caught the mystery and complexity of life itself. By intuitive sympathy we understand something of the character, and are thereby helped to understand ourselves; but we are aware that we have not plumbed it to its depths or exhausted its significance for others or for ourselves.

In later centuries the place of the drama is to a large extent taken by the novel. The basic intent of the two art-forms is the same—to depict the evolution of the character and destiny of human beings caught as we all are between certain unchanging realities of the universe and the vicissitudes of the chances that befall us. But the list of novels universally acclaimed as great is even shorter than the list of great plays—an indication of the extreme difficulty of achievement in this form. The principles of construction of a novel as of a picture are three—limitation, simplification, and suggestion. The second-rate novelist clutters up his work with irrelevant detail. Through lack of skill in perspective, he fails to make his characters stand out sharply against their background and their surroundings. By trying to tell us all about them, he robs us of the imaginative education involved in getting to know them for ourselves. When the three essential elements are held in balance, the result is a masterpiece.

Here again we are confronted by the paradox that that which is in itself limited, provincial, and individual can apparently clothe itself with universal significance. This may be illustrated from one of the novels that would perhaps be universally recognised as great, Flaubert's *Madame Bovary*. Here the characters are few and the action is limited to the narrowness of an insignificant town in

18

France. Slowly and relentlessly, stroke by stroke, the background is painted in. The characters are almost horrifying in their mediocrity, in their total lack of originality. And yet tragedy emerges on the grand scale. Flaubert has himself recorded that he composed the scene of Madame Bovary's suicide with the taste of arsenic in his mouth; many readers must have shared the author's experience as they read. Here is represented, with the concentration of art, the tragedy of a million lives; the conflict of the human spirit that can neither reconcile itself to the limitations within which it must live, nor find a way of release that is honourable and that is release indeed.

The Russian novelists of the nineteenth century added a dimension of awareness that was outside the compass of their contemporaries in England and France. The reader accustomed to classic restraint and order experiences considerable irritation in reading the Russians. He finds himself confronted by a group of people who appear to behave with endless inconsequence, and whose relations with one another change with the rapidity and instability of cloud castles. But the very inconsequence is part of the drama, of the three-dimensional representation of human nature. It serves as a clue to those inner contradictions and conflicts which so often we do not admit to ourselves, and which determine far more of our conduct than we are pleased to recognise. It is his profound acquaintance with the depths of the disturbed human spirit that makes Dostoevsky incomparable as a diagnostician, if not as a surgeon, of the soul. His basic themes are always the contrasting pairs—good and evil, sickness and recovery, sin and redemption. The writing of Dostoevsky, like that of Shakespeare, is often very bad. But the progress in understanding and compassion manifest from *Crime and Punishment* through *The Idiot* to *The Brothers Karamazov* suggests that, if Dostoevsky had lived to complete his own designs and if his own life had been less haunted by misfortune and ill health, he might have produced in the end the great Christian novel of the human spirit and its redemption. As it is, the best of what he has written is so splendid that any reader less insensitive than a stone finds that his own understanding of human existence has been indefinitely enlarged.

There is no reason to suppose that wisdom has been limited to the Western world and the Near East or that the final revelation was granted to the nineteenth century. But, accepting for the moment the limits of this brief survey, it is evident that the art and the literature of the Western world offer us an enormous store of wisdom, based on close observation of human nature in action in its three-dimensional totality, and on that inner understanding that is the fruit of sympathetic intuition. The wise preacher and the wise psychologist alike will return constantly to these treasures as sources for the increase both of understanding and of compassion. Here is offered to us the possibility of an endless process of education. Our relationship with this world of art is of the nature of a dialogue; as we ourselves grow in wisdom and experience, we bring new questions and are rewarded with new and profounder answers.

Yet this inexhaustible treasure satisfies only one of the needs of the questing human spirit. The answers given in this realm to our questions cannot be exactly formulated; they are apprehended by intuition and cannot be expressed otherwise than in symbols. Another part of our nature demands precise formulation. It wishes to analyse, to classify, to reach general conclusions such as are verifiable and readily communicable from one to another; and by this means to master and to control the material with which it is concerned. This is a different approach to human nature from that which we have been considering, but in its own sphere it is equally legitimate and rewarding.

It has to be admitted that, in contrast to the extraordinary wealth of the gains in the intuitive realm, the results of a more reflective and scientifically analytic approach to human nature have been a little disappointing. But if we remember how slow man has been in the discovery of the elementary principles of his own physical constitution, it is not surprising that he has been even slower in mastering the far more complex material offered by mind and spirit. Yet here too there have been solid gains and real progress to record.

In the history of the scientific understanding of man and his nature, the first memorable names are those of Socrates and his disciple Plato. Like the thought of the Old Testament, Plato's thought often takes wings and moves in the vivid realms of poetry and imagination. But it never loses its firm footing on the prosaic earth. If Plato does not always teach us what to think, he does teach us how to think—to follow the argument whithersoever it may lead; and the legacy of his thinking is a contribution of permanent scientific value. It was the lasting service of Plato that he asked the right question: "What is the Good in relation to man? What does it really mean to be a man?" This is in essence the same question as that posed more theologically in the Shorter Catechism: "What is the chief end of man?" The word "good" has been used in so many different senses that it is necessary briefly to elucidate what it meant for Plato. It is not primarily a question of virtue, as is commonly the case in the use of the word "good" in modern English. It is to be thought of rather in terms of effectiveness in relation to function. The practical Greek genius expressed this rather prosaically as "being what it was to be," functioning perfectly in accordance with the laws of its own being. A *good* knife is one which cuts well. But what does it mean to be, in this sense, a *good* man? What are the laws of human existence? Plato concentrated his answer in the term "justice," which he may have derived from his predecessor Heraclitus.

It is the glory of Plato to have realised that the true being of man cannot be apprehended at all, if he is considered in isolation from his fellows; it is only in society that man can both be and express that which he is. This basic truth is one to which we shall have occasion many times to recur in the course of this study. So, having asked the primary question as to the nature of the "good," Plato must accomplish the long roundabout journey of the *Republic* before he can find the answer to his own question. So many and so brilliant are the ideas developed in that greatest of all philosophical writings that it is hard to keep in mind the essential question, and to spot the essential answer when it comes. Justice, according to Plato, both in the individual and in society is a harmony, an equilibrium, of diverse and potentially conflicting elements. And so the definition of human nature emerges in terms of the four cardinal virtues—fortitude, equity, prudence, and temperance. The terms may change; but Plato has in fact laid a permanent foundation for the analytical understanding of human nature. Later the Christian Church added to these natural virtues the three theological virtues, faith, hope, and charity. These too were intended to denote qualities in the absence of which human nature cannot function effectively according to the laws of its own being. Far more than we sometimes recognise, all our Western thinking about ourselves and about society is conditioned by these ancient insights.

Aristotle almost wholly lacked the poetic genius of his teacher Plato. But he made up for this defect by a remarkable power of accurate observation in many fields, and great ability in the organisation of the material that his observation had gathered. In his psychological writings he recognised, as Greek medicine was always to do, the close connection between the body and the mind of man. In his book commonly called *De Anima*, for which perhaps the nearest English translation would be *On the Vital Principle in Man*, he distinguishes clearly the various levels on which life manifests itself, and the diverse functions which it performs on each level. But much of this is of only historical interest. The more permanent contributions of Aristotle to the understanding of. human nature are to be found rather in his writings on man in society, and particularly in his *Ethics*.

The *Nicomachean Ethics* of Aristotle is one of the greatest works in the literature of the world. Based on patient and acute observation of human nature in action, it poses in its sharpest form the problem of what it means to be really human. Plato had already observed that the perfection of human nature can be attained only when certain contrasting qualities are held in equilibrium; the excess of any one among them can destroy the balance of the whole. Aristotle developed this principle to the point of interpreting all genuinely human excellence as the middle point between two extremes; either excess or defect can make real excellence impossible. This law of the Golden Mean, "nothing in excess," is easily misunderstood. It has sometimes been taken as recommending compromise as the highest of all virtues, and thus of excluding the high and the heroic from human existence. To take it in this sense is entirely to misunderstand Aristotle's meaning. On his view, to take one example, courage lies midway between timidity and reckless rashness. But this courage is not to be thought of simply as a point of balance. It, and the contrasting defects by which its true nature are thrown into relief, are rather to be thought of as three diverging lines. If a man has found his feet on the central line of true courage, in which, as Aristotle rightly sees, an element of prudence and cool common sense is generally to be found, no objection can be raised to his advancing along that line to the utmost limit of heroism and self-sacrifice, if circumstances demand it.

And yet Aristotle's picture is a little too much that of the Athenian gentleman, the dignified, high-minded man who will walk but not run, because to run is beneath his dignity. And paradoxically, just because Aristotle is talking in general terms, though within the limits of one single society, his insights into human nature and its problems are of less universal validity than those of art and poetry. The same perhaps is true of the almost contemporary and profound insights of Confucius in China. Here once again we meet the idea of the gentleman, the sage who understands the true order of society and the place of man in it, and who is therefore concerned to preserve the ancient values against disorder and the chilling hand of time. Confucius helped to provide the cement that made Chinese society one of the most durable and resistant that the world has ever seen; he did not offer an understanding of human nature that could be of universal validity for those called to other vocations than that of a Chinese gentleman.

The first five centuries of the Christian Church were largely devoted to working out in doctrinal form the implications of Christian faith. It might be thought that those strictly theological operations, by means of which the nimble Greek intellect produced the ever more complicated creeds of Christendom, had little to do with the theme of genuinely human existence. But even from this point of view those centuries of intense labour were not in vain. In wrestling with the problem of the relationship between the divine and the human in Christ, those great thinkers were compelled to ask anew and in fresh form a number of fundamental questions as to what it means to be a man. Greek philosophy had no concept exactly corresponding to that which we try to express by our modern term "personality." Nor did the great thinkers of the early Christian centuries arrive at any such general concept; but their courageous wrestling with the problem of the *Person* of Christ did open up lines of thought that have continued to be fruitful in man's long attempt to understand himself.

The incursions of the barbarians put an end for a time to creative thinking in the West. And even the Eastern Church was content rather to repeat what it had learned from the past than to think new thoughts. Life was hard and dangerous. Man's sense of inner need tended to find satisfaction in action rather than in reflection, in the liturgical solemnities of a Church that had learned to link its worship with every aspect of his outward life. Even in the great monasteries, those splendid guardians through that dark time of the things that make life human, the emphasis seems to have been rather on the accurate performance of a complicated round of duties than on a deeper understanding of the inner complexities of man's existence.

With the great awakening of thought in the eleventh century, the attention of man once again begins to be directed to himself and to the workings of his own inner being. In this development the leading part was played by the two greatest figures of the early Middle Ages, Anselm and Bernard. The thought of Anselm laid the foundations of what later developed into scholasticism; that of Bernard lies behind much of the mysticism of the later periods. The two men were alike in that both were deeply concerned to understand the inner spiritual experiences of men as they attempted to relate themselves to a divine law. As Mr. Southern has written:

> They are more interested in analysing states of mind and in distinguishing the motions of the will than any writers since St. Augustine. This psychological interest is especially strong in St. Bernard; when he writes of the stages of humility, he is not simply interested as St. Benedict had been in the means of arriving at the state of perfection but in all the hindrances and distractions which draw men away from it—in *curiositas, levitas, jactantia, singularitas*, and many other states of mind about which the Rule is silent.*

The monasteries afforded ample leisure for patient thought on these as on other questions. The practice of hearing confessions provided the thinker with unlimited stores of material on which

*R. W. Southern, *The Making of the Middle Ages* (London 1953), pp. 230–1.

24

to work, and laid the foundations of that great empirical understanding of human nature which is one of the treasures of the Christian Church. There is always a danger that one who is specially concerned with human nature in its aberrations and its sins may come to take a somewhat jaundiced view of it; in the great Christian thinkers this is counteracted by their sense of the infinite redeemableness of that nature, and their writing is marked by a broad generous humanity rather than by the narrowness of purely ecclesiastical thinking.

The power of Aristotle over later generations is nowhere more clearly seen than in the manner in which even the greatest of Christian thinkers tended to organise their material. His interpretation of the soul as the "entelechy," no distinct entity separable from the body, but rather the natural completeness of an organism when all its parts are united and active, lives on in scholastic discussion of the nature and service of the soul as the "form" of the body. The *Ethics* lie behind the standard medieval treatment of human nature in terms of the virtues that are to be aimed at and their opposite vices. Such a method does not exclude the possibility of acute psychological observation, as is evident on page after page of the sections of the *Summa* of Thomas Aquinas that deal with these themes. There is, however, the ever present danger that the spirit of systematisation may win a victory over the laborious task of accurate observation, and that the result of the study may be no more than the formulation of accurate rules for human conduct. It may be thought that, by the end of the Middle Ages, this method had reached the limit of its usefulness, and that further progress in understanding was impossible without a new approach and the adoption of different techniques.

We find a pagan or semi-pagan echo of the classical Christian study of human nature in such writings as the *Characters* of La Bruyère (1688) and the *Maxims* of La Rochefoucauld (1665). But, whereas the inclination of the Christian thinker towards pessimism was always mitigated by the doctrine of redemption, the sceptic had no such counterbalancing factor at his command. Once the belief in redemption had been lost, the tendency towards pessimism or cynicism was extremely strong. Cynicism is perhaps a useful weapon in the armoury of those whose interests lie in the less desirable aspects of the human mind and character; it tends to be blind to certain other aspects. We may look to these seventeenth-century writers for brilliance of observation and analysis in detail; we shall be disappointed if we expect that wholeness of understanding which has been noted as characteristic of the greatest Christian thinkers.

The period that followed the Renaissance contributed curiously little to the scientific understanding of man's nature, in contrast to the immense advance that was made in the accurate understanding of the physical universe and of the "laws" which are discernible in its working. The dominance of mathematics and physics was doubtless of service in making man master of the world around him; it tended to withdraw attention from the inner world, and from those aspects of life which are hardly susceptible of mathematical formulation. It was not until the end of the eighteenth century that the new methods of strictly scientific enquiry began to be extended to the study of man, the microcosm.

One of the turning points in man's understanding of himself was the recovery of a knowledge of the significance of the brain in relation to thought. Hippocrates had been on the right lines and Plato had followed him. Aristotle, unfortunately, had disregarded this insight and had supposed that the heart was the centre of thought and feeling. The authority of Aristotle remained almost unquestioned even after the end of the medieval period. It was only in 1789 that Pierre Cabanis, in his *Rapports du physique et du moral de l'homme*, set forth the true relationship in his picturesque phrase that "the brain secretes thought as the liver secretes bile." It is true that incorrect ideas of human physiology did not prevent the accumulation of a great deal of knowledge of human nature along both the intuitive and the more analytic line. But all human existence has its physical basis, and physiology and psychology cannot be completely unrelated studies. Changes in the functioning of the brain result in marked changes in the personality. We still know very little about the relationship of what we call our minds to our bodies; it is good that we should be periodically reminded that there is such a relationship, and that it is one constant factor in the human nature with the study of which we are concerned.

Since the beginning of the modern scientific period, psychological knowledge seems to have advanced in three main directions.

The first has been the accurate observation and study of animal and human behaviour under controlled and regulated conditions. This work has to a large extent been carried on in laboratories, and has concerned itself with stimuli and human response to stimuli. The stimuli can be almost indefinitely varied, and the human response can be seen to cover an almost equally wide range of variation. The value of these studies lies in their objectivity. The accompanying danger springs naturally from the limits within which they have rightly been carried on. The physiological psychologist is primarily concerned with observable behaviour; he is always in danger of going further, and affirming that behaviour is all that there is, and that, when this has been scientifically observed and classified, there is no remaining mystery about human nature.

This inadmissible step seems to have been taken by some at least among the Behaviourists. Thus, in his famous article in the *Encyclopaedia Britannica*, J. B. Watson wrote: "So far in his objective study of man no Behaviourist has observed anything that he can call consciousness, sensation, imagery, perception or will. Not finding these so-called mental processes in his observation, he has reached the conclusion that all such terms can be dropped out of any description of man's activity."* The Behaviourist thus excludes the possibility of finding any answer to our deepest questions about ourselves by denying that the questions themselves have any meaning or relevance. It is certainly good that all our presuppositions should from time to time be questioned; and at least this negative service to human thought has been rendered by the Behaviourists. Most students of their works would perhaps be content to ask one question: What was the process by which Professor Watson reached the conclusions set out in the article quoted above? They would seem to have been sufficiently close to what is generally understood under the term "mental process" or "consciousness" for it to be possible to hope that the words "mind,"

*14th Edition, vol. III p. 328.

"thought," and "consciousness" may continue to be used with some agreement as to their general meaning.

The second approach is that which, starting in the comparatively humble field of intelligence tests, has now taken to itself the more august title of psychometry. Here once again the aim is perfect objectivity of approach. We are to approach human nature with the minimum of presuppositions, to observe it exactly as it is, to apply to it those methods of experiment, control and generalisation from observed phenomena, by which accurate knowledge has been built up in the other sciences. There can be no doubt as to the fruitfulness, within its own limits, of this approach. It is comparatively easy to plan tests of intelligence in the narrower sense of the term. But the experts in this field of study claim that it is possible to develop also tests of personal qualities, of reactions, and of abilities or potentialities, in relation to every possible quality or activity of human persons. Many difficulties have to be overcome. It is not easy to establish such exact controls as are usual in scientific experiments dealing with less complex phenomena than those of human nature. Tests found suitable in one set of circumstances may not prove to be relevant in another; as the qualities to be proved become less obvious, the tests have to become more elaborate. But those who are committed to this approach are convinced that there is none of these difficulties that cannot be overcome by patience and forethought.

The pragmatic test of a scientific method is its ability to provide reasonable prediction for the future on the basis of the phenomena brought under study. The psychometrists can already claim a considerable measure of success. It is affirmed, and the affirmation can be supported by a considerable weight of evidence, that well-worked-out intelligence tests supply a more accurate estimate of the present and potential ability of children than can be made even by teachers who have taught them and had them under personal observation. It is further claimed that the use of intelligence and personality tests provides a more accurate guide to the suitability of candidates for certain forms of employment than the older methods of interview and personal observation. A beginning has been made in the much more complex task of trying to correlate "personality traits" with the kind of political, social and religious

28

views that those under observation hold or are likely to hold. The aim of all these studies is gradually to built up a scientific knowledge of human nature as accurate and reliable as that which we possess in other fields.

It is possible both to recognise the great significance of this approach, and to feel that in some quarters rather too rosy a view is taken of its possibilities.

In the first place, it must be borne in mind that this study is only in its infancy. Almost all the experiments so far made have been in the West and against the background of Western culture. In all such studies the danger of too rapid generalisation from too narrow a range of phenomena is present. It is possible that what is valid in the West will be valid also in the East, and that what is true of "civilised" peoples will be true also of "primitive" peoples. But this assumption can be made only tentatively in advance of the evidence by which it may be verified or disproved.

Secondly, the method of intelligence or personality tests can never give us a picture of a single individual as a whole. If a garment is to be made so as accurately to fit the human frame, an astonishing number of measurements has to be taken in all directions. Fortunately for the tailors the Western world is content with loosely fitting garments, and a comparatively small number of measurements will be enough to produce the suit which will pass muster among the "men in a grey flannel suit." But this will not do when a perfect fit is required. If this is true of the human body, far more is it true of the mind and personality. A few simple tests may suffice to indicate the suitability or unsuitability of a particular person for a particular appointment. To give a complete account of him, many thousands of tests would be required. And even when all this had been done, the resulting picture would fall very far short of the complexity of the living being of flesh and blood.

Thirdly, there is the danger that if the phrase "laws by which human nature is governed" is used, a meaning may be read into the word "law" which has long since been discarded in the physical sciences. The scientist knows well that what he is dealing with is not laws which have as it were a substantive existence of their own, but with statistical generalisations from observed phenomena. With this the physicist is content; the generalisations serve him

29

well for the purposes of his study. He has no reason to feel perturbed, if later study should show the generalisation to have been insufficiently precise, or to have been prematurely formulated; corrections can always be made. If this is true of the physical sciences, much more must it be true of the sciences which deal with human nature. There are no laws of human nature. This does not mean that no generalisations can be made. They can be made and can be useful within their own terms of reference, if their necessarily approximative character is borne in mind. But the element of individual variation is bound to be large; and the individual has a habit, infuriating to the systematic and orderly mind, of escaping from the generalisations under which it is supposed that he had been subsumed.

It is for this reason that the knowledge of human nature obtained by scientific and analytic methods can never supplant or render obsolete the knowledge which is obtained by intuitive apprehension of the individual in his distinct and irreplaceable uniqueness. This particular tree is the representative of the more general term, the species to which it belongs, and for purposes of illustration any other tree of that species, provided that it is well developed, will serve as well. But this is never true of human beings, or only within very narrow limits. The individual is always unique, and therefore his experience may have significance far beyond himself, in certain cases may even be of universal significance. This is the truth of which poets and artists have caught hold in their interpretation of what human nature is. Even though the "science of human nature" were in the future to make far greater progress than in the past and were to present us with a range of knowledge immensely wider than is now available, that knowledge would not be of the same kind as that which is derived from the vision of the poet, the artist, and the prophet. To the end of time we shall need this kind of knowledge, and no other kind will ever render it superfluous. Each kind has its value; each may, indeed, be regarded as indispensable, if the human picture is ever to be complete. Opinions may differ as to the relative value of the two, and as to the seriousness of the consequences that may flow from a defect in either direction.

The third great new approach to human nature is that historically associated with the name of Sigmund Freud. There has been a tendency to exaggerate the originality of Freud. His work would have been impossible without that change in the attitude of men towards insanity which transformed it in the course of the nineteenth century from a thing of horror into an object of patient and sympathetic investigation. Freud did not originate the concept of "the unconscious." F. W. H. Myers before him had done a considerable amount of work on what he called the "subliminal." Janet in France had anticipated a number of Freud's discoveries, though he failed to work them out in detail, as Freud was later to do. Yet, when all this has been recognised, it is still possible to regard Freud as one of the great discoverers in the history of human knowledge. He was endlessly patient in observation, brilliant in some of his clinical methods, fruitful in suggestion. His understanding of mental illness as the result of conflict below the level of consciousness marked a revolution in the treatment of some of the most grievous ills from which the human race has suffered since the beginning of recorded time. Even those who profoundly disagree with many of Freud's philosophical views and religious speculations need not hesitate to regard him as a good gift of God to the human race.

Psychotherapy is as yet a very young adventure; little more than sixty years have passed since Freud put forth the earliest of his results. Since then there has been a rapid proliferation of schools both of thought and practice. Alfred Adler claimed, probably rightly, to have been the first to work with the concept of the inferiority sense or complex. C. G. Jung in Switzerland developed the theory of the "collective unconscious," and gave to the term "spirit" a very wide extension of meaning. Freud, Adler, and Jung were the founders of what are probably the most widely influential schools of psychological thought and psychotherapeutic practice. But every country of the West now has its own separate developments, sometimes in line with those of the pioneers, sometimes diverging from them, sometimes combining the insights of several schools. In view of the extreme difficulty of achievement in a field of study which aims at nothing less than the penetration of the deepest secrets of the inner constitution of man, this variety of approach and understanding is not to be wondered at. What is disturbing to anyone trained in any of the exacter sciences is the large amount of confident affirmation to be found in the writings of the representatives of the various psychological schools, as contrasted with the very small amount of anything that can be called demonstration of that which is affirmed.

If no more were involved than differing techniques for the treatment of mental sickness, there would be no ground for anxiety. Rather more serious are the affirmations by some schools, and the rejection by others, of certain fundamental psychological concepts. For instance, as is well known the Freudian school lays much stress on the "superego" and has devoted much effort to the elucidation of this concept. Others have found it convenient to accept the concept as a working hypothesis, without committing themselves to any judgment as to the real existence or otherwise of the "superego." Yet others regard the concept as false, or at least as superfluous. This is confusing. Far more disturbing, however, is the possibility that some of the theories and explanations put forward by the psychologists and psychotherapists may in fact rest not upon observation and the analysis of observed phenomena, but upon certain fundamental presuppositions and views with regard to human nature which are in fact derived from very different sources. Unquestionably, it is the purpose of the psychologist to remain objective, to observe his material with the same detachment, the same scientific reserve, as is maintained by the student of other realms of reality. But when human nature itself is the object of study, the maintenance of this detachment is far more difficult than in other fields, just because the observer himself is part of the field of observation, and is more personally and directly engaged with the objects of his study than most of his colleagues who are engaged in other branches of scientific research.

The psychologist's formulations and his practical applications of them cannot remain unaffected by his basic presuppositions and convictions. He does not, of course, stand alone in this situation. Very few would now be found to defend the view that history, for example, can be "objective." The historian must stand at a certain viewpoint, and by that the whole of his interpretation of events will be conditioned. He may feel it right to make clear what his viewpoint is, and thus himself to put into the hands of the student the instrument by means of which his work can be intelligently criticised. But he cannot really detach himself from his own convictions and criteria of judgment. History, like psychology, deals with human beings. The analogy between the two approaches must not be pressed too far, but it really exists.

The argument can be carried further. The psychologist works under the same limitations as the ordinary man. We all have our presuppositions, our viewpoints and our prejudices. We parade our intellectually held convictions; we are often unaware of the existential affirmations that underlie them. Most men start from the simple existential affirmation that on the whole it is a good thing to be alive. The famous Clerihew indeed asserts that "There's a good deal to be said/For being dead"; and the Greek poet in a moment of pessimism may remark that the best thing of all is not to have been born, or if born, to return as soon as possible to that which we were before we were born. But the ordinary man does not usually assent to this; he is of the opinion that a live dog is better than a dead lion. But how does he know? Can this be logically proved, or is it simply a deeply held conviction, an obscure and almost automatic affirmation of the life force within us?

Most of these existential affirmations lie below the level of consciousness; they are taken for granted, and never questioned. As we shall see later in this study, a large part of education consists in helping people to bring these unquestioned presuppositions into consciousness, to look at them, and to consider whether they will really bear the searching light of day. And this, after all, is to a large extent what the psychotherapist is trying to do—to bring to light the unconscious mechanisms, to help the patient to be aware of them, to criticise and perhaps to correct them in the light of fuller knowledge.

But at this point the ordinary man has a right to ask the psychologist to stand and deliver. He too has his existential affirmations. He has his own general understanding of human existence, his own standard of values. What are they, and how has he arrived at them?

The point may be illustrated by the attitude of some psychologists and psychotherapists to the problem of religion. Some, and not the least competent among them, have affirmed in plain terms

33

that the alleged "religious" feelings and experiences of men stand in no relation to any objective reality. Religion is, in fact, illusion, as Freud suggested in the title of his book *The Future of an Illusion*. But how do they know? The psychologist has a perfect right to take up an attitude of complete agnosticism; to state that he is not interested in questions of objective validity, and that he will concern himself only with the phenomena of "religion" as they manifest themselves in the minds that he has under observation. He may state that he himself has no experience of the alleged transcendental realm, just as others will admit that they are tone-deaf or colour-blind. But, if he goes beyond this and denies altogether the existence of the transcendental and eternal realm, is he not in fact making an existential affirmation of the kind that can neither be logically justified nor logically disproved? Unbelief is, in fact, a kind of negative faith; it moves in the same world as faith, though it reaches different conclusions on the basis of the same evidence.

We have another question to ask of the psychologist and we can formulate this most clearly by limiting it temporarily to the field of the psychotherapist. The question, simply phrased, is this: What is he trying to do? Various answers may be given; but they will probably all be related to the general idea that his purpose is to heal or to cure one who is mentally sick. But what does this mean? If he is trying to restore mental health, he must have some concept of what health is. But how has he come by it, and how would he define it? He may answer in terms of a reasonably good adaptation of a man to his environment, physical and social. He may answer in terms of a machine that works efficiently and without undue friction; and perhaps he does not regard it as within his province to answer very exactly any question as to the kind of work that man the machine is intended to accomplish. Or he may simply say that we know pretty well from observation what normal human nature ought to be like, and that for all practical purposes that is a quite sufficient guide.

If the word "normal" is once pronounced, it must at once give the scientific thinker pause. He is bound to ask at once whether we do, as a matter of fact, know what normal human nature is,

34

and whether we can assign any precise or accurate meaning to the
phrase.

The word "normal" has been so abused in common speech that
it has become almost impossible any longer to use it in its correct
sense. It is constantly used in the sense of "average." We do know
fairly well what average humanity is; looking at our fellow human
beings, we can perhaps echo the cynical remark of Macbeth to his
hired murderers, "Ay, in the catalogue ye go for men." But this is
not what "normal" means. It is the adjective of the noun "norm,"
and "norm" means a standard, a criterion, that against which something else can be measured and judged. The norm of human
nature should be human nature in its highest and fullest manifestation. It is tempting in this connection to use the word "ideal."
Yet against this valid objections can be urged. An ideal, as the
word itself makes plain, is something created by our minds, by a
process of thought or imagination; and the ideal may bear little
relationship to the reality which it is supposed to express in its
finest and fullest form. What we are looking for is human nature
that, under favourable conditions, has attained to full and free
development in every aspect of its being; and, since human nature
is to be understood not statically but in terms of action, that has
been able unhampered to act creatively over such a period as is
required for the attainment of full human maturity.

It is clear that, the higher we move in the scale of being ("higher"
being here used in the sense of "more complex," and not as a
value judgment), the more difficult it is to find the specimen in
which the full reality of a type or species is incorporated. In the
inanimate world hardly any difficulty arises; one crystal will do as
well as any other for the purposes of observation. In the living
world, the possibilities of malformation or imperfection are far
greater. Yet, given reasonable conditions of climate and soil, any
forest is likely to produce a considerable number of trees in which
all the characteristics of a given species are so highly developed
that each could stand as the representative of the species. Almost
any tiger, unless its growth has been hindered by disease, lack of
prey, or accident, is likely to be fit to serve as the illustration of the
meaning of the word tiger. But is the same true of the human
race, if we pass beyond purely physical and biological definitions

35

or representations? Have we ever seen human nature raised to the highest possibilities of its development, in the unimpeded, creative exercise of all its powers? In a word, do we know, in the true and accurate sense of the word, what normal human nature is?

The Christian answer is plain and simple. Human nature has once been seen in its fulness—in Jesus of Nazareth. In him is seen the answer to the profoundest questions that every man inevitably asks about himself. This is the way the machine ought to work. This is what it looks like when it is working properly. Here it is possible to see the kind of work which human nature was intended to accomplish. Here is the secret which makes sense of all the strange long process through which human existence, as we know it today, has come into being.

This secret is presented to us not in the form of a series of propositions but in the illimitable richness of a life that was actually lived, that is presented to us in the three-dimensional concreteness of actual existence. When we have done our best with Hamlet, we are likely to feel that Shakespeare has put into him mysterious depths that are beyond our power to sound. When we have done our best with Jesus of Nazareth the man, we shall almost certainly find that there is a mystery which eludes us, and that there will never be any end to the questions we may ask about him. Moreover, Jesus moves in the society of men. Man cannot be understood in the isolation of his individual experience. Here is laid bare for us the fundamental significance of man's relationships to himself, to his fellows, to his environment, and to the transcendental dimension that lies beyond him.

What has so far been written corresponds to the extension and fulfilment of what we have agreed to call the intuitional approach. But Jesus not only lived, he also taught. In his words are to be found, though not systematically arranged, a clear affirmation of certain principles and values that are inseparable from human life in its reality. These may serve as clues to guide us through the labyrinth of psychological study. Mere observation results in the accumulation of an enormous mass of undigested data. If these are to acquire form and meaning, some principle of arrangement and classification is necessary. The Christian claim is that only the understanding of human nature set forth in the words of Jesus supplies principles sufficiently comprehensive to give meaning and significance to the whole range of possible observation.

The whole of the rest of this book will be devoted to the exposition of this point of view, and it is only in the concluding chapter that the arguments adduced in its defence can be summed up. But it may be well to face at once one *a priori* objection that may be raised.

This is to the effect that no individual can present the fulness of human nature, since no one individual can pass through all the experiences which are possible for man. In the case of Jesus, it was obviously impossible that he should be both male and female, both married and unmarried; and, as a matter of history, he did not pass through the experiences of old age and failing strength. This objection seems to rest on a failure to distinguish between the particular in relation to the general and the individual in relation to the universal. It is precisely the characteristic of the individual that it can have universal significance. For the individual to have significance beyond himself, it is not necessary that he should have passed through an unlimited number of human experiences. All that is required is that he should be completely himself, a real person, wholly and entirely distinct from any other, and that he should remain creatively free in relation to the circumstances in which he is called to act. This is true originality. It is this, and not similarity of circumstances or experiences, that makes the life and experience of one man significant for many.

An illustration may be given from a familiar and very human sphere. Marriage is a common phenomenon, and a number of generalisations can readily be made about it. But in point of fact every marriage is different from every other, since each is a continually changing relationship between two people, each of whom is unique and unlike any other. And yet it is possible for one marriage, highly individual and incommensurable with any other, to attain to something approaching universal significance. The marriage of Robert Browning and Elizabeth Barrett brought together two exceptionally gifted and sensitive people. It was an unusual marriage. When it took place, both partners were on the frontier of middle age. Robert was several years younger than Elizabeth. But, for all that, it is likely that any pair of lovers or any young married people, reading the love letters of these two, will recognise that they are reading about themselves, though they would never have found such terms in which to express their experiences. Almost certainly their circumstances will be entirely different. Their own marriage may show up rather shabbily by contrast. Yet this record of perfect devotion and mutual self-giving may help them to see the reality of that after which they have half blindly and unsuccessfully striven, and may open before them the way to new and as yet unapprehended depths of happiness. It is in this sense that one human life may become significant for another. There is no logical ground on which we can exclude the possibility that one human life might be significant for all.

One who has, by one route or another, come to faith in Jesus Christ should not find it difficult to recognise the validity of this approach, though he may at first find it strange and different from that which is generally adopted by theologians. The central concern of Christian theology is the question whether Jesus is the final and definitive revelation of God to man, the decisive act of God in the world of men. This book is concerned with the hypothesis that what man encounters in Jesus Christ is also the revelation of man to himself, the disclosure of the true and full reality of human nature. Our present study may best be considered as the first part of a trilogy. It should be followed by a consideration of Jesus as the revelation of God to man, and then by a study of the practical conclusions, with regard to the education of the well and the pastoral care of the mentally sick, which will follow, if the arguments and conclusions of the first two parts of the exposition are found to be acceptable. This book limits itself as strictly as possible to the first of the three themes, Jesus as the revelation of man to himself. It is never possible entirely to separate related themes; and at certain points allusions will be found to matters which belong more strictly to other parts of the subject; but these are no more than incidental. This is primarily a book about human nature in the light of the Gospel.

One who is not a Christian will naturally find himself less at home with the standpoint here adopted. But it may be argued that the hypothesis is one that deserves the consideration even of those who are in no way committed in advance to the acceptance of it.

38

Even a non-Christian historian might find himself led to the conclusion that Jesus of Nazareth is more important in history than any other man who has ever lived. He brought into being a movement which is still in motion today. His message has found adherents in almost every country in the world, and on every level of intelligence from the brilliantly intellectual Brahman in India to the most primitive pygmies in the African forest. Many of the most intelligent men and women in the world today are actuated by a reasoned faith in him and by devotion to his ideals. Western civilisation is very far from being purely Christian either in origin or in practice; but Europe and America as they are today would be inconceivable without the steady influence of Christian ideas and ideals on the life of the Western nations. It is not necessary to be a Christian believer in order to take seriously this remarkable complex of phenomena.

The non-Christian reader may take note at the outset that this book is not a dogmatic exposition of the Christian faith. It is a serious attempt to state a hypothesis, and to test it in the light observable phenomena. This is the normal method of scientific working. Indeed, it is hard to see in what other way knowledge could be advanced. It is inevitable in every field that we should start with some postulates, presuppositions, or existential affirmations. What is important is that these should not be concealed and that their character should be recognised. When this has been done, it is useful to formulate an hypothesis in relation to a number of phenomena. Then follows the attempt at verification through observation, experiment and control, the nature of these varying according to the subject of study. Finally it may be found necessary to modify, to restate, or to reject the hypothesis. It has sometimes happened, in the field of psychological research as elsewhere, that presuppositions have been left concealed instead of being brought out into the light of day and recognised for what they are; and that hypotheses have been treated as established truth instead of as tentative pointers that may guide us through the confusion of the phenomena. In this book a serious attempt has been made to avoid both these errors. Presuppositions have been stated as clearly as possible; if any remain concealed, that is only through inadvertence. The main thesis of the book is treated as an hypothesis in need of verification, until the last chapter in which a rather more positive form of statement is adopted. The Christian reader may find that this leads to an irritatingly tentative way of stating things which he himself believes to be absolute truth; but this is inseparable from the way in which, in the light of the initial approach, the material must be handled.

At this point the objection may be raised that what after all is really intended is an appeal to authority. If Jesus is accepted as the final revelation to man of man's nature, then all questions are answered and free enquiry is at an end. Nothing could be further from the truth. It is the acceptance of true principles that makes free enquiry possible and profitable.

An illustration may be given from the history of physics. The publication of Newton's *Principia Mathematica* in 1687 was one of the landmarks in the emancipation of the human spirit. Newton was remarkable among the sons of men for a rare combination of three faculties, each raised to the highest degree—intuitive insight into the realities of the physical universe ahead of scientific verification; unexampled power of concentration on the problem in hand, until it yielded up its secrets; unwearied patience in working out the scientific proof of those things which he had intuitively seen to be true. The result of his discoveries was to set the study of physics free from false theory and idle speculation, and to make possible two centuries of advance along the lines that he had laid down. He had made possible the correct formulation of the questions; and, until the questions are rightly framed, there is little possibility of correct answers being found. When Newton set forth certain truths, inevitably a great deal of error was set aside. Truth was seen to lie within certain limits and not beyond them. In this sense and in this only he imposed certain limitations on human thought. But to bring the human mind back to its proper direction is really to confer on it its freedom; and there is no restriction on the discoveries that may be made once the mind is set in the direction of the truth.

The application is obvious. If Jesus Christ is in truth the key to the understanding of human nature and destiny, certain solutions of problems are necessarily excluded as falling outside the limits of the truth. But this does not mean that all questions have been answered or that further discovery is impossible. Provided that the central direction is maintained, there is no limit to the questions that may be asked. Countless hypotheses may be put forward and tested in the light of the phenomena. New phenomena, such as those of extrasensory perception, may challenge us to a reconsideration of certain convictions that had appeared to be firmly established. But, if the basic principle is sound, it makes possible the correct formulation of the questions, and that is always half the battle. It may be that in taking Jesus Christ as "the truth," as the groundwork of our thought, we shall find that for the first time we are on the way to the understanding of ourselves.

Jesus: Model of Maturity

II Genuinely Human Nature

THE NEXT STAGE in our enquiry must be a study of human nature, as it is manifest in Jesus of Nazareth. This means that for the moment our concern must be with history.

History deals with men and women who have actually lived and with events that have really happened. These, it is true, are only the raw material of history. If an event has more than trivial significance, the mind of man sets to work upon it and produces interpretation. The mistaken ideas that men have held about events in the past may in certain circumstances be as important as the events themselves. Emotional reactions may inflate certain events, such as the storming of the Bastille at the opening of the French Revolution, with a significance greater than that which strict historical science would attribute to them. Conflicting reports may make it difficult to ascertain exactly what was said or done on any particular occasion. But behind interpretation, symbolic magnification and contradiction, lies that which really and truly did happen. *Magna Carta* is a real document which is still in existence and can be seen and handled. King John really did once sign it, on a certain day in 1215, in a fit of violent and perhaps pathological ill-temper. And once that has happened, neither God nor man can cause it not to have happened.

This is the special characteristic of history. It flows only in one direction. Once a thing has happened, it stands fixed for ever as an event; time will move forward from it, but the clock can never be put back. There is a sharp contrast between the fluidity of the

42

future and the frozenness of the past. The future is full of un-determined possibilities; but once the decision has been made and potentiality has become actuality, all the other possibilities have ceased to exist, and nothing remains but that one which has become frozen in fact. Before I write the next sentence in this chapter, I have open to me the inexhaustible riches of the English vocabulary. But if I wish to write it, I must choose one set of words and no other. Once it is written, every other form of words is excluded and one of the many possibilities has become fact. It is true that I may later cancel that sentence or revise it; that can never alter the fact that it was once written in that particular form and no other. The same is true in history. A later event may trammel up the consequences that seemed likely to flow from an earlier. From a later standpoint the significance of an event may be seen to be other than was supposed by contemporaries. But all this does not alter the fact that King John signed *Magna Carta*.

From this it follows that there is a great gulf fixed between history on the one hand, and pure thought and imagination on the other. Both thought and imagination tend to find their starting point in some tangible existence or event in the visible world. But their development is free. Thought can be followed out to the furthest point of logical development. Imagination can create new and wonderful worlds of beauty or of horror. Neither is impeded in its development by having to take account of the hard, rocklike resistance of the things that men and women actually do, of the things that have actually happened. History can make use of both thought and imagination; but only in so far as these are willing to submit themselves to the discipline of the-thing-that-really-happened.

None of the great religions of the world is a system of pure thought or imagination. Each is in some way related to history, to things that happened; and this is specially true of the three great monotheistic religions of the world, Christianity, Judaism, and Islam. This is a point that must be reckoned with in any attempt to work out the significance of religion in human life.

The practising psychotherapist constantly encounters religion in the form of convictions, ideas, prejudices, or fancies in the minds of his patients. He may have reason to think that these

Psychiatrist : religion Ok.

43

inner experiences have no direct relation to objective realities outside the mind of the patient. But he is aware that they are intensely real to those with whom he has to deal; and he is right to study them patiently and sympathetically, and to weigh the possibility that they may be no more than symptoms of conflict or disturbance in the patients' minds. The danger inherent in this approach is that the psychotherapist may come to think that no other explanation of religious phenomena is necessary, that he may exclude the possibility that religious experience is related to some objective reality, and that he may forget to take serious account of the basic historic facts to which some of the major religions of mankind claim to be related. This may result in a misleading, or at best a partial, understanding of the nature of religion.

An illustration of this danger may be drawn from an admirable book, one quotation from which has already been used in this study. On page 16 of *Before Philosophy* we read: "Of the dramatization of myth, Holy Communion is a well-known example." It would hardly be possible to set forth a larger number of misleading ideas in a smaller number of words.

Part of the trouble resides in the use of the word "myth." Much confusion has been caused in contemporary thinking by the introduction of the word in contexts where it is inappropriate, and in senses different from those which it has traditionally borne. Thus we encounter fairly frequently such expressions as "the Christian myth," without clear definition of what the phrase is intended to mean. It has to be recognised with regret that the use of the word "myth" in several different senses has established itself in modern speech and writing; it is necessary that these senses should clearly be distinguished from one another. (1) "Myth" is sometimes used as an equivalent for pure fantasy, fantasy unrelated to any reality outside the imagining mind. It may be doubted whether this is ever a legitimate use of the word. (2) "Myth" may be correctly used to designate a particular presentation of certain historical events or traditions in the light of the ideas, the ideals or the self-consciousness of a people. (3) The term "myth" is also used frequently and aptly of the personification of natural phenomena. Such myths express vividly man's interpretation of nature,

44

his understanding of the universe in which he lives and of his relationship to it. They no longer have significance, when man had passed on to another and more scientific phase in his understanding of his world. (4) The term "myth" can be used of the expression in imaginative form of profound experiences of the human race, such as perhaps could not be so well set forth in any other way. Such examples as the opening chapters of Genesis, like the intuitive insights of art and poetry, are of permanent significance, since they are related to permanent and unchanging factors in human nature, or to something fundamental in man's understanding of the universe in which he lives.

Now it is at once obvious that the word myth cannot rightly be used in any of these senses of the Christian observance of the Holy Communion. That observance is related directly to a well-known historical fact. Absolute certainty can rarely be attained in historical research. But few events in ancient history are as well attested and as little open to doubt as the crucifixion in Jerusalem, in or about the year 29 A.D., of a young Jew named Jesus of Nazareth. It is almost equally certain that on the night on which he died, he took supper with a group of friends, and that in the course of the meal, he took bread and broke it, and blessed a cup of wine, and in some way identified these simple physical elements with his body and his blood. The earliest account of these happenings comes to us from the first Epistle to the Corinthians, written by Paul less than thirty years after the events that he is recalling, and well within the lifetime of some of those who are affirmed to have been present with Jesus on that famous occasion. This first account is confirmed by others, which are to be found in the first three Gospels. There are differences in the accounts, and in the words which Jesus is recorded as having spoken. These suggest that we have to do with two independent traditions, both of which must have grown up within a very few years of the death of Jesus. Finally there is the unquestioned fact that we have no record of any time in which the breaking of the bread was not the centre of the life and worship of the group which in course of time came to be called Christians.

In giving a full account of what Holy Communion has meant across the centuries, we have to reckon with the element of inter-

45

pretation which always attaches itself to every significant historical event. But when we have made the fullest allowance for this, there is really no ground at all for the statement that Holy Communion is the dramatization of a myth. Behind interpretation and adoration and fancy stands a sober fact of history, a real meal which was actually eaten, a real death which actually occurred. Christians observe this rite only because they believe that these things really happened, and that they are the central events of the world's history. They do not observe it in order to procure for themselves pleasant inner experiences—in fact most Christians find that such experiences are notably lacking. They do not observe it as the symbolic expression of certain ideas. They are concerned with a person who lived and died at an identifiable point of history and in an identifiable area of the surface of the world.

Attempts have, indeed, been made to show that the Christian ideas are valid in themselves, and would continue to be valid, even if it could be shown that Jesus had never existed, or that we have no certain information about him at all. If this were true, it would perhaps be correct to apply the terms "myth" and "mythical" to the Christian faith. But in that case the entire character of that faith would be changed; it would become one of the religions of ideas, and would no longer be one of the religions of history. And if such a view were accepted, this book could not be written. For the three propositions on which the argument of this book are based are these: that Jesus was a man who really lived; that we have sufficient reliable information about him to form an estimate of what he did and what he was; and that in him we see the reality of our own being and of our destiny.

First, then, we must consider briefly the nature of the historical evidence on which our knowledge of Jesus is based. How much do we know, and with what measure of certainty? Many men are asking this question at the present time, some with scepticism, and others with an urgent desire to believe. There appear to be three main sources of hesitation. In the first place, Jesus himself wrote nothing. Secondly, the records of the New Testament are not supported by the independent testimony of contemporary non-Christian writers. Thirdly, the books of the New Testament were written by disciples, uncritical people, who were prone to use every

46

means at their disposal to magnify their master, and to hide the historical reality under legendary and mythical accretions.

It is not necessary to pause long over the first two difficulties. If Jesus wrote nothing, he stood in the regular tradition of the Jewish teachers. They too wrote nothing, and their teaching was handed on by word of mouth among their disciples. The careful training of the verbal memory among the Jews made possible an astonishingly accurate transmission of an elaborate body of teaching over many years. Our knowledge of the Roman Empire in the first century A.D. is curiously limited. Only those who have worked in detail in this field know how slowly and painfully the picture has had to be built up from many and varied sources, and how many gaps there still are in our knowledge. It is not surprising that events in the obscure subprovince of Palestine have left few echoes in the writings of such Greek and Latin authors as have survived to our day.

The third difficulty is more serious. No books in the world have been subjected to such minute examination and cross-examination as the four Gospels. One theory after another as to their origin and reliability has been propounded. Their authenticity and accuracy have been challenged and defended in ma: y different ways. It is impossible to give here even the briefest outline of all the study that has taken place in the century and a half since the rise of the critical method, though it can be stated with confidence that the results of New Testament criticism are on the whole reassuring to the Christian mind. But three lines of approach can be suggested, along which any serious student without special theological training can do a little investigation for himself and can form an independent judgment as to the value of the historical evidence for the life and doings of Jesus of Nazareth.

In the first place, it is generally recognised today that behind great movements the influence of great men can be discerned. In a slightly earlier period historical study concerned itself largely with movements of peoples and ideas, and with changes in social structure. Of late there has been some reaction against this method, and a new recognition that movements need leaders, and that leaders impress their own personalities on the movements which they direct. Certainly movements come into being and prosper only when time and circumstances are favourable; but the personal factor is never absent. Thus Hitler could not have called National Socialism into being, if the despair into which the German people had been plunged by the consequences of the First World War had not created a situation which was favourable to his ideas. But it is equally true that National Socialism was Hitler's movement; if the German national revival had been under other direction than his, it would have taken on a very different form.

Given the movement, it should be possible to infer from it the character of its founder, even if direct historical evidence concerning him were entirely lacking. One of the greatest movements in the history of the world is Buddhism. We have considerably less historical evidence about the founder of it than we have about Jesus of Nazareth. But if we had less even than we have, it would still be possible to work back from the characteristic features of the movement, and to reconstruct a picture of the gracious and gentle Indian prince Gautama, who under the Bo Tree became the Enlightened One and went out to preach to mankind his gospel of deliverance from suffering. From the middle of the second century onwards we have an enormous amount of evidence, from friends and enemies, about the Christian movement. We may well ask ourselves the question, with considerable hope of being able to answer it, as to what kind of a person he must have been who could call so gigantic a movement into being in such generally unfavourable circumstances.

But after all, we are not left to the resources of such backward inference alone; we have the New Testament. We shall at once recognise that all these books were written by disciples, and therefore coloured by the faith of the writers. We shall further take account of the fact that in all of them there is an element of interpretation—what we meet here is portraiture and not photography, an attempt to understand and not merely the intention to delineate. We shall recognise different strata in the tradition, and shall see that from the strictly historical point of view not all of them are of equal value. If we look for such minute biographical detail as is available about George Washington or Abraham Lincoln, we shall look in vain; it was not the intention of the Gospel writers to provide such detail, and there are a great many gaps in our knowledge of Jesus. On the other hand, we shall note that the earliest of the traditions were written down within fifty years of the birth of Jesus, and that the greater part of the New Testament had been written within fifty years of his death. As those of us who are getting older know well, fifty years seen in retrospect are a very short period of human experience.

What emerges, however, most strikingly from the New Testament writings is the mutual consistency of the various pictures of Jesus with which we are supplied. There are in the New Testament at least six different presentations and interpretations of Jesus, to be found respectively in the Gospel of Matthew, the Gospel of Luke, the letters of Paul, the Gospel and Epistles of John, the Epistle to the Hebrews, and the Book of Revelation. These differ markedly in detail and in point of view, and in the present state of our knowledge some of the differences are hard to reconcile. But the impression left overwhelmingly on our minds is that all these writers are trying to depict the same person, and that that person was unlike anyone else who has ever lived in the world. For all the gaps in our knowledge, there are very few characters in history of whom we have such a clear and distinct picture as we have of Jesus of Nazareth.

If the picture of Jesus as it has come down to us is not historical, it must be due to invention, deliberate or unconscious, on the part of one or more among those who called themselves Christians. This view has been plausibly argued by distinguished scholars. The early Christian communities, we are told, read back into the life of their founder a number of their own experiences, combined with a number of mythical elements drawn from the climate of thought of the Mediterranean world in which they lived. In that case, our picture of Jesus depends far more on the creative faculty of these early communities than on verifiably historical tradition. Certainly we must allow for both these factors—the growth of tradition and the influence of the environment. But perhaps those who maintain this view have underestimated the greatness of the feat which they attribute to the early Christian communities. To invent so complex a character is in fact exceedingly difficult, so difficult that it has very rarely been accomplished in the whole literature of the world. The books of the New Testament are works of genius, but not perhaps of that particular kind of creative genius. It is even more important to notice that, if the early Christians were inventing, the character of Jesus as we meet it in the New Testament is not at all the kind of character that we would expect them to have invented. Jesus is not in the least like any of the great figures of Jewish history. He did not fulfil any of the messianic expectations that were current among the Jews of his day. He is not in the least like any of the saviour-gods of the contemporary Mediterranean mythology. As Paul himself so frankly tells us, what the Christians preached was absurdity to the intelligent Greeks, and a scandal to the tradition-minded Jews. The very unexpectedness of the figure that confronts us in the Gospels tells most strongly against the idea that it is the product of creative invention. If they were going to invent, it is not this that they would have invented. If they set things down as they did, it is hard to resist the conclusion that they did so because they could not escape from a reality that they had not created and that imposed itself upon them.

That reality was the reality of a man. When we have recognised all the limitations of our knowledge, and made all our critical reservations about certain aspects of the story, there is still ample ground for believing that what confronts us in the New Testament picture of Jesus is a real person who really lived, a towering character, the study and analysis of whose life and teaching is not likely to prove a waste of time for any intelligent man.

What, then, is the first quality that immediately strikes us in the character that meets us in the pages of the Gospels? The answer is such as to dispel for ever the pale images of stained-glass windows and sentimental hymns. That answer is *power*. The Jesus who strides through the Gospels is a man of immense and terrifying power. He is the master of every situation. He speaks with authority and not as the scribes. He is never at a loss for an answer. His glance can quell and put to flight the crowd of buyers and sellers in the Temple. He knows how to draw men and women to himself in a devotion which will prove stronger than persecution and death. And all this is seen as the authority of a man. Part of the admirable dramatic quality of the first three Gospels is that, though the writers themselves believed Jesus to be the Son of God, they

50

take us back to the atmosphere of doubt and questioning among those who saw before them only the carpenter of Nazareth and yet were aware of the immensity of his power.

Why, then, are we so different from Jesus? Why is weakness as characteristic of us as power was of him? No doubt there are among men great differences in natural endowment and ability, and on the evidence that we have we may suppose Jesus to have been rich in natural gifts and endowments. But is this all? Must we not consider the possibility that Jesus was strong because he lived every moment with the full intensity of all that he was, whereas most other men live most of their time on only a fragment of their capital? It is certain that we all have great reserves of physical strength, which are called on only in moments of crisis, when the natural checks of prudence and self-preservation are in abeyance. May it not be that we have reserves of other kinds of strength, that are hardly ever called on, but are waiting to be set free? We are hampered by uncertainty of purpose, timidity, inner conflicts, and irresolution; these things inhibit our strength and cause our weakness. From all these things Jesus was free. All that he was and all that he knew was at every moment available for his purposes; hence he manifested at every moment power such as is only rarely seen in other men. This is a question to which we shall return. But first we must study more closely some of the areas in which the power of Jesus was most conspicuously manifest.

A man is known by his speech as an author is known by his style. Most of our speech and writing is imitative and slovenly. We use words and images without a clear and sharp sense of their meaning. The result is the tame, flat, and conventional form of expression which generally passes muster in the modern world. Those who are repelled by this flatness easily fall into the error of seeking a strained and contorted originality. The great writer or speaker has no need of such methods. He can use the simplest and most familiar words, and in his hands they become as new. The most evident characteristic of the speech of Jesus is its integrity. With him every word is a living word, and words are immediately related to things.

There is a quality in the speech of Jesus such as is still observable in the contrast between the speech of the countryside and that of the town. The utterance of the countryman is usually direct, vivid, racy, pictorial, drawn from the soil and related to the concrete and visible realities of everyday life. Jesus spoke Aramaic, an unliterary but flexible form of speech, enriched in his case by the Hebrew of the Old Testament, of which he seems to have had a profound knowledge. His thought flows on in a steady stream of metaphor and illustration, drawn in the main from the commonest sights and scenes of country and village. Most of his utterances are couched in the simplest of words, and to a remarkable extent can be reproduced in English in monosyllables. One of the evidences for the astonishing purity of his language, its complete freedom from literary artifice, is the fact that it can be translated into the most diverse languages without noticeable loss of power. In his hands the commonest words shine as though new-minted, and through the force of his personality behind them acquire vividness and biting power: "Go and tell that fox." When commands are given, they are comprehensive in their directness: "Go thou and do likewise." A whole discourse is summed up in a phrase: "So is everyone that is not rich towards God." A whole parable is contained in less than a hundred words. But in the hundred words, more or less, of the parable about the Pharisee and the publican at prayer, two common types of men are caught and fixed forever with the precision of a cameo.

This is not to say that the words of Jesus are always easy to understand. He was an Oriental, and there is in his words an element of oriental hyperbole and paradox. Some obscure sayings have been the cause of great perplexity to commentators, and of controversy among the followers of Jesus. In some cases the obscurity may be due to confusions in the tradition. But such factors are not the real cause of the difficulty. Simplicity is compatible with unlimited depth. This is true of all great thinkers; they challenge us to learn their manner of speech, and when we have tried our hardest we are likely still to feel that they reach out beyond us and have secrets that it has been beyond our power to penetrate. This is more true of Jesus than of any other. When we have done our best with his sayings, we are likely to apply to ourselves words which were spoken to him in another context: "Sir, thou hast nothing to draw with and the well is deep."

What is true of the words of Jesus is also relevant to our understanding of his character. To that character also the word "simple"
may be applied. There is in him complete integrity, unmarred by
the subterfuges and evasions of which we are conscious in ourselves.
There is the transparence of absolute sincerity. There is the simplicity of a single all-embracing purpose, pursued with undeviat-
ing fidelity. But the simplicity of the whole must not be allowed
to blind us to the great complexity of the elements out of which
that simplicity is built up. The character of Jesus is simple, as the
blending in perfect proportion and equilibrium of a number of
characteristics which we can single out and identify, just as clear
light is the result of the blending of those seven colours into which
it can be broken up by the prism. What is most remarkable in
this character is the way in which we can see held together in it,
in harmony and in tension, sharply contrasted and almost con-
tradictory traits such as are rarely combined in the less perfectly
rounded characters of lesser men.

Nothing is more evident in the Gospels than the courage of
Jesus. But equally every page is marked by the evidence of his
extreme imaginative sensitiveness—to atmosphere, to the needs
of others, to the inner reality of situations. Some men are brave
just through the lack of this sensitiveness; they have not the
imagination that makes men acutely aware of danger, and this
obtuseness serves usefully as a kind of screen between them and
fear. Other men are imaginatively aware of all the realities of
danger, of suffering and of death; in them courage is the expression
of a calm inner resolution, which asserts itself at great cost over
the natural instinct of self-preservation. Most men would probably
agree that the second is the higher form of courage; no reader of
the Gospels can doubt that this is the kind of courage which is
manifest in Jesus. His decision to go up to Jerusalem and to face
almost certain death was taken calmly and without haste, and was
carried through dispassionately without the aid of those heats
and excitements that keep men unafraid amid the perils of battle.
The story of the garden of Gethsemane, considered as we should
in this context consider it on the purely human level, makes it
clear that Jesus, like other sensitive men, had to pay a heavy price

for his victory over himself. It was no easier for him to die than for any other young man in the prime of life.

The next paradox in the character of Jesus is the combination of an unlimited capacity to exercise authority with unlimited humility and willingness to serve. Both these traits are admirable. Without leadership the world could not go forward at all. But the exercise of authority tends to mislead men into arrogance and disregard of the rights of others. Humility is not to be confused with that timid self-distrust which is not prepared to take the risk of bearing responsibility; it implies complete self-forgetfulness and disregard of personal interest in the carrying out of duty, and strict consideration for the well-being of others. Leadership and humility are both admirable things; history and experience alike show that they are only rarely found together in the same individual.

Jesus has both, and in the very highest degree. He gives commands and he expects them to be obeyed. He makes demands on men for total surrender to his purposes, and doubts no more than Garibaldi in somewhat similar circumstances that they will count the world well lost in order to follow him to the ends of the earth. Moreover he has that mysterious magnetism of the true leader, which inspires men to live above their natural level and to find fulfilment in total self-commitment to another's cause. But in all this there is not a trace of personal self-assertion; his demand for obedience to himself rests on his own total obedience to One higher than himself. When he claims that he is meek and lowly in heart, the common judgment of mankind has affirmed that he was speaking the truth. When the people were anxious to come and make him a king, he withdrew himself beyond their reach, since the kingdom that they could offer him was not the kind of kingdom he had come to seek. He would not be a judge or ruler among his people. He laid it down for ever that the principle of leadership in the fellowship that he founded was to be the principle of service, and that he who would be great must take the position of being least. He was entitled to lay down this condition, since he himself had taken the position of servant in the midst of his friends.

Jesus combines extreme severity of judgment with an almost womanly gentleness in personal relationships. His denunciations

54

of the scribes and Pharisees are terrifying in their severity: "Ye
serpents, ye generation of vipers, how can ye escape the damnation
of hell?" But there is no trace of personal rancour or venom in
these diatribes. They are one expression of that grim realism, so
terrifying to our sentimental minds, that runs through all the
words of Jesus and is an essential component in all genuine Christian faith. In a general sense, Jesus in denouncing "the hypocrites"
is doing no more than to stress the call to decision in favour of
reality that every man must face at every moment of his waking
life. But in his particular historical situation, he, unlike his hearers,
is aware of the appalling catastrophe that must break upon his
people unless they will change all their ways of thinking. He is the
watchman on the walls, who almost despairingly tries to awaken a
sleeping people before it is too late. But this is only one side of
the picture. The stern prophet is also the loving shepherd. He
who proclaims the alarming judgments of God is also the one
who would gladly have gathered the young of Jerusalem together
as the hen gathers her chicks under her wings. He who has no
place for the self-righteous makes friends with the outcasts and is
criticised by the respectable as the man who eats with publicans
and sinners. The sinful woman who has found new life through
his appeal is welcome at his feet.

Jesus is at the same time the most accessible and the most
withdrawn of men. The records make it plain that he really enjoyed
the society of ordinary people. He is no remote ascetic like John
the Baptist; and once again criticism is ready with the complaint
that he is a gluttonous man and a winebibber. He is perfectly at
home at a banquet, though host and guests alike may find the
plainness of his speech a little disconcerting. He knows how to
speak to ordinary people in terms that they will understand. He
always has time for the individual, for Nicodemus who comes by
night and for the woman of Samaria at the well. Even the agony
of the cross leaves him inner freedom to speak a word of comfort
to one of his fellow sufferers. But this abounding friendliness is
balanced by an urgent need at times to be alone. There are depths
of his being which he cannot share with any other living being,
though as intimacy develops he tries more and more to admit his
closest friends to the secret of his hidden life with God. There are

problems in his work which he cannot discuss with others; even when the multitudes press in upon him, he withdraws to a mountain and spends the whole night in prayer. And yet, when his solitude is disturbed, he is once again gracious and friendly and ready to receive those who seek his help.

It is important to note that Jesus does not make a compromise between the contrasting needs for fellowship and for solitude. Each is felt in full intensity, and for each provision must be made. The suggestion may be hazarded that it is precisely the loss of this dimension of intensity that is at the root of many of the ills of modern society. Modern man is a little afraid of being alone and of being still. He does not care to look too deeply into himself for fear of what he might find. But this curtailment of human experience in one direction takes its vengeance in another direction. Because we are afraid to know ourselves, we find difficulty in knowing one another. Because we do not know how to withdraw into ourselves, we find it hard fully to go out to other people. In consequence human relations tend to remain superficial and unsatisfying. The recovery of the rhythm of life as it is seen in Jesus, both in its withdrawnness and in its open-heartedness, might be the first step towards the deliverance of Western society from a number of the ills that so heavily oppress it.

These are some sample measurements of the human character of Jesus. The list could be almost endlessly prolonged. Yet this small selection should be sufficient to make plain that each quality which we can isolate is present to the highest degree, but that none excludes or inhibits the presence of the apparently contrary quality, equally in the highest degree. It is this that gives its complexity, its richness, and its power to the character, and also its capacity to disturb and to perplex our lesser minds.

Here attention should be drawn to one common quality in these apparently contrary characteristics. Through sixty generations and more both men and women have found their example and their ideal in Jesus Christ. This is simply a fact of history. Now this would hardly be possible unless Jesus had succeeded in combining in himself those qualities which are seen as admirable in man and those which are seen as admirable in woman. This is in fact what we do find in him. And this is achieved, not by some

56

kind of compromise, by such a refusal to develop contrasting qualities as would lead to a kind of hermaphrodite or emasculate humanity. On the contrary, each quality is developed to the fullest possible extent. The strength is that of vigorous and uninhibited manhood; the gentleness is that of the tenderest of women. The two aspects are held together in a tension, which is itself one of the sources of the balance and stability of the resulting character.

It is interesting that, over the centuries, large sections of the Christian Church have failed to hold together that which is held together in the Gospels; in these there has been an ever-increasing tendency to supplement devotion to Jesus by devotion to his Mother. It is evident that what lies behind this dissociation has been overemphasis on certain aspects of the character of Christ, and a comparative failure to give adequate attention to other aspects. In *Dies Irae*, the greatest of all medieval hymns, Jesus is Saviour as well as judge; the elements of sternness and of mercy are still both present. But as the Middle Ages moved forward, Jesus became ever increasingly the remote and austere judge, and Mary was brought in to satisfy man's need for gentleness and tenderness in his idea of the divine.

The most conspicuous service rendered by the Reformation was that for all its weaknesses it brought together those things that ought never to have been separated, and gave us back the integral reality of the Christ. It was not a Protestant but an intelligent Italian Roman Catholic who recently pointed out that, whereas in Protestantism the central point of dogma has remained constantly the person of the Redeemer, in Roman Catholicism in spite of most emphatic affirmations to the contrary there has been a steady and ever more evident displacement of the centre towards the person of Mary. One side is marked by Christocentricity; what is most clearly marked on the other side is Mariology. The best Christian piety has always been marked by deep reverence for the Mother of Jesus; the Christian consciousness has to raise its protest only when such reverence tends to obscure the full reality of Jesus as he is depicted in the Gospels.

But Protestantism also has not been without fault. It too, and in two directions, has tended to hide or to disregard the human reality of Jesus. When it has dwelt on his humanity, it has often

57

sentimentalised it, and has obscured the strong hero behind the picture of a gentleman of kindly appearance carrying a lamb. At other times it has been so absorbed in dogmatic and theological interests as almost to have overlooked the fact that Jesus really was a man, who lived a human life among other men and cared for them. It is the supreme service of the scientific study of the Gospels over the last century that it has given us back Jesus, that it has taken away the scales from our eyes and enables us to see him again in all the simplicity and splendour of his humanity. The liberals were blind to some things; they failed perhaps to see the tragic depths in the story of Jesus and his death. We have had to learn other things from later teachers. But it will never be possible to go back on the rediscovery of the Gospels as the picture of a man.

We have completed the first part of our study in the depiction of a man of rounded and balanced character and of immense power and authority. We have now to consider the way in which that power was used, and the purpose to the fulfilment of which it was directed.

Comparison may usefully be made between Jesus and one of the outstanding figures of modern history, concerning whom we have most minute and detailed information. What was it that made Napoleon Bonaparte for a whole generation the central figure of world history? He started with few advantages as the younger son of a not very distinguished Corsican family. No doubt the French Revolution gave him opportunities such as he would not have had in quieter times; but such men as he have a way of rising even in the face of most unfavourable circumstances. Napoleon had a quick and restless intellect; without much formal training he had used occasion to read widely and to make himself well informed on many subjects. He possessed immense powers of concentration, could work long hours, and do with far less sleep than ordinary men require. He was quick in apprehension, confident in judgment, and firm in execution. He had a peculiar flair for judging the exact moment at which action should be taken; this was the secret both of his military genius and of his rise to political power. All his great gifts were constantly at the disposal of a steady, resolute, and unswerving will; and that will was directed to one

58

unchanging purpose. It was his misfortune that so much genius was directed to a purpose that lacked lasting splendour—the glory of Napoleon Bonaparte. Real greatness was offset by the pettiness of self-centredness, a defect that the cynical Talleyrand perfectly hit off when after a long interview in which Napoleon had excelled himself in the art of vituperation, he quietly remarked, "How regrettable that so great a man should be so ill-bred."

It is not difficult to recognise in Jesus certain Napoleonic traits. Here once again we find fearlessness in decision and execution, resolute firmness in the face of opposition, quickness to see the significance of occasion and to make the best use of it. Here too are a profound knowledge of human nature and the power to make use of other men for his own purposes. In Jesus also all the powers of thought, of imagination, and of action are at the service of a concentrated and inflexible will. This will also is directed to one single, overmastering purpose. But it is here that the parallel breaks down; the purpose of Jesus was related to something outside himself. The fulfilment of his purpose is intimately connected with what he is and what he does. But he is always the servant, the messenger, the one who can command only because he first obeys.

The term by which Jesus describes his purpose is "the kingdom of God." This phrase had had a long history before Jesus began to use it, and is rich with a variety of meanings. It points forward beyond the end of human history to the fulfilment of all the purposes that God is believed to have taken in hand, when first he made his universe. But for our immediate purpose it is necessary to draw attention to one aspect only of the kingdom as Jesus understood it. It is to be the great revolution as a result of which God will exercise immediate sovereignty over men. Under that sovereignty man will be restored to that which from the beginning it was God's intention that he should be; in fellowship with God he will be set free to be himself. It is the task of Jesus to bring in the kingdom; in him it is already present.

It is in the light of this concept that the miracles of Jesus are to be understood. There are few subjects on which greater changes of thought have taken place in recent times. Traditionally, the miracles were one of the chief weapons in the armoury of Christian

59

apologetic in its attempt to demonstrate the truth of the Christian faith, and in particular to maintain its claim that Jesus was himself divine. Few apologists are likely to pursue that line of argument today. Then followed the period in which physical science was almost wholly dominated by mechanistic concepts of the nature of the universe, and scientists were inclined to affirm, first that nothing like a miracle could ever happen in this closed universe of physical causation, and secondly that, if ever a miracle had taken place, convincing historical evidence of its truth could never be produced. The miracles of the New Testament seemed to be a source of weakness rather than of strength. Still more recently, thought seems to have begun to settle down in a mediating position. The physical scientists are less confident in their pronouncements than they were, and more prepared to recognise the existence in the world of other than purely physical realities. The clearer knowledge that we now possess of the interaction between mind and body, between spirit and matter, makes possible a changed attitude towards some at least of the miracles of Jesus as recorded in the Gospels. Some of the mighty works of healing attributed to him resemble phenomena that have come under scientific observation in recent times. This does not mean that the phenomena have explained the miracles, or that Christians are absolved from the difficult task of explaining exactly what they mean by a miracle. But at least there is some common ground for reasoned discussion of the problem.

Our concern here, however, is not with the miracles in themselves, but with the part that they play in relation to the purpose of Jesus. It is easy in the first place to say what the miracles are not. Jesus is not a wonder-worker, who uses these means to draw attention to himself or to extract a reluctant faith from the spectators. He attaches little importance to a faith based on signs and wonders. At times he seems to act almost unwillingly, and to deprecate the excited attention that he himself has been responsible for provoking. He never uses his powers for his own advantage. There is no doubt a purely human element of compassion in his actions; he pities humanity in its bondage and its sufferings and is impelled to do what he can to relieve them. But this is not central; the miracles are signs that the kingdom of God is here, or at least that it is near at hand. The watchword of the kingdom, as Jesus quotes it from an ancient prophet, is the proclamation of liberty to the captives. It means the liberation of man from those alien powers that have invaded his life, have inhibited his free development and frustrated his good purposes; it means the restoration of human nature to normality and the recovery for man of the fulness of his powers. Almost all the miracles of Jesus are directed precisely to this recovery of the full and normal working of human nature. The sick are healed. The leper is cleansed. Men are delivered from the strange infirmities which in those days passed as possession by evil spirits. The whole is summed up in the indignant protest of Jesus when an attempt was made to check his healing activity: "Ought not this woman, being a daughter of Abraham, whom Satan hath bound, lo, these eighteen years, to be loosed from this bond on the Sabbath day?" His message is a message of liberty to men now living; his concern is with fulness of life available for men today.

Jesus could not carry on his work alone. It was not long before he gathered round him a band of associates, to whom in the end he would hand over the responsibility for completing that which he had begun. Nowhere is his work as a liberator more splendidly manifest than in the kind of influence which he exercised on those whom he most closely associated with himself.

Close contact with so powerful a personality is always dangerous for weaker men. The wrong kind of leadership can be disastrous in that it can still further weaken those who are defective in independence and in the power of decision. The naturally dominant man imposes himself on those around him, and makes them all into pale shadows of himself. The bad teacher imposes his ideas and his methods on his pupils, and such originality as they may have had is lost in the second-rate art of imitation. The good teacher, on the contrary, discovers the natural gifts of his pupils and liberates them by the stimulating influence of the inspiration that he can impart. The true leader makes his followers twice the men they were before.

Here as in so many other fields, the truth about Jesus can be expressed only in paradox. He makes as stern demands for total obedience as have ever been made by any leader; yet the effect of

61

this obedience is to make men free; his service turns out to be perfect freedom. His demands are unconditional. Those who follow him must leave home and friends and occupation. He does not for a moment conceal from his disciples what is involved in his demands; if they follow him they must be prepared to face obloquy and scorn and persecution and perhaps death. But he will have no unwilling followers. If a man has not counted the cost in advance, it is better for him not to start to follow. If later on he finds the cost too high, he is free to leave. The question addressed to the disciples, "Will ye also go away?" is, as the original Greek makes plain, not a pathetic appeal for loyalty; it is a frank and honest question: "If you feel that the time has come to leave, you are free to go whenever you wish." When one of the twelve chosen friends proves to be a traitor, every attempt is made by trust, by patience, by affection to win him back from the evil way; but when all fails, he is allowed to go out into the night, though Jesus knows perfectly well what it is that he has gone out to do.

In the end Jesus reaps his reward for all the gentleness and consideration with which he has treated his friends. At times his patience must have been sorely tried. These men were often stupid, often infuriating. They failed to understand their master; they brought into the intimacy of his circle the pettiness of their own feuds and ambitions. And yet in the end they grew into real men. Almost all of them soon disappear from history as individuals; but the movement that Jesus had initiated survived. The astonishing variety of the testimony to him that we encounter in the New Testament, the courage and persistency of the witness that his followers bore to him, are evidence of his power to release in men their individual gifts, and not to stifle originality but to foster it.

The will of Jesus was set on one single purpose, the bringing in of the kingdom of God. This was so all-absorbing, so overmastering a design that it involved him in a total disregard of all his own interests, a total surrender of himself to the fulfilment of his purpose. He tells his followers that it cannot be otherwise with them. They too will be required to renounce themselves, to deny, as we may put it, their right to their own existence. Is this a demand that can justifiably be made? The great Bishop Butler has taught us that reasonable self-love is one of the foundation

62

principles of ethics. Does not the demand for total self-renunciation run counter to this? Does it not indicate a pathological element in the Gospel?

In some recent writing there has seemed to be a tendency to confuse renunciation of self with hatred of self. It may be prudent at this point to make clear certain distinctions, which are of importance for the development of our argument.

Hatred of self is akin to despair, to a denial of the significance and the value of life. It can take various forms. One of these is dislike of the body, resentment that man, who is apparently capable of intellectual and spiritual being, should be tied to this coarse and crude conglomerate of flesh and blood. In such an attitude there is certainly a pathological element. But nothing of the kind is to be found in Jesus. He was perhaps more aware than any other man of the ills to which human nature is subject and of the extent to which evil can distort it. But he never for a moment doubts that it is a glorious thing to be a man. He never for a moment suggests that the body itself is evil; rather he quite calmly accepts it, in all its operations, as a good creation and gift of God. If it had not been so, would the restoration of man in both body and spirit to that which he is capable of being have played so large a part in his plans? It is to be regretted that the followers of Jesus have not always managed to live up to the large-hearted sanity of the Master.

There is a quite different range of experience to which the term "hatred of self" can also be applied. It does happen that, when men are confronted with the pure majesty of Jesus, they awake to a horrified sense of what they have made of their own humanity, a drear awakening powerfully described by Francis Thompson:

> Grimed with smears,
> I stand amid the dust o' the mounded years—
> My mangled youth lies dead beneath the heap.
> My days have crackled and gone up in smoke. . .
> My freshness spent its wavering shower i' the dust;
> And now my heart is as a broken fount,
> Wherein tear-drippings stagnate, spilt down ever
> From the dank thoughts that shiver
> Upon the sighful branches of my mind.

The years the Locust has eaten

63

This is the experience of the prodigal son when in the far country he came to himself. The utterances of those who have passed through such an experience may well seem exaggerated and unbalanced to those who have never had occasion to pass that way. But in many cases they are simply a dispassionate appraisal of a lamentable state of things that actually exists; and the Christian answer to such distress is given in what follows later in that same parable of the lost son who was found.

Self-renunciation, as set forth by Jesus, has nothing to do with either of the states of mind that have just been described. It is simply the necessary condition of all human achievement. This is well known to every writer and artist; to achieve anything, he must give and hazard all he has. It is not fame, as Milton wrote, that constrains the writer to scorn delights and live laborious days—such self-centred ambition never leads to anything higher than the second-rate in art. The artist is not so much master of his craft as its servant. Sometimes he would fain be delivered from this power that is stronger than himself. When the inexorable necessity of creation is upon him, he must forget all else, as during the composition of the *Messiah* Handel lived for three weeks almost without food or sleep. He is with child; until the work of art is brought forth, he must suffer the pangs of labour, often prolonged. And when he has sacrificed everything to his art, it may bring him nothing but poverty, ill-will, or neglect; what Western man can think without shame of the end of Mozart or of Schubert? And yet, knowing all this, the true artist will cling to his agony and martyrdom, rather than sell his birthright for the endless years of bourgeois bliss that self-interest offers to those who make it their god.

This is the extreme case, and not all men are called to be artists. But any man who has married and brought up a family is likely to have encountered and accepted the principle of self-renunciation. Happiness and fulness of life do not come by seeking them directly; it is only in the renunciation of himself in love for wife and children that a man can find the fulness of adult happiness. Every realm of life confirms the truth of the saying of Jesus that he who seeks to save his life shall lose it, whereas he who is willing to lose his life shall find it.

64

An immediate consequence of this sane and rational acceptance
of the principle of self-renunciation is to be found in the attitude
of Jesus towards suffering.

In later times there have been manifest among Christians traces
of that unhealthy interest in suffering for its own sake which in
modern speech passes under the name of masochism. The various
historical reasons for this are not difficult to trace. Ascetic influences
from the non-Christian world pressed in upon the Church. In
times of persecution, tempers tend to become strained, and nervous tension may drive some unquiet spirits to go out and look
for martyrdom if martyrdom will not come to them. Cases are on
record in which Christians deliberately brought upon themselves
the fury of the non-Christian world by desecration of idols or
similar acts of public contempt for the established religion. The
Church, wiser than the individual, laid it down officially that in
such cases the victims of the vengeance of the Church's enemies,
however great their sufferings and however courageously borne,
were not to be regarded as martyrs. If suffering came unsought,
it could be accepted as something sent by God; and in that case
should be accepted patiently, or rather joyfully; but in no case
was it to be deliberately or willfully sought. Here the Church was
faithful to what it had learned from its founder.

For in the Gospel picture of Jesus there is no trace at all of any
pathological interest in suffering. He regards his life as a precious
possession, to be safeguarded up to the point at which it becomes
clear that the choice lies between suffering and unfaithfulness to
the task which he believes to have been committed to him. The
Gospels make no mention of any physical suffering that he had
endured before the final crisis in which he lost his life—he was
not practised in it. Yet when suffering comes, he meets it with the
quiet resolution of balanced and adult human nature.

The reaction of most of us to suffering is infantile or adolescent.
The three commonest methods of dealing with it are evasion, self-
pity, and rebellion. Even grown men are known to postpone to
the last possible moment an urgently necessary visit to the dentist!
If undeserved suffering comes upon us, we are all too liable to
whimper and complain, and to wonder why we of all people should
have been selected to bear this visitation of the injustice of the

world. In the darkness of profound or long-continued suffering we are likely to shake our fists in impotent rage against a universe in which such things are possible and against "whatever brute or blackguard" rules the world. When we observe such attitudes in others, we know that they are neither dignified nor adult. We are aware that it is better not to complain. We are even dimly aware that suffering borne in the right way has a strengthening and purifying effect. But it is easier to give good advice to others than to bear these things in mind in the moment of our own trouble. *True*

In contrast with all this, the manner in which Jesus meets suffering is a perfect expression of the attitude of the full-grown man. As long as suffering can be avoided, he avoids it. When his hour has come, when in his judgment it is necessary for him to confront his enemies, he waits for them quietly in the garden of Gethsemane. He had often seen crucified men—it was impossible to avoid the sight in Roman Palestine—and he knew perfectly well what was in store for him. But this does not turn him aside one hair's breadth from his chosen path. He repeatedly rebukes the injustice with which he is treated and reminds his judges of the responsibility which they bear in the sight of God. But he utters not one word of complaint or of self-pity. He rises above his sufferings so completely as to show more concern for others—for his mother, for the dying thief, for the soldiers who crucified him—than for himself. More important still, he is convinced that suffering itself is something that can be turned to creative purpose in this strangely confused and troubled universe. It is in cheerfully dying for the truth that human nature reaches its own most authentic greatness. All history confirms his judgment. The immediate gain may not be evident, but in fact the willing sufferer is the servant of all mankind. So much that we can recognise as gain in the human story has been won only at the cost of suffering willingly accepted. We who have lived through the Nazi tyranny and the Second World War are not likely to forget our benefactors.

The last point that must be considered relates to the immense claims made by Jesus for himself and the calm assurance with which these claims were made. Citing certain provisions of the ancient law, he quietly puts them aside with the words, "I say

66

unto you . . . ," thus putting himself at least on an equality with the divinely inspired lawgiver of the Old Testament. Such words as, "Heaven and earth shall pass away, but my words shall not pass away" fall from his lips. His own operations were limited to the small field of his own country and his own people; but a number of hints even in the first three Gospels suggest that he regarded his work as having a world-wide significance. The vivid imagery of the discourses about the last things and the coming of the Son of Man may owe a good deal to contemporary Jewish ways of speaking and to interpretation and expansion by those who later set down the sayings of Jesus; it is almost impossible to eliminate from the record all that gives the impression that Jesus did regard himself as the central figure in history, and his life and death as the all-important events on which the whole future destiny of mankind would turn.

Such claims inevitably pose certain questions. Are they the mark of an unpleasant megalomania, a further stage of that defect of character which in the end led to Napoleon's undoing? Are they the dreams of a crazy fanatic, the fancies of an intellect disordered by its own powers? These and similar views have been held. They are not new, and traces of them are to be found in the Gospel record itself. His family, disturbed by the enthusiasm and the commotions aroused by his mission, sent to restrain him, thinking that he must be beside himself; others, less kindly, affirmed that he was possessed by a demon, or in more modern speech, that he was mad. Some modern writers have held that, sane as he may have been at the beginning of his ministry, by the last week of his life he had become deranged by his own apocalyptic visions of future glory. How far does such an interpretation seem to correspond to the recorded facts?

The picture in the Gospels is that of a man and not of a superman. Jesus does not pass unscathed through the vicissitudes of life, untouched by its sorrows and its joys. In fact we may suppose that his special gifts exposed him to a depth and range of emotional experience that are closed to men of less sensitive mind and spirit. It is hardly possible to read the last six chapters of the Gospel of Mark straight through without becoming aware of the mounting strain and tension as the narrative moves towards its climax. No sane man likes to be hated. Jesus, by doing what he believed to be his duty, had brought upon himself the murderous hatred of the leaders of the people. They were about him all the time, trying to entrap him in his speech. It was essential that he should keep so strict a guard upon his utterance as not to utter a single word that could be twisted even by malice into a just ground for condemnation either by the Jewish or by the Roman authorities. He was aware of the presence of the traitor in the inmost group of his followers; he knew well how confused were the ideas of the others and how little they had really entered into the purpose for which he was to die. It is not surprising that even his serene spirit shows signs of strain in those last days. If it were not so, we should find it hard to believe that he was truly man and to feel that as man he is our own kinsman.

But to be exposed to strain is not the same as to be thrown off balance by it. Of such loss of equilibrium there is not a trace in the closing chapters of the Gospels. There are indeed two moments of intense conflict—in the garden of Gethsemane, and in that part of the sufferings on the cross that is marked by the word, "My God, my God, why didst thou forsake me?" But each of these dark moments is followed by tranquillity, in the one case by the calm self-control with which Jesus comes to meet those who are about to arrest him, in the other by the quiet peacefulness which surrounds the actual moment of his death. Apart from these two moments, in the last days of his life he seems to be if anything in heightened possession of all his abilities. In his discussions with those who test him by hard questions, his mastery of the situation is unfailing, his repartee particularly apt and brilliant. Indeed repartee is hardly the right word, since his answers travel far beyond the petty limits of the questions to throw light on some of the darkest questions that have perplexed men since the beginning of time. His words to his disciples take on a new dimension of tenderness and penetration. There is no sign whatever of failing powers or of hysterical emotion. The claims of Jesus may be staggering. But they are not those put forth by a megalomaniac or by a victim of ill-balanced fancies.

The most astonishing thing about the claims of Jesus is that history has to so large an extent proved them well-founded. We

68

are for the moment excluding the divine dimension and reserving it for treatment elsewhere. But on the purely historical plane, what followed on the death of Jesus is perhaps the most surprising reversal of fortune of which history anywhere has record. Everything seemed to have failed. His own life had been thrown away in a desperate venture; the disciples had scattered and were sitting idle amid the shattered fragments of their hopes. And yet what he so confidently affirmed has come true. A great many things have passed away. The Jewish faith as it was in his day and the Roman Empire under which he died are no more than memories. But his words have not passed away. They have been translated into more than a thousand languages. Jesus can still arouse the passionate hatred of men, as well as their passionate loyalty; but there is no sign that his influence on history and on human thinking has as yet reached its climax. It is more widespread and perhaps more effective than it has ever been before. And as each generation comes to weigh those words and to ponder that life, it contributes something of its own in the new questions that it asks and is perhaps able to discern answers that were hidden from earlier generations. There is no indication that this process has as yet come to an end. Our own period is marked by fruitful discovery in the realm of the social implications of the Christian Gospel.

It is perhaps imprudent to ask exactly what picture Jesus himself had formed of the success that would follow on his work. Here too we meet paradox, the paradox of the Galilean artisan, who shows no sign of possessing any general information beyond that which we would expect to be within the range of such a man, and is at the same time the prophet who can make his own the prophecy from the Old Testament that "his dominion shall be from one sea to the other, and from the flood unto the world's end."* It is, however, relevant to our purpose to ask on what Jesus relied for the immense extension of his work across the world. There can be one answer only. He relied on human nature, that is, on what he was convinced that God could make of human nature. He had looked on human nature with the eyes of a patient and unsparing realism. He knew very well the worst and the weakest

*The prophecy in Zechariah 9: 9–10 that must have been closely associated in his mind with his triumphal entry into Jerusalem, Matthew 21:1–9.

that it could be. And yet his message was a message of hope. He was assured that for those who were prepared to be completely honest with themselves and to put themselves into the hands of God there was a possibility of transformation, of recovery of the lost reality of their own being. He always looked on men not only as they were but also in the light of that which he was convinced that they could become. He alone had discerned in Simon son of Jonah, impetuous, unstable, and overconfident, the elements of that character that would one day enable him to be true to the name that Jesus gave him, Peter, the Rock. Human nature can be delivered from its servitude. The lost image of God in man can be restored. But before it can be restored, that true human reality into which man is to be transformed must be visibly set forth before his eyes. This it was that was accomplished in the life and death of Jesus of Nazareth.

III Order against Freedom

IF THE ARGUMENT put forward in the preceding chapter is found generally acceptable, something definite has been gained; we have a working picture of what human nature in its perfection looks like, and of how it works. But is the gain in reality very great, if Jesus as the norm remains unique and incomparable, if he is no more than a standard against which the extent of individual and racial failure can be measured?

It is hardly necessary to labour the situation of imperfection of which we are aware in ourselves and which we observe in other people. On the whole that highly complex entity the human frame proves itself to be remarkably tough and stands up surprisingly well to the rough and tumble of its actions and reactions with its environment; but few of us are likely to claim that we have always enjoyed perfect health, or that in our case the human body has worked with maximum efficiency. Grave cases of mental disturbance are not rare; but in general we get on pretty well, and in most of us the departures from what we are accustomed to regard as normal balance do not go beyond the limits of those pleasant eccentricites that make us interesting to one another. But will any psychiatrist maintain that he has ever encountered the perfectly balanced type, the perfectly integrated individual? If we admit the existence of a moral sphere, the sense of imperfection is likely to be even more keenly felt. People on the whole are fairly "good"; but it is unlikely that anyone will affirm that he has always done those things which he ought to have done, and that he has never done any of those things that he ought not to have done. The moralist, observing human behaviour from his particular standpoint, will certainly not admit that he has ever seen any individual whose conduct at all times has come up to the standard that he regards himself as entitled to demand.

That is the situation. What, if anything, can be done about it?

The physician, the psychologist and the moralist are all, each in his own separate way, concerned about the same thing—the recovery of human health, the restoration of that state in which the human entity can act with the highest efficiency of which it is capable. The approach of one must not be confused with the approach of the others; but it is becoming increasingly difficult to regard them as completely separate and unrelated to one another. All three fall, so to speak, within the same area, all are related to the same existent. Physical health, mental health, and moral health are not the same thing. But man remains a unity. In recent years there has been an increasing tendency to recognise that, if a man is in any way ill, if any part of his being is not working properly, then it is the man himself, the whole man, that is sick.

Is it possible to find one general term under which all these various forms of sickness and imperfection can be subsumed? It would be premature at this stage of the argument to attempt to arrive at any such general term. But attention may be drawn to one observable factor, which seems to be present in a great many human troubles. That factor is conflict.

This has for ages been part of the small change of the moralist. He has been accustomed to speak in picturesque terms of man wrestling with the devil, encountering Apollyon straddled right across his path, and so on. He has contrasted man's "higher" with his "lower" nature and seen the two in perpetual warfare against one another.

It is the abiding service of Sigmund Freud that he was the first to realise in full the relevance of this familiar observation to another field, and to relate the phenomena of mental ill-health to those of inner conflict. Wherever mental strain or suffering is found, there we may expect to find the traces of conflict, often below the level of the conscious mind. This is not without its interest to the physician, whose primary concern is with the working

72

of the human body. It may be taken as firmly established that mental states have their effects on physical conditions. Just why or how this should be so remains a little obscure, and medical opinion is divided as to the range of diseases in which such psychic factors play their part; the general principle can hardly be called in question.

Conflict —use

A little space must be given to elucidating the sense in which this word "conflict" is used. Inevitably man experiences his natural environment as in part hostile to himself. We have not been put in a world in which it is easy for us to exist, and it continually threatens us with famine, earthquake, and flood. But this warfare with nature, if that is not an extravagent term to use, is not conflict in our sense of the word. Man is constantly at loggerheads with his neighbours; he finds it difficult to live comfortably with others of his species. This is a matter which will come before us in many contexts in this book. But this too does not fall within our definition of the word. Man's real warfare is against himself. He does not know how to live with himself, and therefore he is in a perpetual state of conflict. Our main concern here is with that which the Epistle to the Hebrews calls in a dramatic phrase "the contradiction of sinners against themselves."* If man is to live as man should live, he needs to be reconciled to his environment and to his neighbours. But first and foremost he needs to be reconciled to himself. The nature of that reconciliation is the main subject of this book. *We experience not God, but ourselves as our enemy today*

Conflict is not to be understood simply in terms of such situations of uncertainty as inevitably come our way in the world in which we have to live. This is a world in which choices and decisions have to be made. This will always be so, and no one, however well balanced, is likely to pass through life exempt from situations in which choice is difficult and the necessity of decision is painful. Choice may be difficult, just because there are so many possibilities; or because two alternatives are almost exactly balanced; or because there is a large factor of indefiniteness which cannot be eliminated;

*Hebrews 12:3. There is considerable variety of testimony in the Greek manuscripts; but a number of excellent manuscripts give the reading quoted in the text, and many good scholars believe that this is what the author of the Epistle actually wrote.

73

or because awkward questions of "right" and "wrong" insist on obtruding themselves. Before reaching a decision we may have to pass through a period of hesitation and uncertainty, and such a period is always painful. But the endurance of uncertainty without undue distress of mind is just one of the lessons that we have to learn in life; and this has no necessary connection with the anxiety or conflict that are signs or accompaniments of mental ill-health, though in certain cases it may be an accompaniment or symptom of it.

An excellent illustration of this situation of necessary choice is provided by the life of Jesus himself. The dramatic story of the temptations, which must come from his own lips since there was no one else there to see, is in fact a story of choices and decisions that he could not avoid making, in view of his special gifts and powers and of the vocation that he judged to be his own. The poetic features in the narrative—the forty days' fast, the wilderness, the wild beasts—picturesquely represent the complexity of the problems, and the long period of inner travail through which he had to pass before the questions could be rightly formulated, and the right answers given to them once and for all. In what way should he use his supernatural powers? May they be used for immediate and personal advantage? The answer comes clearly that he has been sent to bring in not the welfare state, but a kingdom of God in which it may be necessary for men to act in defiance of their own apparent interests. As God's appointed messenger, can he count on God's special protection in all circumstances? The reply is that there are to be no "spiritual adventures," no unnecessary risks; life as a good gift of God is to be carefully preserved and used as long as that is possible, and not jeopardised to no purpose. Are there circumstances in which force may be used in bringing in the kingdom? No; for this is to be a kingdom of free men; and it cannot be that unless men's freedom either to accept it or to reject it is scrupulously preserved. From the ordeal of this long conversation with "the devil" Jesus emerges weary but unscathed, and with a fresh endowment of the power of the Holy Spirit.

We are all in one way or another certain to be called to make similar choices and decisions, though not in quite such dramatic circumstances. We often increase our own difficulties by an im-

74

patience which will not wait to see clearly what the questions at issue really are, or by a timidity which hesitates to face the possible consequences of decision. These are signs of an immature spirit. The ability to face such situations tranquilly and undismayed, to wait patiently, to see clearly and to decide effectively is one evidence of adult manhood. The grown man emerges from such times of stress with courage enhanced, and the inner spirit tempered.

Outward conditions—the pressure of events, exacting demands, the pressure of other selves upon the self—can produce situations which are favourable to the production of conflict, but they cannot of themselves produce conflict. That can happen only within the inner sanctuary of a man's own life, only through some inner schism or dislocation by which the man is in some way set at warfare with himself. In a complicated machine, every part must be accurately adjusted to all the rest, and all must work together in perfect time. If there is loss of adjustment or of precision in timing, the machine will continue to work up to a certain point, but with loss of efficiency and greatly increased wear and tear. If things are not put right, it will in the end wear itself out. Man is not a machine; but the parallel is sufficiently close to make the illustration relevant. He too is composed of many parts, all of which are intended to work together harmoniously. If this delicate machine is not working as well as it should and showing signs of undue strain, it is a fairly safe conclusion that the dislocation is not in the time, which Hamlet so sadly declared to be out of joint, or in circumstances, but in the man himself. In some way he has become divided within himself, or at least some aspects of his being are not working in timing and adjustment with other aspects. We may all have felt occasionally that several warring selves dwell together within us; and when we feel that we are fighting ourselves, perhaps this is more than a metaphor or a symbolic expression for what is really going on.

The multiplicity in man's inner being has been described in various ways. The classical psychology worked in terms of feeling, thinking, and willing—sensation, intellection, conation. This is an indispensable classification, and we shall never be able to do without it; it is just the fact that the self makes itself known to us

75

under the three aspects of feeling, thinking and doing; though it must be observed that these three operations tend to be all going on simultaneously rather than successively or in separation from one another. Another classification was worked out by Sigmund Freud in terms of the id, the ego, and the super-ego. This was a brilliant achievement. It drew attention to real factors in the problem of human experience and provided a technique which has proved its usefulness in the handling of certain forms of mental trouble. These and other analyses of experience will be in the background of our minds; but they will not provide exactly the categories within which we shall work.

We may start from a simpler principle of classification, the fact that we do all experience ourselves and the world around us in two different ways—the first in which we apprehend things and persons directly as wholes; the second in which we take things to pieces, analyse them, and reflect upon them. The one approach is synoptic, the other is analytic. We all constantly use both methods, so constantly that we may be hardly aware of the difference between them. But a simple illustration will make clear what the difference is. One man, looking at a primrose, is quite content to see it as a whole, and to carry away the immediate impression of life and beauty that it conveys. Another man, or maybe the man in a different mood, wants to understand the primrose, literally to take it to pieces, to determine the botanical family to which it belongs, to study the harmony of its different parts and the way in which they contribute to the whole, and so on. Perhaps he may go on to ask the far more difficult question, "Why does this flower present itself to me as beautiful, and why does it give me pleasure to look at it?" In the former case, he is analysing the object presented to his senses; in the latter he is trying to analyse his own experience of that object. It is clear that both these types of approach, the synoptic and the analytic, though different, are legitimate as approaches to reality. A combination of both is indispensable to fulness of human experience. And human nature certainly will not work well unless they are co-operatively adjusted to one another.

It is a little difficult to find an agreed terminology in which to express the exact nature and work of these two different approaches.

The difference is not that between intellect and emotion, for emotion can be felt on both levels, though in rather disparate ways. Perhaps the most correct terms are "ratiocination" for the more reasoned and analytical handling of the material, though that is rather a heavy and cumbrous term for something that we are doing without thinking about it all the day long; and "intuition" for that immediacy of experience for which it is more difficult to find a precise and satisfactory term.

This immediacy was undoubtedly what D. H. Lawrence was after, when he used his unexpected but strangely powerful language about the blood: "My great religion," he wrote, "is a belief in the blood, the flesh as being wiser than the intellect. We can go wrong in our minds. But what our blood feels and believes and says is true." That is an observation of genius, though we may feel some hesitation about adopting Lawrence's use of terms and about following up the deductions that he made from his observation. But in principle he was right. That inner self, which is the subject of immediate apprehension, always speaks the truth. If we can overhear its voice we shall know exactly what at a given moment we experienced or felt. This does not mean that that experience necessarily gives us a true and objective transcript of the world around us and of the people with whom we had to do. This truth is an inner truth; this voice will tell us the truth about ourselves, about our experiences and our feelings at a given moment.

"The blood" will not serve us for all purposes, but we may be tempted to follow up Lawrence's physical analogy by another drawn from much the same realm. It is possible to speak of "the higher" and "the lower" self; and this is permissible, provided that no moral connotations are read into the phrase. All mental process whatever seems to be directly linked with the brain, but the results of such process can be felt in various parts of the human anatomy. When we are thinking, thought seems to be going on inside our heads. But many people, when suddenly exposed to fear or crisis, find that their reaction to it is registered in the solar plexus. Some sensitive people find that a sudden revelation of beauty is felt in the same region. The ancients believed that the liver was the seat of love; the Hebrews associated compassion with the bowels—with painfully ludicrous results when the Hebrew Scriptures are literally translated into English. If we simply mean that "thinking" is generally associated with the head, and "feeling" with other areas of the body, the use of the terms "higher" and "lower" will do no harm. But in our overintellectualised age there is so strong a tendency to identify ourselves with the thinking brain, and to attribute superiority to its operations, that probably it is wiser to avoid altogether the use of such terms.

In the field of education, we are inclined to contrast the scientific and the aesthetic factors; but this is a distinction that must not be pressed too far. It is true that physical science works in the main in strictly intellectual categories, from which the personal equation, feeling, is as far as possible excluded. But the strictest science itself cannot dispense with the other, the more intuitive, approach. The great mathematician G. H. Hardy has written of the *beauty* of certain mathematical equations or proofs, and even the non-mathematical reader can understand something of what he means. It has been observed, apparently with truth, that no great scientific discovery has ever been made purely by the use of the analytical reason. The great scientist is one who *sees* something ahead of proof; a faculty of intuition gives him the answer to a problem before he is able to prove the truth of what he knows. We have already noted that Sir Isaac Newton seems to have had this faculty in supreme degree. But he does not stand alone. The Indian mathematical genius Ramanujan, who died in 1920, left behind him at his early death notebooks full of mathematical equations which he could see to be true but which he had not yet had time to prove. The conclusion cannot be avoided that, though we can distinguish the two kinds of mental operation, we cannot allocate spheres in which one or the other of them will be exclusively operative.

Perhaps we shall come nearest to the terms we need, if we are willing to take a leaf out of the old book of the Aristotelian philosophy and to think in terms of *matter and form*. Matter, in the Aristotelian idea of it, was there all the time as the raw material, shapeless and indeterminate, of reality; but it did not become real until joined with form; whereas form remained a mere principle of organisation—formal in the strict sense of the term—until it found the matter on which it could impose itself. Immediate im-

78

pressions, especially when accompanied by strong emotion, are very powerful but often almost formless. We can feel without words. But can we think without words? Is an experience really our own, until we have found some approximately accurate way of expressing it to ourselves? And can we communicate it to others, unless form has been joined to the original impression? It may help us at this point to recall Wordsworth's account of the poetic process as emotion recollected in tranquillity. One day the poet sees daffodils, "ten thousand at a glance." The impression of beauty is immediate and profound; the sensitive observer is deeply stirred by the experience. But it is only later, when he reflects calmly on the experience, when the analytic intellect gets to work on it and finds the suitable form in which it can be expressed, that it can become the permanent possession of the experiencing subject. In this case the observer was a poet. A poem was born, and the mystery of the communication of experience was added to the understanding of it. A mysterious trinity—experience, reflection, communication—with which we shall have a good deal to do as our argument unfolds.

We may find it useful, before turning to the daily problems of human experience, to consider a little more in detail the nature of artistic experience and artistic production. The artist is one whose capacity for direct and intuitive experience of reality is in one direction or another a particularly sensitive instrument, and who at the same time is master of a technique through which that experience can find memorable expression, and can so become available to others than the artist. Genuine artistic production is not possible unless both aspects of the self, the intuitive and the intellectual, are active, unless there is a true marriage of matter and form. Achievement is rarely easy in any of the various fields of art. Often it is a matter of intense labour, even of agony. This does not necessarily imply, as has been affirmed, that every work of art is simply a means for the resolution of the artist's own inner emotional conflicts, though this may on occasion be true. More often the labour is that of finding the appropriate form in which the vision can be expressed. The greater the vision and the more significant it is felt to be, the greater the difficulty the artist is likely to experience in finding that form in which it can be worthily

79

and adequately set forth; the more likely he is to feel, when he has done his best, that that part of it which he has managed to express is less than that which has failed to find expression.

The greatest works of art can be produced only when intuition and intellect, matter and form, are held in perfect balance in relation to experience or vision, which is itself of great significance by reason of its depth or amplitude. This perfect balance is only rarely achieved; and it is not difficult to foresee what the results will be if one or other of the members of the team is predominant.

If the initial impulse in experience is somewhat weak and the gift of form is exceptionally strong, the result is likely to be something on the level of the poetry of Alexander Pope. Few English poets had so perfect a mastery of the English language and of English verse forms as Pope. The element of feeling, of immediate experience, is not absent; but what strikes us at once is the flawless perfection of the form. Any cultured person must derive considerable pleasure from the reading of his works.* But it is only occasionally that the depths of human feeling are touched; and the vision of reality is not in itself so significant and stirring as to communicate to the reader the feeling of moving in new and hitherto unrealised worlds.

Where the initial inspiration is extremely strong, but the capacity to relate form to matter is limited, we are likely to encounter such monuments of genius as the poetry of William Blake. Here is a volcanic power, profound intuition accompanied by great intensity of feeling; but it all pours forth with something of the impetuosity of lava and something of its disorder. The wealth of raw material, welling up from the deepest levels of human experience, has been only imperfectly passed through the discipline of intellectual travail; form has only in part been imposed on matter. In reading Blake, we move in a cloudlike world, only in part perceptible. But so much of his power resides precisely in this realm of mysterious suggestion that many of his admirers would not have him other than he is; much of the magic might have disappeared, if the labour of imposing form on matter had been

*Mr. T. S. Eliot has informed us a little pontifically, that unless we are able to enjoy the poetry of Pope, we cannot arrive at a full understanding of English poetry.

carried one stage further than Blake himself felt it necessary to carry it.

Similar observations can be made in the field of painting.

Perugino is a painter of considerable merit, who left behind him a small number of frescoes that rank high among the treasures of Italian Renaissance art. The trouble with Perugino was that he became the servant of his own technique instead of its master. Before long he was really re-painting his own pictures instead of drawing afresh from observation and experience and wrestling with the unfamiliar problems that are presented by every new experience. As a result, the figures in his later work are always charming, airy, competently presented, and almost completely null. They do not, so to speak, stand firmly with both feet on the ground; they are not the fruit of direct contact between the artist and the vivid realities of life.

As a representative of the other type of artist, the one in whom intensity of experience is always breaking through the limits of his acquired technique, we may take Vincent van Gogh. His work is too recent for us to be able yet to judge with certainty what rank he will eventually take among the world's artists. But to stand in front of any of his canvases (unfortunately even the best reproductions largely fail to reproduce the impression) is to be convinced of the sterling integrity of the man in every stroke of his brush. The rapidity of his development during the brief period of his productivity, his constant dissatisfaction with what he had done, are confirmatory evidence of this. Here was a man who was increasingly sensitive to reality in many directions, and who in the end wore himself to death by the ceaseless and ever unsatisfied yearning to find the last and consummate expression for his vision.

From time to time in human history a man appears in whom intense sensitiveness in the intuitive apprehension of reality is married to perfect mastery of form. Then the incomparable work of art is born.

In the field of literature the mind turns at once to Dante Alighieri. To most people the *Divina Commedia* is known only through a few specially famous incidents, such as the meeting of the poet with Paolo and Francesca near the beginning of his descent into the infernal regions. But it is only when the great poem is

81

read and studied as a whole that the magnitude of the poet's achievement can be understood. No work in the whole range of human composition manifests a greater power of sustained imagination than the *Divina Commedia*. The theme is grandiose—nothing less than the whole nature and destiny of man. Every height of possible human feeling is attained, every depth is sounded. The worlds through which the poet leads us are as different as could be imagined from that in which we lead our daily lives. But such is his power over us that, open the book at any point, and we are immediately in Dante's world; we stand by the glowing red-hot tombs in the *Inferno*; we share in the exultation of the spirits when the whole mount of Purgatory shakes for joy that one more of the redeemed has come to the end of his purgation. Almost with a sigh we come back to the dusty world of use and wont.

And yet for all the intensity of the vision, form has been wedded to the matter with which the poet's brain is teeming. Over the many years through which, in his own words, the labour of producing it has made him lean, it has been patiently fashioned and chiselled, the proportions and the mutual relationships of the parts determined; so that, though apparently Dante died before it had received its final revision, it stands before us as a majestic whole. Dante is a writer who makes great demands upon his readers. He is our judge, and what we make of him is the measure of our own artistic and aesthetic faculties. It is unlikely that he will have more than a few readers in any generation; but perhaps those few are the elect of that generation. Those who have come to know him return endlessly to the great poem, and never fail to find refreshment in this immortal manifestation of the powers of the human spirit.

Most of those who have directed their attention to Jesus have been so much interested in him as a teacher, or in the significance of his religious message for mankind, that there has been a tendency not to recognise or to attribute to him that place among the supreme artists of the world that is his by right. But this is an aspect of his genius, of his typical and representative character, that ought not to be overlooked. Even a cursory reading of the Gospels will suggest that we find in him the same openness to every kind of human experience, the same vividness of apprehension, the same mastery of form as we have found to be characteristic of the greatest artists.

82

In one respect Jesus suffers under grave disadvantages. As far as we know, he wrote nothing down, and we do not possess a single one of his poems in the language in which it was originally spoken. We are dependent on the recollections of friends, who were not always well equipped to grasp the meaning of their master. The poems have come down to us only in translation into a Greek which was long past its literary prime. And yet, even in translation and through imperfect tradition, the nature of the poems stands out in perfect clarity. Jesus never finds it necessary to go beyond the simplest forms of speech, the ready-to-hand images. The words that every child knows are all that he needs to give expression to his most memorable sayings. Page after page of the Gospels in the King James Version consists almost entirely of monosyllables. And passage after passage falls almost directly into the classical form of Hebrew verse—the parallelism of two clauses in which the second balances the first with a delicate interplay of repetition, change, or antithesis:

He that findeth his life shall lose it; ✓ *case of antithesis ?*
And he that loseth his life for my sake shall find it.

Where shall we find a simpler and more direct transcript from life than the following:

> *And the rain descended*
> *And the floods came*
> *And the winds blew*
> *And beat upon that house;*
> *And it fell not,*
> *For it was founded upon the rock.*

But what is indicated in these extremely simple words is the whole mystery, and the possible tragedy, of human existence.

Most of us are not artists, but most of us have some appreciation of art, and we can understand what it is that the artist is after. He takes a slice of time and space and sets it within a framework. His work has beginning and end. Within the limits that he himself has chosen, he sets himself to work out the possibilities that are inherent in his material. When he has finished his job, it is there, complete and still; we can examine it and learn from it at our leisure. The artist is of value to us partly because he draws our attention to things that otherwise we would never have noticed; but also because he does as it were in slow time and with limited material what we have to do continuously, without rest, and working in a far more difficult material than any that the artist has to handle—the very stuff of life itself.

We too are confronted continuously by the problem of matter and form. The outside world and the people in it are pressing in on us continuously through all our senses. We are subject to innumerable stimuli, and to each stimulus there is some kind of response. Unless there were some principle of organisation and selection, life could be nothing but an illimitable series of almost unconnected experiences. In point of fact, in every sane person a considerable number of systems of organisation are at work. From a large number of objects within the field of vision, the eye concentrates on a small number, in relation to the purpose in hand, and thereby excludes all the others from the centre of attention. Patterns of life are imposed upon us by temperament, by family circumstances, and simply by the necessity of living. To these we must submit more or less passively, though even within these predetermined fields the need for discrimination, arrangement, and choice persists. But the individual is not likely to be very effective in the business of living, unless there is some inner and conscious principle of organisation, or perhaps more than one, so that some coherent pattern can emerge out of the interaction between the raw material of experience, and the reflective process through which the raw material can be brought into some kind of order.

We may judge that the most successful and genuinely human life would be that in which the two components were working each in full strength and co-operatively one with the other—in which, that is to say, the individual is perfectly open to every kind of experience that comes his way, and perfectly sincere in his reaction to it, but where the inner principle of co-ordination is sufficiently strong to sort out all this experience, and to build it up into what we may call, in one connection or another, conviction, character, disciplined habit, balanced relations with other people, or creative self-expression within the limits of the possibilities provided by the natural gifts of that individual. This would constitute fulness of experience and of life.

No large stage is needed for such fulness of life to be possible. Tolstoy's *War and Peace* and Jane Austen's *Emma* are both great masterpieces. *War and Peace* takes the whole of a great epoch of European history and the clash of empires as its theme; the story of Emma unrolls itself in the quiet scenes of a single English village (with modest excursions outside it). Tolstoy could not have written *Emma,* and Jane Austen could not have written *War and Peace;* we may be thankful that each produced the classic to which the genius of each was suited. But Jane Austen is right. A small village offers to the sensitive and receptive self the whole gamut of experience. Nazareth itself was, after all, only a small country town; and it is not necessary at this point to stress what came out of it. It might well be argued that, the smaller the community, the more intense the experience it offers—in love and hate, in self-assertion and self-distrust, in co-operation in the face of urgent need, and violence of dissension over what to the outsider would appear to be trivial matters.

Almost all of us must have known some fortunate people in whom the two aspects of the inner life have seemed to be almost perfectly harnessed together, in whom, so to speak, the two cylinders work in perfect timing. They are open to every experience that comes their way. They live with gusto and enjoyment. They are open-hearted with their friends, who are many, and honest in their dislikes, which are few. Without trying to impose their will violently on events, they discern a direction and follow it with resolution but without inflexibility. No one can pass through the whole of a life without encountering the experiences of loss, bereavement, and suffering. When these come their way, they feel them to the full, but do not allow them to become sources either of bitterness or of lasting depression. If they live long, they gradually acquire the mellow wisdom of old age; and, when vigorous activity is no longer possible, they live contentedly with their memories, and experience vicariously through the lives and enterprises of children and grandchildren and younger friends. When they die, it is just, in the exquisite phrase of the Book of Job, "like as a shock of corn cometh in his season."

85

Not many lives, perhaps, come up to the full level of this idyllic picture. When they do not, it may always be suspected that the two great divisions of the inner nature have not been working in balance or in harmony, that the cylinders have somehow fallen out of timing.

This can happen in various ways, and the maladjustment can take various forms.

The extreme case is that in which the two levels, the intellectual and the intuitional, appear to become entirely detached from one another. Each goes its own separate way, without communication with the other. This finds its result in those strange cases, some of which have come under careful medical observation, in which two entirely distinct and separate personalities seem to inhabit a single body. In a number of cases the one personality has been of a different sex from the other (as in a rather painful short story by Aldous Huxley, and in one well-written but rather horrifying murder mystery). The two seem alternately to take control of the body which they inhabit, and each to be unaware of the activities of the other. Clearly such extreme cases of derangement must be the concern only of the expert alienist; and even he may be perplexed as to what can be done to restore unity to so gravely dislocated a human being.

Other cases are observable in which one part of the self is acting in contradiction to the other. One part, so to speak, is saying Yes, and the other No. In the endless tussle between them, a great deal of strain and friction is generated, and the consequent waste of creative energy is considerable. We shall come on to consider such cases in the next chapter.

The third main possibility is that one aspect or the other—matter or form, the intellectual or the intuitional, the spontaneous or the controlled—should dominate the other. The result is likely to be a character which is highly developed in certain directions, but is markedly defective in others.

Our Western world is on the whole dominated by the intellect. This is perhaps in part because it is a man's world. In men the purely intellectual and analytic function seems to be in general more highly developed than in women, and society reflects the attitude of the dominant partner. Prizes are offered for intellectual achievement. It is only of very recent years that the technologist has come into his own—previously such work was regarded as "banausic," artisan, and the technological institute was considered to be much inferior to the humane university. The artist was generally suspect until he had been dead for a good many years and had had time to accumulate posthumous respectability.

One curious manifestation of this emphasis may perhaps be found in the poverty and abstractness of our speech. We tend to write and to speak allusively rather than directly, to use a jargon from which sap and freshness have long since been drained away. Anyone who has lived among a primitive people, or even among simple people in a Western country, must become aware of the freshness and vigour of their speech, a vigour paralleled sometimes in the picturesque argot of the underprivileged classes in great cities, and faintly reflected in the slang phrases which the elect sometimes permit themselves to use. Simple speech flows along in a steady picturesque stream, adorned with proverbs and fresh metaphors drawn from direct observation. The African telling a story mimes the whole thing; he is himself in succession all the characters in his story and speaks as each in turn. Nothing is abstract; everything is personal. I well remember an Indian market woman, indignant at the way in which a possible customer was fingering the fruit set out on her stall, crying out, "If it had a mouth it would cry." When Jesus, looking darkly forward, sees the disasters that are coming on his people, he does not speak of the menacing character of the political future; his phrase is, "Wheresoever the carcase is, there will the eagles be gathered together."

This is not to say that abstract speech is never in place. Technical and abstract terms form an admirable shorthand, and make possible the rapid exposition of a number of complex ideas. They are in place where precision of thought rather than imaginative suggestion is required. In fact they are an admirable medium for the communication of information. But if we wish to meet one another on the level of genuinely personal exchange, it is almost certain that we shall have to get back to another and more creative form of speech.

Now this general tendency of society is paralleled in a psychological tendency that is observable in a certain number of people. In them the reflective, intellectual element is dominant, and they seem to shrink back from the rough and tumble, the inevitable disorder of direct experience of life. They prefer, as it were, to experience everything at second-hand, by taking it into the intellect where it comes under control. All problems are visualised as problems in the intellectual realm, where they can be worked out correctly, without any of those awkward and unassimilable remainders that are so often left over, when problems have to be dealt with on the level of genuinely personal encounter.

This type of character is familiar in a variety of professions.

If such a man takes to literature, he is likely to be more successful as a critic than as a creative writer. Since his own experience of life is muted and softened, he has little power to infuse life into the characters that he attempts to create. On the other hand, he may have considerable gifts of critical analysis and appreciation. He can classify and organise; there is hardly a writer or a musician whom he cannot fit into his proper pigeonhole in the scheme of literary or musical development.

Such a man is the very type of the perfect civil servant. The world passes before him in the procession of files that move across his table. He may have an acute and real knowledge of the world, but it is of a world strained of its noise and its urgent immediacy. He can penetrate to the heart of problems, and find the answer to complex questions—though it does not always follow that his answers will work out when transferred from his silent world to the disorderly concerns of actual administration. In business, he will be the perfect executive in the lower echelons of the profession—always reliable, punctual, and unimaginative. It is unlikely that he will rise to the top of the ladder, where gifts of courage, flair, and decision are more required than those of prudence and of an orderly mind.

If he takes to teaching—a profession to which he is likely to be inclined, as providing partial protection against the roughnesses of the adult world—he is likely to be admirably efficient, precise, a little dull, a little impersonal in his relationships with his pupils. He is probably known as a strict disciplinarian, insisting on perfect order all the time—for an obvious reason: he is very uncertain of his own capacity to deal with a situation of chaos, and any breach of order seems to him to threaten the irruption of total chaos.

Another type of teacher can permit a great deal more freedom, amounting at times to positive disorder, because he is not afraid of the rougher elements in reality and is convinced of his own ability to deal with the demands of any situation that may arise.

If our man is religious, he is likely to be rather rigid and puritanical, not, as is often supposed, through an unconscious desire to take it out on other people for committing the sins that he would like to commit himself if he had the hardihood to do so (this is not an unknown reaction, though hardly in this connection), but simply from the feeling that in religion, as everywhere else, all should be decorous, orderly, and controlled. The eighteenth century, with its dislike and distrust of "enthusiasm" in any form, may serve as the perfect illustration of the type. People like St. Francis or John Wesley or General William Booth are disturbing; they remind us too plainly of areas of life that we would prefer, if possible, to ignore.

It is not impossible, on these terms, to lead a reasonably happy and useful life. Such a man may well have friends; but, if so, his meetings with them are likely to be concerned with the exchange of ideas rather than with any warmer or deeper personal exchange. For the fact is that such a man is rather a spectator of life than a participant in it. He is a little like a man who watches the unrolling of a drama on the screen. He is perfectly aware of the figures on the screen; he can observe their doings, and in a measure enter into them with sympathy. But the figures are still two-dimensional. They cannot walk out of the screen, and challenge him to enter into a three-dimensional relationship with them. They are strictly under control. This is almost exactly what such a man tends to do with those whom he does meet in the flesh and blood of everyday experience. They do not really exist for him in three dimensions and in their own right; they exist for him only as figures in his brain or in his dream. He does not meet them in all the three-dimensional richness of their personal lives. As an observer, he may have considerable knowledge and understanding of human nature; but he is liable to be singularly ineffective in direct personal dealings, when human beings fail to move in orderly fashion in the predestined grooves that his imagination has provided for them, and insist on moving in highly eccentric and arbitrary orbits of their own. At this point he is likely to feel himself in the position of the schoolmaster whose class has got completely out of hand.

The parallel from watching a film proves itself to be at one point singularly apt. It is not unknown for those whose own lives are most prim and orderly to take considerable pleasure in the reading of thrillers, and the most unlikely people are sometimes found completely absorbed in the enjoyment of a Wild West film. The reason is not far to seek. The spontaneous and disorderly element which is in us all may be discouraged and ignored; but it is certain that, if it is merely ignored, it will find its compensation somewhere. Emotion and excitement can be vicariously enjoyed—but always at one remove, so that the inner being of the spectator is not directly, or in current jargon, existentially, involved in the emotion that he is feeling.

It is an observable fact that those who live mainly on the intellectual or analytic level often complain of feeling tired, or of having to make a special effort when they become involved in any situation that is three-dimensional in its nature. It may be that the reason for this is not far to seek. Intellect can go on working unimpeded in its own sphere, provided that it is dealing with concepts and can bring all the problems under its own control; the pure mathematician sits so to speak at the switchboard, and the figures on his paper will go where he wants and do exactly what he intends. But strength for real living is in the main derived from the other part of human nature, the more spontaneous or intuitional level. If this has been cut off, or for some reason or other is not operative, to live without it is rather like running a car on the battery—it can be done, but the battery soon runs down, and it takes a long time to be charged again.

An illustration may be taken from the art and work of preaching. Some ministers are completely exhausted after the effort of preaching the Sunday morning sermon. This may be due to a variety of causes, and another will be indicated later in our study. What suggests itself here is the inadequacy of the analytic and intellectual self to deal with a three-dimensional and properly existential situation. Preaching is always hard work, but there are two ways in which it can be done without any approach to spiritual or emotional exhaustion. One method is that of purely intellectual communication. Mind speaks to mind, and there is no question of contact with the hearers on any other and more personal level of experience. It is possible to preach excellent sermons on this level; and if nothing more is desired than the enlightenment of the mind and the clarification of intellectual conviction, the intended purpose has been fulfilled. Another type of preacher puts the whole of himself into his sermons. He is accustomed to meeting his people three-dimensionally in personal contact; when he speaks to them from the pulpit, he is simply extending to a larger scale a kind of contact that is already familiar to him and can be largely effortless. His sermons are what John Oman so aptly called "educated conversation." To preach in such conditions is a stimulating experience, and need be no more exhausting than a quiet conversation with a group of friends around the fireside. The difficulty arises when that which is provided is on the intellectual level, but the aim is to produce an emotional or existential result. Then the preacher has to strain and strive. If he does succeed in producing emotion, it is likely to be of that sentimental kind which leaves no lasting effects—and all the time his own resources are wasting, because he is making emotional demands upon them to which they are inadequate.

So far we have been considering overemphasis or overdevelopment in one aspect of human personality; but the exaggeration can equally well be on the other side, in an excess of unregulated spontaneity, and a lack of respect for the organising and controlling power, for that part of the self the task of which is the imposition of form on an always more or less recalcitrant matter.

In moderation, uncontrolled liberty for the spontaneous self may be good rather than bad. It is a good thing that most of us sometimes act on impulse without time for reflection. "Second thoughts are best" is in most cases a sound maxim, but not in all. It may well be that our spontaneous reaction to a situation, our intuitive analysis of it, is correct, and that to act upon it will lead to the best results. Reflection can sometimes take the form of rationalisation—the provision of good reasons, for instance, for not doing things that impulse tells us we ought to do—and so good impulses become "sicklied o'er with the pale cast of thought/And lose the name of action."

But if carried beyond narrow limits, response to intuition without control can clearly be dangerous. It tends to make impossible a planned and ordered course of life, and the brilliance of occasional improvisation is no substitute for a settled purpose. It is curious that so often artists, who have been amazingly successful in wedding matter to form in their artistic creations, have been strikingly less successful in the ordering of their own lives. For this a variety of reasons can be suggested. It is certain that the artist is more sensitive than ordinary men to the immediacy of experience, and more than other men he lives by the renewal of that immediacy. It is doubtful, however, whether there really is any such thing as "the artistic temperament"—that greatest of all artists, Johann Sebastian Bach, was conspicuously regular in his habits and happy in his domestic life. Yet the lives of many artists do suggest that the disorder of their own inner lives was in some intimate way related to their need for artistic creation and to their power in achieving it. Baudelaire is an example that at once leaps to mind. If he had been a happy and balanced man, perhaps he would never have been a poet; and the chronic disorder of his own inner life seems to find its balance in the bold and imaginative perfection of his writing.

At a certain point this reaction to the immediate and this inability to control or organise it becomes a serious mental disease such as may tax the skill of the most skilled and sympathetic doctor. We all know unfortunates who work only by fits and starts as the mood takes them; who are always making fresh beginnings, yet always slipping back to what they were before. Neither kindness nor severity seems able to help them to keep a steady line, or a steady pace, for more than the shortest span of time. In the extreme case of the so-called psychopathic personality, the unfortunate man may be a danger to himself and others. When an impulse is upon him, it fills the whole heaven and earth, and he is really unaware of other people as people. He may be conscious that the things he is impelled to do are judged wrong by other people, and that society will take vengeance on him if he is caught doing them. But this seems to make no difference to the compulsive power of the spontaneous instinct or desire or to his inability to control it. We are all at moments aware that such a man lives inside us. We may well be thankful that there are very few moments in which he takes control.

Now, it is evident that each of these types of human imperfection is due to the partial or total exclusion from consciousness and consideration of certain aspects of reality. As we shall have occasion to remark more than once, unwillingness to face the fulness of reality is a recurring characteristic of mental illness and strain in all their forms.

On the one side is a desire to exclude all that is violent, unpredictable, and tempestuous in nature, and to leave only the orderly and the controlled. To return for a moment to the world of art, we may think perhaps of the eighteenth century with its love of light and order and proportion. We speak, of course, of the eighteenth century as experienced not by the trulls and the highwaymen of *The Beggar's Opera*, but by the civilised and possessing classes. That was an age of dignified and well-proportioned architecture, without adventure and without irregularity; of formal manners and formal gardens. It was convinced that there was nothing expressible in poetry that could not be better and more lucidly expressed in prose; the wayward imagination was not in favour, and the cool and critical intellect was allowed to reign supreme. That was a great age, but one that by its very disregard of certain elements that cannot be eliminated from human nature was preparing for the revolutions in politics and literature that were to usher in the nineteenth century.

On the other side, we find resentment against those forces of order that impose restraint on the immediate freedom of self-expression. Again the illustration from art is illuminating. We may think of those young poets who try to express themselves in that most difficult of all literary forms, *vers libre*, when they ought to be learning to write Spenserian stanzas in order to accustom themselves to the values of English rhythm and form.

When we meet individuals in whom one or the other of these two tendencies is strongly marked, it is usually possible to infer, and perhaps to ascertain, that something in the outside world has had a great deal to do with producing this condition. One man has been badly hurt or frightened as a child, and had ever since tended to withdraw as far as possible from the dangerous outside world into the safer world of his own inner experiences. Another has suffered in early years from excessive and senseless restraint, and by reaction manifests a tendency throughout life to resent any form of restraint whatsoever. He is not prepared to admit that, if people are going to live together at all, each must recognise that the existence of other selves with their claim to living room necessarily imposes some limitations on an unconditional claim to self-expression on the part of the individual.

External situations may have much to do with the production of problems; but this is never the whole story. We may encounter two individuals who appear to have passed through almost exactly the same experiences and yet have developed two entirely different types of character. In every situation there are two factors—what happens, and the person to whom it happens. Even when we know exactly what happened, we still have to ask what was made of it by the one to whom it happened. In a word, we have to look to the inner self as well as to the outward circumstance.

In the case of the one type we have pictured, it has been suggested that he has rejected from his consciousness, or as far as possible from his direct experience, certain aspects of the outside world—those that are dangerous or incalculable or uncontrollable. But it is probable that what he has in reality been rejecting is one part of himself—a part that is in all of us, and in its spontaneity of reaction is unpredictable, immensely vigorous, sometimes even violent and difficult to control. The other appears to be rejecting the restraints of society and of a moral code. He too is in all probability rejecting a part of himself—that part which tries to draw order out of chaos, and to weave the raw material of immediate sensation and impulse into a recognisable and constructive pattern of living.

Nothing that happens to us from outside is really of any great importance unless it is taken inside and becomes part of our own inner selves. Hurtful outward experience becomes really hurtful only if it takes advantage of or reinforces a tendency towards inner schism which was already present in the soul. A full and joyful acceptance of outward reality in all its forms is a necessary precondition of all full mental health; but we are not likely to make much progress in this direction unless we have taken the first and more difficult step of accepting the whole reality of ourselves. We must go on to consider rather more intimately the nature of those inner conflicts through which human development may be impeded or turned in unprofitable directions.

OK chapter

IV Meet Mr. Hyde

THE PROCESS OF THE DISCOVERY of human nature is very much like *psycho analysis* the experience of going down a spiral staircase. The same points recur, but each time they are encountered on a different level and have to be looked at in rather different perspectives. This means that a certain amount of repetition is unavoidable; but the point of view is constantly changing, even though the material considered may be essentially the same.

In the last chapter we considered the possibility that two different aspects of the self might operate each with an almost total disregard of the existence of the other. We must now go on to ask what may happen if these two aspects of the self should be locked in conscious or unconscious hostility to one another. *inner conflict*

A great many readers have been made sharply aware of this possibility for the first time not through psychological disquisition but through Robert Louis Stevenson's famous story of Dr. Jekyll and Mr. Hyde.

The theme of the story is simple. Dr. Jekyll, an elderly physician, respected, upright, and urbane, finds that by the use of a certain drug he can separate out certain hidden parts of himself and transform himself into Mr. Hyde. Mr. Hyde is small, strong, and reckless. Nothing is allowed to stand in his way, and he will not stop short of violence if the impulse to violence comes upon him. The story ends in tragedy when Dr. Jekyll finds that the drug which should restore him to his respectable and virtuous self no longer works, and that he is condemned to be for ever Mr. Hyde.

The story is a work of pure genius, and will serve admirably as a text for what we have to deal with in this chapter—except for one point. Most readers interpret Dr. Jekyll and Mr. Hyde in terms of the "good" and the "evil" self. We shall consider later the sense in which the terms "good" and "evil" can be regarded as appropriate, but for the moment will deprecate the use of any abusive or pejorative terms about any part of the self. It will be prudent at this point to go no further than to say that Dr. Jekyll is the conformist, and Mr. Hyde is the nonconformist; and we shall remind ourselves that conformism is not always good and nonconformism is not always evil. It was the arch-conformists, the scribes and Pharisees, who brought about the crucifixion of Jesus on the most virtuous principles of the safeguarding of the order of society. And Jesus himself showed a clear and marked preference for the society of the nonconformists—the publicans and sinners. He seems on the whole to have preferred Mr. Hyde to Dr. Jekyll.

At two points, however, we shall find no occasion to disagree with Stevenson's presentation of the other and hidden self.

He is right in making Mr. Hyde extremely strong. Here his picture is borne out by all contemporary psychological study. Our actions are far less controlled than we imagine by the purely rational processes of consideration and choice, and much more than we like to think may be at the mercy of instinctive and perhaps unconscious drives, of the force of which we may be ourselves unaware.

Secondly, Stevenson is right in presenting Mr. Hyde as considerably younger than Dr. Jekyll.

It is just the fact that very few of us grow up to a regulated pattern or all of a piece. We differ very much from one another in our rate of growth, and the various parts of our complex nature seem to vary a good deal among themselves. Most people have reached their full physical stature, though not their full physical strength, by the age of sixteen; but it can happen that young men drafted for military service grow an unexpected further four inches between the ages of eighteen and twenty. Study of mental development suggests that few people enlarge their mental capacity after the age of fifteen, though of course there is no limit to the acquisition of knowledge towards which that capacity can be directed. But emotional growth is altogether a slower business. It is unlikely to be complete

96

before the age of twenty-five, and in a sense the process of growth into emotional maturity is one that never comes to an end. Almost every case of mental ill-health seems to present features of emotional immaturity.

We shall have occasion, as the argument proceeds, to suggest a number of reasons why this may be so. At the moment it is enough to note the fact. The trouble about Mr. Hyde, if we become aware of him, in many cases is not that he is particularly wicked but that he is rather young—his spontaneous impulses and desires are unrelated to the physical and mental age of the Dr. Jekyll with whom he has to work in double harness. It is not so much that these impulses are harmful as that they are incongruous, and if yielded to might result in raised eyebrows in the conformist part of society. A brilliant young lawyer found that a previously unknown part of himself was impelled by a strong desire to build sand castles—the expression, no doubt, of some part of the self that had not found its natural expression in childhood. Very wisely he decided to indulge in this simple, harmless, and in his case undoubtedly releasing and health-giving pastime—but equally wisely he chose a remote and unfrequented shore, where his doings would not attract the attention of sensible grown-up persons unlikely to understand their purpose.

Most people are dimly aware of the existence of Mr. Hyde, and this awareness is the source of a considerable measure of discomfort. What is to be done with this unwelcome tenant in the basement? There are several wrong ways, and one right way, of dealing with the situation.

Some try simply to ignore him, and to pretend that he is not there. This may work very well for a time; but he does not like being ignored and is liable to take his revenge by making his presence all too plainly manifest at awkward and ill-considered moments.

Others believe that Mr. Hyde should simply be excised—the evil self should be got rid of. Fortunately, this is not possible; and, if it were, it would be a thoroughly bad thing. For Mr. Hyde is our strength, our vigour, our power of initiative. His strength and energy may be misdirected and misapplied; but if they were altogether withdrawn, we could not hope for more than a rather shadowy and etiolated existence.

97

Yet something very like this is set forward as the goal in certain forms of Christian teaching. Those who have undergone a sharp and sudden form of conversion experience sometimes imagine themselves to have been entirely relieved of their "evil nature." If events prove all too plainly that this is not so, if old "bad habits" reassert themselves, some conclude hastily that the conversion experience was a mere passing emotion of no lasting significance—a conclusion which does not by any means follow necessarily from the evidence. Others may pass the matter off by a too easy application of Paul's words, "So then it is no more I that do it, but sin that dwelleth in me"—a refusal to recognise the essential unity of human nature, which may be harmful as separating supposedly "spiritual" progress from the true development of an emotionally mature personality. The only right way to face this situation is to recognise that Mr. Hyde is the person in whom God is really interested, but that the discovery of the correct way to handle him may be a much longer process than is suggested by the immediate feeling of release that comes with an experience of conversion.

The commonest way of dealing with Mr. Hyde is that of simple suppression. If he makes suggestions that are incongruous or unsuitable, these are at once to be thrust out of consciousness and treated as though they had not existed. A great deal of Christian teaching on "evil thoughts" is along these lines; if they come, they must at once be thrust down below the level of consciousness, which is of course the very best way of giving them explosive or compulsive force. This refusal to accept the reality of Mr. Hyde may result either in repression, in the technical sense of the term, the process through which something is so completely thrust out of consciousness that even the experiencing subject cannot readily recall it; or simple suppression, in which by an effort of the will what are regarded as the less desirable elements in the personality are kept below the level of consciousness. In either case, the result is certain to be strain and tension. Two parts of man's being, which ought to work in harmony and co-operation, are failing to work together, or, it may be, are working in direct opposition. An emphatic "Yes" from one side is met by an emphatic "No" from the other. Since the hidden or half-known forces are very strong, a great deal of the energy that ought to be available for creative living is wasted in this

98

inner conflict; where the "Yes" and the "No" are almost equally balanced, the result may be an almost total loss of the power of decision and resolute action.

It is possible almost completely to suppress Mr. Hyde; but he has a tendency to escape and express himself at inconvenient and ill-chosen moments. His presence may become manifest in a sudden burst of uncontrollable anger or the sudden blurting out of an unpalatable truth that courtesy would rather have kept concealed. Such outbursts are startling because they seem out of character; and the one who has been guilty of the lapse is likely to say, "I can't think why I did that; I can hardly have been myself at the time." But this may be almost exactly the opposite of the truth; this may have been the occasion on which the carefully built-up and artificial self for a moment cracked, and a very much more real self, which has been all the time living down below, for a moment showed through.

For we have got to start by recognising that Mr. Hyde is a part of our real being, an indispensable part. He is not our enemy; he is our friend. It may well be that, when we first start seriously to make his acquaintance, he may prove to be a rather dishevelled friend, and one with whom we should hardly wish to be seen in the streets. Indeed, there is no reason why at present we should introduce him to our friends. His habits may be unpleasant and his morals poor; his strength may have been directed to confused and ill-chosen ends. Yet it remains the fact that we cannot be real people, unless he is brought back into the family and encouraged to make his own special contribution to the well-being of the whole.

Is it surprising if at present he is not very well fitted for respectable company? Almost from the start he has been given a bad name and treated in accordance with the bad name. It has even been affirmed that he is uneducable, and therefore in many cases no provision has been made for his education. He has not been introduced into decent society, and therefore he has tended to retain the manners of the coal hole and the garbage heap. It is not to be wondered at that poor Mr. Hyde is not a very reputable member of society. But we must not conclude in advance that nothing can be done about him. Before we decide anything at

99

all, the first thing is to make his acquaintance—the acquaintance of this so largely unknown self that dwells somewhere in all of us.

This is old and good advice. "Know thyself" was the first word of the ancient Greek gnomic wisdom. One of the greatest revolutions in human thought took place when Socrates, basing himself on this sphinxlike word of wisdom, turned the enquiring mind away from speculation on the mysteries of the physical universe to the mystery of man himself. About the same time the Hebrew Psalmist was making the affirmation, "Thou desirest truth in the inward part." In the presence of God, only the most relentless sincerity can stand—the willingness to know the reality of the hidden self, to experience feelings in their intensity without attempting to tone them down, to recognise impulses and desires for what they are without disguise, to accept our just measure of responsibility for what we are and for what we have done. The Christian tradition takes up exactly the same injunction, with perhaps the addition that the inner nature of man is so intricate and complex that only God can know it in its fulness, and that therefore it is only with the help of the spirit of God that a man can truly know himself. At this point the psychiatrist finds himself in goodly company. For, after all, his primary purpose is just to know what is really there and to help the sick person to know himself. The aim is healing; and analysis will naturally precede reconstruction. Although the term "psychoanalysis" is reserved for one set of techniques and one group of therapeutic procedures, in point of fact every psychiatrist starts, to use the military term, with an appreciation of the situation, an analysis, before he can begin to consider what can or should be done about it.

It is at this point that every kind of helper—the pastor, the counsellor, the moralist, the psychiatrist—begins to encounter opposition. Does the human race wish to know itself? The answer may perhaps be a modified affirmative, provided that the process of knowing does not cut too near the bone and does not involve too disastrous an undermining of self-esteem. As at the dentist, when it begins to hurt, most people wonder whether it is necessary to carry the operation any further.

A number of different motives can underlie resistance, and it can take on a considerable variety of forms.

Any priest who is in the habit of hearing confessions is aware that it is easy even for a sincere penitent to confess the wrong things and not the right ones. This is not to be confused with the "bad confession," in which deliberate concealment is made of things that are acknowledged to be wrong. What is meant here is the tendency to admit to symptoms without the willingness to go behind the symptoms to what may be much more serious causes—to own up to occasional lapses of temper without being willing to recognise the deep disturbance of family relationships which may underlie them, the ocean of resentment from which the occasional lapses pop up like scattered coral islands. The frank acknowledgement of that which in itself is not very important may serve as the perfect excuse for not going forward to face the far deeper reconstruction that may be needed, if steady spiritual progress is to be assured.

The religious sphere will afford another example of similar reluctance to face a reality that may prove to be menacing.

A sincere Christian becomes aware of questionings within himself. Does he really believe the things which he professes, which have come to him sanctioned by the authority of revered parents and touched with the glow of early religious experience? If such doubts arise, the only right course is to let them come out into the open, to look at them, to ask advice, and then with perfect sincerity to decide what changes, if any, are necessary in the structure of faith. But this takes a great deal of courage. A natural instinct is to strangle the monster doubt, as the infant Herakles is supposed to have strangled the serpents. And this can be done, but at a price. The price that has to be paid is the strain of maintaining the precarious balance of a faith that no longer rests on the total consent of the believing self.

A young officer on active service feels within himself the stirrings of fear. The right way to deal with this situation, as we shall have occasion to remark in another context, is to let fear come out into the open and be looked at. When so looked straight in the face, given a certain amount of resolution and self-discipline, fear can usually be kept in his proper place, and duty be done in spite of him. But our young man may feel that he must deal with the situation in a very different way. He is an officer and a gentleman, and he has probably been brought up to believe that officers and gentlemen are not afraid. Therefore fear must be driven down so deep that it can never be identified as fear. In such circumstances also duty can still be done; but when the pull between a consciously asserted "Yes" and an unrecognised and unadmitted "No" is so intense, it is likely that a heavy price will have to be paid in inner strain and nervous tension, over and above the inevitable strains that result from becoming engaged in human conflict.

During World War II, whenever a young friend of mine was about to be sent up to the front line, he went down with acute dermatitis. It is unlikely that he was in reality more afraid than a great many other young men in similar circumstances; but in this case fear that had not been dealt with in the right way found this method of expressing itself round the corner. The army doctors conscientiously dealt with what was truly and unmistakably a physical ailment; in this case they appear not to have detected that the ailment from which their patient was really suffering, the inner cause that underlay the purely physical symptom, was one that needed to be dealt with in a very different way.

A man, let us suppose, has always passed himself off as a devoted and affectionate son. He has maintained in every respect the traditions set by his father and always speaks of him with the utmost veneration. But the reality may be entirely different from the appearance. The man may really have feared and hated his father. The fear may have resulted in the policy of close imitation as the best safeguard against the possibilities of retaliation and disapproval. The hate may have been concealed by apparent transformation into something very different. Nice boys do not hate their fathers. If, therefore, the hatred was strong, it would be necessary for it to be completely concealed by a specious transformation into its exact opposite; hate must become an almost exaggerated affection, and no trace of disloyalty must ever be allowed to appear. If a man has built up a great part of his life on the denial or conversion of the reality of his own most intimate feelings, it is unlikely that he will welcome the disclosure of that reality. If a slight lifting of the trapdoor suggests the presence of

102

the unpardonable sin underneath, far better to let the trapdoor fall quickly and firmly back into place.

Another man has masked an intense inner need for self-assertion and dominance over others under the form of self-forgetful and public service. A willing horse will be offered plenty of work in any community; he is likely to find endless means for the exercise of influence and for the satisfaction of his need for the sense of power. And he is making the best of almost all possible worlds. He may have irritated a number of individuals who feel that he takes too much upon himself; but in general he will have the approval of the community as a model of unselfishness; and his many acts of unrewarded service will bring him the reward of the approval of his own virtuous conscience.

If some sign of lack of equilibrium should bring such a man to the consulting room of a psychiatrist, it is fairly easy to see what will follow. "Thou desirest truth in the inward parts"—and the last thing that the man is likely to want is the real truth about himself. As the enquiry proceeds, he is likely to become aware that the whole of his carefully developed and integrated life has been built upon an unstable foundation, may be in fact no more than a house of cards. Perhaps after three or four interviews he will depart and be no more seen. If he desires to continue, he will almost certainly have to pass through that agonising period that has been noted by almost all those who have recorded the experience of being deeply analysed—the sense of a dissolution of the entire personality, without any assurance that Humpty Dumpty can ever be put together again. What had been counted on as the strongest supports seem to crumble at a touch; the motives that underlie action are seen to be very different from what they have given themselves out to be. But if health is to be recovered, there is no other way. A tower has been built. If it rests on an unsound foundation, there is nothing to do but patiently to take it down brick by brick until the flaw in the foundation has been uncovered. It is probable that many of the bricks are good bricks; once rebuilding has started, they can probably be put back with very little delay. But the rebuilding cannot begin until the original defect has been repaired; and the process of taking down the tower will certainly be tedious and will probably be painful.

Whether we are sinful and in need of a pastor, or sick and in need of a physician, the process of getting to know ourselves is difficult and troublesome. It demands patience, courage, and relentless sincerity. Because in most of us these virtues are not highly developed, we oppose resistance to the process of discovery. The kind of resistance, and the strength of it, to a large extent determine the kind of help that we need.

It is clear that there is a great range of possible techniques and approaches. If resistance is strong, if what is needed is the baring of long hidden tendencies or the facing of thoughts and memories that are unbearably painful, nothing may suffice except the expert technique of the psychiatrist and the patient sympathy which is able and willing to continue until the deepest wounds have been probed. In other cases, the need is for the experienced pastor, who through long years of service has come to know the secrets of the human heart, the mixture of splendour and misery which is the make-up of most of us. All that is needed by many is the help that can be given by a patient and sensible friend, who is prepared to listen patiently, not to be shocked by anything, and always to remain "your considerate stone," impenetrably discreet in regard to everything that he has been told. As is now increasingly recognised, there is a great deal that we can do for ourselves, given certain guidance as to the kind of questions that we should ask and a willingness not to be afraid of anything that we may discover. Such "self-analysis" does not lead, as might be feared, to morbid introspection; rightly practised, it has exactly the opposite effect, since it helps to bring out into the open those inner tensions which always have the tendency to turn the self unhealthily back upon itself. But here, as in so many areas, the biblical principle that no man liveth to himself seems to be valid. None of us can see the back of his own throat without the help of a mirror; most of us do not make much progress in self-knowledge without the help of the candid and intelligent friend. It may seem that the part he has to play is no more than the passive role of the mirror, but it is none the less important for that. As long as problems are churning around in our own minds, it is very difficult to get sufficiently far away from them to be able to see them in perspective. The very necessity of putting them into words, perhaps with the help of sympathetic questioning, gives them a certain objectivity. Once they have, as it were, been put down on the table between two friends, they begin to fall into proportion, and then it is time to raise the question as to what, if anything, can be done about them.

Techniques may vary; but in principle the aim of all of them is the same—to encourage the individual to listen to that other voice, which from time to time we hear express itself in fragmentary utterance, which we so often try to suppress, to which so often we are extremely unwilling to listen. We vary greatly in the extent to which we can hear this other voice; but with a little practice considerable progress can be made; and, in conditions of reasonable physical and mental relaxation, almost anyone can begin to hear that voice speak. When it authentically speaks, it always speaks the truth—not in the sense of giving an objective transcript of reality outside ourselves, but in the sense of telling us what we actually experienced inwardly and what we felt about the experience. In the phrase of D. H. Lawrence, it is the blood that is beginning to speak. *Ch 3*

It has been convenient to refer to the hidden self as "the inward voice"; but the moment we begin to consider what the voice will tell us, the inadequacy of the term becomes apparent.

The first and most evident characteristic of this other experiencing self is its astonishing power of memory and actual visualisation. *1.* When once it begins to work, scenes of a distant past can be reproduced in the utmost perfection of detail, even to the accompanying smells; indeed, it is the sense of smell more than any other that seems to have this strange faculty of recalling the past, transporting us back over a couple of generations to a long-forgotten situation or incident, bringing it back to life with all the vivid colours of the original experience.

Secondly, this other self has an almost unlimited power of re- *2* covering and recreating emotion. A young man once told me that eighteen years before his father had beaten him severely and un- *lu* justly; it was evident, as he told me, that the very fact of speaking of it had brought back in almost full measure the mental and physical pain of the original experience.

But most important of all the characteristics of this other self *3.*

is that, at its most authentic, it invariably speaks and thinks in pictures. This was correctly observed by the great eighteenth-century German thinker Johann Georg Hamann, who was in many ways far ahead of his own time. The same observation was made more than a century later and independently by Sigmund Freud. We have now moved on from that other well-established characteristic, the pictorial faculty of accurately remembering what has actually happened; our concern now is with the mythopoeic faculty of representing in pictorial or mythological form an inner emotional experience or state. If a direct question is asked as to the nature of an emotional conflict, the answer is likely to be hesitating and uncertain. If the question is changed to the form, "What does it look like? How do you see it?" the answer is sometimes astonishingly clear, brilliant, and illuminating. No one can foretell what another's mythological forms are likely to be, and it is most important that the questioner should not attempt to impose his own mythological pictures on the answerer. It is the very unexpectedness of the replies that constitutes their interest.

Clearly, we have here moved near to the world of dreams. In dreaming, a part of our personality that is usually kept under control walks abroad and expresses itself in vivid and sometimes disconcerting images. Those who dream regularly and are able to recall their dreams must often feel regret that their waking self seems to manifest so much less creative brilliance than the self that takes its exercise during the hours of sleep. From the earliest times (we need go no further than the Book of Genesis) dreams have been regarded as having the greatest significance. Some have interpreted them as being always symbols of internal conflicts; but this seems to be unnecessarily narrow. They may equally well be the expression of inner reconciliations. "Swift as the radiant forms of sleep/From one whose dreams are paradise/Fleet, and the fond wretch wakes to weep," writes the poet, putting into memorable words what must be equally the experience of many of his readers. What is certain is that dreams afford clues, such as cannot always be come by in any other way, to states of inner experience that lie far below the level of ordinary consciousness. It is equally certain that the interpretation of dreams is an extremely delicate and risky business.

In the Bible the interpretation of dreams is regarded as a province that belongs to God alone: "Do not interpretations belong to God?" Joseph answered Pharaoh, saying, "It is not in me: God shall give Pharaoh an answer of peace." "There is a God in heaven that revealeth secrets" (Gen. 40:8; 41:16; Dan. 2:28). Even if we do not limit the possibility of interpretation to divine inspiration, we do well to remember the difficulty of the task. Dreams speak in a double or treble cypher, and in many cases it seems impossible to recover the key. The fact that symbols mean something in the dreams of one person gives no guarantee that they will mean the same in the dreams of anyone else. All attempts to assign universal significance to the types and varieties of symbol that appear in dreams have proved to be temerarious, if not positively dangerous. We have always to bear in mind the possibility that the interpreter may make use of his own mythology in trying to understand the dreams of another person, and so may end by imposing his own unresolved inner contradictions on the one whom he is attempting to help.

This does not involve any denial of the importance and value of dream interpretation; it does mean that this is an area which is clearly marked "Amateurs, keep out!" and in which even the expert must move with hesitation.

The use of the pictorial imagination in waking hours is parallel to the study of dreams but moves in a very different field. The one who sees the pictures remains fully conscious. He cannot foretell what picture will shape itself within his inner consciousness, nor what direction the movement of the picture will follow. But he is probably to some extent aware of the problems for which a solution is being sought and has at least some clue to the meaning of the mythological symbols in which inner experience, conflict, or desire, has presented itself.*

More important still, it seems possible for the individual to act in the mythological situation, and for such action or decision to have healing effects in the inner being of that individual in the

*It is possible at once to see a parallel with the use made of drawing or painting in certain schools of psychotherapy. "Draw what you feel" can be a very useful line of introduction to the inner self. But whereas not everyone can draw, everyone can see pictures.

present. In the long distant past, a situation was wrongly faced through ignorance or fear; now, in its mythological presentation, it is rightly faced. Necessary decision or action was evaded; now, in mythological form, it is taken; and the sense of release and renewed strength in the ordinary and prosaic world shows that the action or decision had more than a merely imaginary or pictorial value.

Out of innumerable examples that might be given, a small number may make the point at issue clear.

A student who was conscious of indecision and the inability to follow a settled line of conduct (and quite incidentally was leading a life of sexual irregularity which his own conscience did not approve) was asked to put into words the kind of way in which he saw his own situation. He rapidly produced two mythological pictures. One was of a kind of medieval castle, closely guarded, with himself safely inside it, but unwilling to face the danger of emerging into the outside world. The second was that of a man clutching a post in the middle of a swirling stream that threatened to carry him away. As we have seen so often, all mental strain or sickness is associated with the refusal or rejection of some aspect of reality; it would be hard to arrive at two more dramatic and revealing pictures of a self that had never had the courage to take the plunge into a reality which of its very nature can never come completely under the control of the self. It was suggested to the young man concerned that the time had really come to lift the portcullis, both in order to admit strangers to the castle and to allow the inhabitant to emerge into what was evidently in many ways an attractive outside world. When this had been accepted, it was suggested that something should be done about the second picture of the man clinging to the post; the unexpected answer was, "Oh, I let go long ago, as soon in fact as I realised what he was doing." Such an experience is only a beginning; but observation shows that such a beginning may lead on to the kind of reconstruction of personal experience that is involved in any genuine healing.

Another student, asked to describe his situation, found himself in the very familiar dream situation of a long dark tunnel, with no light showing at the end. Asked whether he could begin to walk towards the outlet, he replied that he could, and began to do so, still of course in the mythological situation. It took him a long time. From time to time comments were made—the beginning of the appearance of light at a great distance and so on. At last he remarked, "Now I'm out." It is simply the fact that, in this case, the kind of depression and sense of isolation represented by the tunnel never recurred.

All mental sickness involves the division in some way of the self against the self—otherwise this kind of conflict and strain could not occur. Often the inner division is disguised under the form of maladjustment to others or to the environment. But occasionally the mythological picture reveals quite plainly the existence of two almost independent and separate selves, and the recovery of health depends on a conscious reconciliation between the two.

A young man, through birth and upbringing, was perfectly bilingual in French and English. Through circumstances that need not be detailed, it had come about that each of these languages had become associated exclusively with one part of his being. His education had been carried on entirely in French. The reasoning or intellectual self, under the influence of this education, had become critical, severely logical, sceptical in matters of religion, inclined to be arrogant and self-assertive in discussion. The whole of his home life, with its gentler and more emotional aspects, had been lived in English. This more intuitive self was kindly, affectionate, and inclined to be religious. Each self was dimly aware of the other, disliked and despised it, and was inclined to resent its presence. But in point of fact there was hardly any communication between the two. It must be emphasised that the young man was not in the least "schizophrenic" in the sense in which that term is often used. He had done well both in school and college and was satisfactorily holding down a job. He was leading to all appearance a perfectly normal life and showed no symptom of any lack of equilibrium other than a certain shyness and hesitancy in personal relationships. But the lack of inner unity kept him constantly on the strain and produced a feeling of helplessness, irresolution, and immaturity. "Shall I ever grow up to be really a man?" was the anxious and unanswered question. It took a long time before the nature of the problem could be understood; the fortuitous discovery of the symbolic role played by the two languages gave the clue. Once the two separated selves had been identified, the reconciliation between them proved to be unexpectedly easy. The extremely happy end of this story is of no interest to anyone except the fortunate young man concerned.

The words "accept" and "acceptance" have already been used more than once. The reality that is there within us must be known in its totality, and in its totality it must be accepted. The word "acceptance" tends to be so much misused and misunderstood that it is necessary to make clear exactly the sense in which it is being used. Acceptance is not the same as approbation. It means simply the recognition of the fact that what is, is; and at the moment it cannot be anything other than what it is. If that is what I am, that is what I am; I may very much hope that tomorrow I shall be something else; but the future is not the same as the present. I may very much wish that I were something different from what I am; but if wishes were horses beggars would ride to town. The first step towards mental health is the willingness to make the simple affirmation "I am I." In the immortal words of Bishop Butler, "Things and actions are what they are, and the consequences of them will be what they will be. Why then should we desire to be deceived?" It may be our concern to work for a very different future; but a rational and unimpassioned acceptance of the present, of that which is already given, is the only ground on which practical planning for a happier future can be undertaken.

But, let us repeat, acceptance is not the same as approbation. We may have learned to accept the reality of that which we are and at the same time find that there is much in that reality which we deplore. A man who has come to know himself may find that he is ashamed of himself, ashamed of the hollowness of the virtue which Dr. Jekyll has displayed to the world, ashamed of the vindictiveness with which Mr. Hyde has taken it out of others for his own unhappiness.

The capacity to feel shame is the most human of all human qualities, and perhaps less attention has been paid to it by psychologists than it deserves. It is observable to some degree in certain animals, but apparently only in those which by long association with human beings have acquired a number of quasi-human characteristics. An animal impelled only by "instinct" would presumably be incapable of that inner discrimination of purposes and motives, that possibility of self-criticism without which shame is impossible. When the prophet Jeremiah wishes to give expression to the extreme degradation of his people, the worst that he can find to say about them is that "they were not at all ashamed, neither could they blush." To have lost the capacity for shame is to have lost one of the qualities without which a genuinely human existence is impossible. *in Blushing*

It is not to be supposed that the word "shame" is to be found only on the lips of the moralists. It expresses an instinctive and apparently universal type of judgment. The things about which men feel ashamed, or expect others to feel ashamed, may vary greatly; apparently the word, and the associated idea, exists in every language. That popular play *The Late Christopher Bean* is a study in the contrast between the simple honesty and loyalty of Gwenny the Welsh maid, and the grasping, scheming hardness of the commercialised people who are trying to make capital out of the assets of a dead man. One of the highlights of the play is the moment at which Gwenny turns to her employer the doctor, and says to him, "You ought to be ashamed of yourself"; the unexpected answer is, "I am ashamed of myself."

A very interesting study could be made of the situations in which a man of today is likely to say "He ought to be ashamed of himself." The word "sin" has come to be regarded as so old-fashioned that it is hardly heard in ordinary conversation except as the name of a fashionable perfume. But the guess may be hazarded that the idea of "shame" is instinctively associated in the minds of most of us with actions which, if they became general, would make life impossible for everyone.

In recent years, we have all become aware of the necessity of conserving the fertility of the good earth which God has given us. It is possible in some areas for a farmer, by reckless harrying of his land, by taking everything out of it that he can and putting hardly anything back, to slip quick and immediate profits into his pocket, and in five years to leave the land so grievously ruined

111

that fifty years may not suffice to repair the damage that he has done. If, as a result of his depredations, erosion sets in, the damage is likely to be literally irreparable. When we have made every possible allowance for economic pressure and every other consideration, there would be general agreement that this is not the kind of thing that men ought to do. Another farmer, hearing of it, is likely to express his feelings in the words, "He ought to be ashamed of himself, doing a thing like that."

Some years ago, a highly imaginative historical work became one of the best-sellers of its generation. This was one of the pioneers in the gentle art of debunking the past, the method being to gather together everything that could make certain eminent people appear ridiculous—and then conscientiously to refrain from laughing. A serious historian, working over the same period, became aware that the popular writer had suppressed a piece of evidence which, from other passages in his work, it was quite certain that he must have had in his possession. He wished to present a picture—a rather malicious picture—of a man who had long been held in general esteem. Because this evidence did not fit in with his preconceived picture, he quietly suppressed it. When we have made every possible excuse we can for the writer, the judgment of every scholar would probably express itself in the same words, "He ought to be ashamed of himself, doing a thing like that." Unless those who write, and thus take it upon themselves to direct the opinions of others, are unswerving in their devotion to the truth, life becomes impossible for everyone.

These are the cases in which a certain type of instinctive judgment is likely to be passed on other men. The same kind of instinctive judgment can be turned on the self.

Sometimes the idea of shame is associated with fear of discovery by others. Something that I have said or done does not come up to the standards generally accepted in the society in which I move; if I am found out, I shall be ashamed in front of them. But this is far from being the only situation in which shame can be felt. It can be related to some act or thought of which no one else is aware, or at any time can possibly be aware, but with which man is left alone in the inner forum of what is commonly called his conscience. He is ashamed of himself. This does not imply a judgment that what he has done is socially disadvantageous and, if discovered, would injure his reputation with others. It is related to some inner and personally accepted standard of conduct in terms of "better" and "worse," or at least of "helpful" and "harmful." It is when a man has seen what he judges to be the better, and without compulsion from without or from within has chosen to do what he judges to be the worse, that he is ashamed of himself, without regard to any judgment other than his own. *guilt; guilt works contrasted*

This may sound rather like the harrowing experiences of what has come to be commonly known as the guilt complex. But in point of fact there could hardly be a greater difference than that between the dispassionate and almost frigid judgment of the man who concludes that he has cause to be ashamed of himself, and the hectic and unprofitable self-tormenting of the man who is suffering from a guilt complex. It is important that the distinction should be understood.

A guilt complex is usually related either to some purely imaginary source of guilt, or to disproportionate feelings of culpability about something that in itself was only trivially wrong, and when once seen in reasonable proportion will cease to torment the conscience of the one who did it. There is no doubt that a considerable part of the human race suffers in health, efficiency, and happiness from carrying a heavy burden of imaginary guilt. No greater service can be imagined than that of freeing those who suffer in this way from their unnecessary burden.

We are now fairly familiar with the kind of situations that can produce a guilt complex, though in detail they vary as much as the individuals who have come to suffer through them.

Sometimes the starting point is nothing worse than a childish peccadillo, which anxiety and fear of discovery have inflated to enormous proportions, the anxiety and the fear persisting long after the originating cause has been forgotten.

A strongly moralistic atmosphere in the home can produce a state of continuous uncertainty and an almost perpetual feeling of being in the wrong. If the parents expect of the children a really unattainable standard of perfection, if every minor failure becomes the occasion of an emotional crisis instead of being dealt with rapidly and summarily and forgotten, the result may be to induce in the children an emotional instability of which later they will find it very difficult to rid themselves. A young friend has described to me the way in which he was brought up. He was never punished. But if in any matter great or small he failed to come up to the expected standard, his father became like a thundercloud. The thundercloud never exploded in anger—in many ways it would have been much less harmful if it had—then after two or three days of anguished suspense, everything would return more or less to normal. There was no sense of perspective in failure or wrongdoing; after all, one can drown as well in six inches as in twenty feet of water. It is not surprising that the boy developed a sense of being always and hopelessly in the wrong. Such a feeling is very hampering in the ordinary business of daily life; and once acquired, it cannot easily be got rid of.

Sometimes the sense of guilt attaches itself not to anything done, but simply to ideas and impulses that are felt to be so horrifying and unnatural that they never ought to be entertained. One who is conscious of such ideas becomes like a man or woman with a guilty secret which can never be shared with anyone and exposes the bearer of it to the perpetual fear of discovery.

A considerable part of the time of the psychiatrist is spent in trying to help people to be free of these bogeys of the imagination or of the past. Since the Christian ideal is that of free, healthy, and effectively working human nature, and the sense of guilt can so grievously thwart or delay the development of that nature, the Christian can only wish the psychiatrist well in this part of his task. Disagreement is likely to arise only if it is supposed that, when we have dealt with the guilt complex, we have dealt also with the problem of guilt.

We shall have occasion later to consider whether moral judgments can be regarded as in any sense absolute. Here it is necessary only to note that the majority even of those who would not commit themselves to any judgment in terms of absolute "good" and "evil" are prepared to recognise a difference between "better" and "worse," between "more desirable" and "less desirable." Some schools of psychological thought seem to come near to the profession of a psychological determinism and to a denial of human freedom; yet almost all seem in practice to allow, at least in some

114

measure, for the responsibility, restricted though it may be, of the individual for his own actions. If this did not exist, it is hard to see how anyone who is mentally sick could ever get well or on what principle the psychiatrist could base his practice of the art of healing.

What are we to do if, when we have eliminated every trace of a guilt complex, we are driven to the conclusion that what we have to do with is a case of human guilt?

The most famous representation of a troubled mind in the whole of human literature is the sleepwalking scene in *Macbeth*. Lady Macbeth has that on her mind which can be suppressed in waking hours, but will out and will find its expression in the hours of sleep. As she walks to and fro wringing her hands, her waiting-woman asks the doctor, "Canst thou not minister to a mind diseased?" In the sixteenth century the answer was an almost categorical "No!" So Lady Macbeth goes on walking endlessly to and fro— "All the perfumes of Arabia will not sweeten this little hand." Today we have changed all that. We can analyse the lady to the roots of her being. We can lay bare the hidden motives of action, the childhood frustrations that had to find their compensation in overweening ambition, all the various pressures that lie behind the existence of a disordered personality. We can make every excuse for the weakness and perversity of human nature. But when all this has been done, every morbid element exposed and healed, have we really said the last word? After all, all this will not bring the king to life again. The king is dead—"Who would have thought the old man to have so much blood in him!" His death was the result of careful planning and preparation. It really was not necessary to kill him. Most people would agree that on the whole a live king is "better" than a dead one, especially when as in this case he is adorned with so many princely and attractive virtues. Is it possible that Lady Macbeth is not suffering from a guilt complex, that she is in fact just a guilty woman?

Most men, at one time or another, turn the same question round upon themselves—am I too a guilty man? If the question is put in the torrid and emotional climate of the guilt complex, or in those anxious hours between two and four in the morning when everything takes on a sable and discouraging hue, the answer may not be particularly true or particularly useful. But the same question can be asked in purely dispassionate and unemotional tones. And the answer may be, "I saw two courses clearly open before me; I saw that one would be helpful to myself and harmful to someone else; I was under no overwhelming or compulsive inner pressure to choose one way or the other; I deliberately chose to do something which I knew would hurt another in order to help myself. I am, in fact, a guilty man."

If this is the situation, what is either psychiatrist or pastor to say?

In many cases, both have to say the same thing. "You may regret it, but you can't do anything about it now. You must learn to let the past be the past." In many forms of mental illness there is an element of inability to let the past be the past, an insistence, conscious or unconscious, that the past with all its emotional entanglements and violences must live on in the present.

Regret is not in any way pathological; it has no feature of the "complex" about it, if it means no more than looking back from the present on the past, judging that past unfavourably, and deciding that the future shall be as little like it as possible. And often there is literally nothing that can be done about that past. "It is true that thirty years ago you robbed your mother's bag, and allowed suspicion to fall on someone else. If you were able to tell her now, probably she would not mind so much after all; but she is dead—you can't tell her, and that is all there is to it. If there was anything you could do about it, you would; but there just is nothing. So it is better to let the dead bury their dead, to let the incident remain where it belongs—in the long distant past."

This is sapient advice. But it is not always so easy to let the past be the past. The dead are not always willing to bury the dead; and the past has a disconcerting way of popping up and disturbing the tranquillity of the present. Is there anything further that can be done about it? The Christian would like, at this point, to be allowed to add two dimensions, which do not fall directly within the sphere of the psychiatrist, but of which the psychiatrist may readily understand the nature and appreciate the healing significance. The first is forgiveness, and the second is grace.

We shall later have occasion to consider the immense significance

116

of the willingness to forgive. We are concerned for the moment only with the willingness to believe in the possibility of being forgiven. True forgiveness has nothing to do with the remission of penalties that have been deserved, though in certain cases such remission may accompany forgiveness. Nor has it anything to do with failure or refusal to recognise to the full the nature and the gravity of the wrong that has been done. If this were its meaning, it would involve a regress into that world of unreality, which under one aspect is mental ill-health and under another is hypocrisy. True forgiveness is the one completely adequate method of putting the past back where it belongs—in the past. It means that the one who has been wronged recognises to the full the wrong that has been done and the injury that it has caused him; and then creates an entirely new situation by accepting the wrongdoer as a friend, setting himself beside him to help him to make a fresh start, and as far as possible to overcome the harmful consequences of the wrong for which he alone has been responsible. In such a situation, even the man who feels that he "cannot forgive himself" may feel that there is hope for him after all.

Suppose that God is able to do all the time what men are prepared to do in certain circumstances. Human folly has some-times pictured God as though he were a jealous tyrant, always watchful to catch his creatures off their guard, and to take it out of them for their misdeeds. Suppose that the exact opposite is the truth, and that it is better expressed in the remarkable metaphor of the prophet, "Thou wilt cast all their sins into the depths of the sea." Suppose that God is in reality the patient friend, who knows and understands everything; before whom no evasion is either possible or necessary; who, knowing the worst about us far better than we know it ourselves, knowing all the gross and mon-strous wrongs that we have done to him, then creates a new situa-tion by setting himself firmly on our side, to make possible a new beginning and to repair as far as repair is possible the harm that has been done by the mistakes and follies of the past. If this supposition by any chance proved to be the truth, it would mean that the whole of the past could be faced without evasion, and so firmly set in the past that it could no longer exercise a paralysing or hurtful influence on the present.

117

Psychiatrist and pastor alike are concerned with the future as well as with the past. Suppose that the past has all come to light and the analytic process is complete. What is now going to give the patient confidence to start the process of reconstruction, to pick up the bits, and to begin to build? The second half of the process is often more difficult of achievement than the first.

"Grace" is not a word that the psychiatrist is likely to have in his vocabulary, but it is one of which he should be able without difficulty to grasp the significance. It means simply, in one particular connection, that helpful and healing influence that one personality can exercise upon another. According to the splendid saying of Ferenczi, it is the love of the psychiatrist that heals the patient. This is a saying that needs a little interpretation. The psychiatrist is usually advised to have no personal relationships with the patient outside the consulting room, and above all not to allow himself to become emotionally entangled with his patient. Indeed, if he allows another's emotional problems to course through his own emotional tracts, he will probably lose that impartial independence without which it is impossible for him to be of service. But is not the word "love" the correct word to use of the deep and lasting concern of the healer for the one who stands in need of healing, of the endless patience that will not allow itself to be discouraged or deterred by any frustrations or setbacks? The psychiatrist starts by accepting the patient just as he is, with all his Dr. Jekylls and all his Mr. Hydes. If he does his job well, he is likely to find himself moved by a deep and increasing admiration for human nature and for the courage with which people bear their almost unbearable problems. He takes hold of the situation with a quiet confidence in the patient's capacity for recovery, which may be the only thing that holds when the patient himself is inclined to despair. All this must be done in the spirit of complete self-effacement and without the least desire to dominate. The delight that the healer feels when the patient shows the first signs of recovery is the highest reward that the exercise of his profession offers him. If this is a true picture, the psychiatrist knows quite well what grace is, though he might be considerably disturbed by the idea of using the term, especially in relation to himself and to his own professional activity.

118

The pastor works under fewer limitations than the psychiatrist. His relation to one whom he is trying to help spiritually can and in many cases should be a more directly personal one. It is to be expected that he will meet his friend in the natural surroundings of home and family as well as in the austere atmosphere of the confessional or of the minister's study at the church. Otherwise the parallel between the two types of ministry is extremely close. It is a little poetical, but not far from the truth, to say that in each case one man is lending his health to bear the burden of another's sickness.

The influence of one human personality on another, or rather the reciprocal influence of human personalities upon one another, is something that we should not wish to deny, and which it would be futile to deny if we wished to do so. The trouble is that the psychiatrist and the pastor cannot be always there. The healer knows how often his work is frustrated because the sufferer has to go straight back into the situation which in the first place brought his neurosis into being and is likely to hinder its resolution. The spiritual guide has so often to send one who is trying to make a fresh start back into the very situation in which he has yielded to temptation, and in which it is unlikely that he will summon up sufficient resolution to resist it if it should recur. Even the wisest doctor sometimes misinterprets the evidence put before him and gives advice that does more harm than good. Even the most sensitive of friends may put his foot wrong, and injure where he is trying to help. And we are all of us so trying that it is a wonder that we do not more often wear out the patience of all our friends.

Suppose, for the moment, that it is part of God's nature to supply hope for the future as well as forgiveness for the past. If he exists at all, he is presumably the One who is always there, whose help can always be counted on when it is needed. He is the One who never misunderstands, but is aware of the most secret thoughts that we cannot make plain even to ourselves. He does not obtrude himself or undertake to do anything for us that we could do for ourselves; but his strength is always available to the weak, his wisdom to the foolish. We cannot wear out his patience, for his patience, like himself, is infinite. It is his love that heals the patient; and nothing can stand in the way of that love except the sheer

119

foolishness of the lost sheep that will not allow itself to be found, the sheer obstinacy of human nature which affirms that, "Of course I am not really ill; I have no problems that I can't solve myself."

This is a charming picture and to those who do not believe in the existence of such a God, it must present itself as based wholly on wishful thinking or on imagination. But if so, it is not on the imagination of the writer that it is based. It is a brief transcript in contemporary language of what Jesus said that God was like.

The question of the relationship between Jesus and God is one that hardly comes before us in this book at all. What does concern us is that, because Jesus believed that God is like that, and that the universe is made in one particular way and not in any other, he himself was led to treat human beings in one particular manner, and laid it down as a universal rule that this is the manner in which every one of us ought to treat his brethren.

We have already noted that, to the infinite scandal of all respectable people, Jesus chose his friends among the poor, the alienated, the underprivileged, and the socially discarded. It was taken for granted that a religious teacher would move in the society of the virtuous, the polished, and the well-to-do and that he would become interested in the others only when they had reached a certain stage in the transformation of themselves into respectability. Jesus swept away all such prudential ideas with the one trenchant maxim, "They that are whole have no need of a physician, but they that are sick." He seems really to have liked his disreputable friends and to have found among them a sincerity and an openness to the realities of life that are often lacking among those whose existence has been cushioned against these harsh realities. He was prepared to accept them in their pathetic contradiction against themselves, in their ineffective absurdity, their alienation from society, and the darkening of their minds and spirits. They could not wear out his patience; stupid, inconstant, and faithless, they found him changeless and always the same. He was prepared to trust them even when they were not worthy of any trust.

Of course, this acceptance did not imply approval. Anyone who was brought into contact with Jesus was well aware that it was hopeless to attempt to hide anything from his ruthless realism. "He knew what was in man." There was to be no compromise with anything that was unworthy of a man, no tame acceptance of anything that fell short of a genuinely human existence. Those who associated with him knew well that they were facing a demand for a complete transformation of their way of thinking and their way of acting. But what he seems to have done for them was first to stimulate in them a desire to be different from that which they were; and secondly, to create in them a confidence that through his help, "the grace of our Lord Jesus Christ," that which had been impossible would become possible. They began to hope.

And among all the drugs in the pharmacopoeia there is none that has a healing power equal to that of hope.

V   I and Thou   *Social relations*

MAN NEEDS TO BE RECONCILED to himself if he is to live like a human being. It is even more true that he needs to be reconciled to society, to the people who live round about him. No doubt Robinson Crusoe had plenty of internal problems when he lived on his desert island—indeed, that can be confirmed from the records of those who have undergone completely solitary confinement in recent years—but at least he was free from the troubles that come from the intrusive presence of other human beings. Not so the rest of us. We have to live with other human creatures pressing in upon us nearly all the time; and that is where many of our troubles come from. It usually starts in the family. Relationships within the family, as experienced by some individual, were not what they ought to have been. Then the trouble has been aggravated by the pressures that come from living in other groups. And so we are faced with all the problems that can arise in the world of personal relationships.

What are personal relationships? It is extraordinarily hard to give a definition which is other than purely tautological. Personal relationships are those which can exist between persons. And what are persons? They are those living creatures between which personal relationships can exist. This is not mere nonsense. It reflects the fact that we are here dealing with a range of experiences which are entirely unlike anything else in the world and cannot be explained in terms of anything else. We all know fairly well what we mean by the terms; we are all baffled by the attempt to find a precise definition for them.

122

There has been much discussion of the problem in recent years, and one of the chief starting points has been Martin Buber's book *I and Thou*, one of those small books that from time to time set going a whole new stream of human thought. Buber draws a very sharp distinction between the relationship I-It and the relationship I-Thou. If we wish to sum up the distinction very briefly, it may perhaps be expressed in the difference between detachment and engagement. I can acquire a certain kind of knowledge, even of other persons, by treating them as objects, by watching and observing them, but without being personally concerned or moved by their affairs. But this is not the I-Thou relationship. To reach that, I must come out from myself, I must abandon the independence of the observer, I must be willing to reveal myself and to receive the revelation that only the other can give of himself. Then *exchange* becomes possible; and short of exchange, no genuinely personal relationship has been established.

To some extent we can enter into such relationships with pet animals, but only to a very limited extent, because their means for the expression of their feelings are so limited in range. All human beings have the immense advantage of articulate speech; we can say more or less what we think and feel, even though often the words at our command fall far short of what we would like to say. Human selves are always in movement, and a true relationship between them is always a moving relationship between moving beings. We can keep an object still for a certain length of time and examine it. But human nature is always in a state of kaleidoscopic reaction to its environment and experiences; it is always changing, and therefore the I-Thou relationship is also always in a state of change. This explains how it is possible to remain happy though married for fifty years. In any real marriage each partner has every day some new and interesting experience to contribute, so that the fellowship is one of endless and delighted mutual enrichment.

Are there laws which are valid throughout this world of personal relationship, and can we find expression for them? That is our problem. If we venture on personal encounter, we come so terribly near to one another. We can enter that world only by a willingness to surrender some of our own autonomy and by taking from the other some part of his autonomy. We can render one another such tremendous service—not simply such service as is rendered by the janitor who carries us in the elevator to the thirty-fifth floor, but in the way of making true human existence possible. We can do one another such terrible injury. Does this not mean that, if we enter into this kind of relationship at all, we are *responsible* for one another? We can no longer regard our actions as though they concerned ourselves alone, or what happens to the other as being no concern of ours. It is for this reason that, traditionally, personal relationships have been expressed in terms of obligation; and that means that it has not been found possible to exclude such terms as good and bad, right and wrong, "ought" and "ought not."

Not everyone of course would accept these traditional terms as relevant or valid. Cannot living together be based on self-interest as well as on mutual obligation? One famous theory of the origins of society took as its starting-point the idea that society developed simply from men's mutual agreement not to injure one another. They came to see that if each followed his own impulses and aggressive tendencies without limit, there would be no possibility of living together at all, and so they agreed to set certain limits to those instincts that man has inherited from the beasts of prey. Certainly there have to be such agreements, even if it be only as to who is to sleep on which side of the bed, if any common life is to be possible; human nature cannot stand the strain of continual altercation on every imaginable subject. In a recent and well-known book on psychology, *Man, Morals, and Society*, the distinguished author puts forward the view that morals is an "orectic" science. "Orectic" is derived from the Greek word *orego*, to want or to desire. Morals, then, would be the organised expression of man's wants and desires, his desire for comfort and his desire to be free from pain, discomfort, or injury, but would be unrelated to any absolute standard external to man and independent of his existence. From the practical point of view, we can get on fairly well with this kind of understanding of the nature of society. But it is not easy to exclude completely deeper questions, such as cannot be answered altogether in these terms.

"Parents are responsible for the welfare of their infant children." That sounds straightforward enough; it becomes difficult, as soon as we begin to ask exactly what it means. Who has made parents

124

responsible, and to whom are they responsible? Does this mean no more than that the state will insist that, if parents have brought children into the world, they must look after them? If they happen to have come to dislike their children, they cannot evade their obligations by just throwing them out on the street. But why not? And what are obligations? Might it not be better, as Plato thought, if the state did bring up all children, out of reach of the dangerous likes and dislikes of their parents? And what is the welfare of children? Do we know? If we try to define it, shall we not find ourselves bringing in the words "good" and "bad," and does not that imply that we know what these words mean?

These are difficult questions. If the answer to them was obvious, they would have been settled long ago, like the question as to the distance of the moon from the earth, instead of being still the subject of lively discussion among moralists, philosophers and theologians. Here we need not go in detail into the theoretical discussions, intensely interesting as they are, but we cannot altogether disregard the subject, since our quite practical answers to a number of questions will depend on our general attitude to the underlying problems.

In the first place, it must be made clear that there are three levels on which these questions can be discussed, and these may be distinguished, for convenience, as the levels of ethics, of morals, and of conduct.

An illustration from a different sphere may help to make clear the difference. There are three ways in which we can approach the problem of putting up a building. There is the theorist, who is concerned with the nature of materials, the strains that they will stand, the best methods of using materials for particular purposes. There is the practical architect, who is responsible for drawing up particular plans according to which a building will be put up; the same plans can be used for putting up a large number of buildings in different places. There is the builder, who is putting up one building on one piece of ground only, and, as he does so, makes impossible the putting up of any other building on that spot. All these three functions may be combined in the same man or they may overlap; for all that, they remain quite different functions.

Now let us apply this distinction to our other problem.

125

theory

What for the moment it will be convenient to call ethics is a high and austere science, remote from immediate human needs and desires. It concerns itself with such questions as: What is the nature and meaning of responsibility and obligation? What do we mean by the words "good" and "bad"? Is there a good life for man, and if so, do we know what it is? The answers given to these questions have no immediate practical reference; but a great many practical consequences may flow from the kind of answers that are given to them.

Morals (though in this field too the word "ethics" can be used) deals with the general principles on which the life of men together can be based. This study may concern itself with such great questions as the rightness or wrongness of war in any or all circumstances. It can also concern itself with such questions as common honesty in commercial dealings between man and man. All of us have inherited certain moral ideas from the society in which we were brought up, and usually we accept them without question. But change in society depends on the willingness of individuals to question these inherited ideas and perhaps to see that what was relevant and useful at one time no longer is so and had better be abandoned; or that these inherited ideas are a very imperfect reflection of fundamental principles.

The third level, corresponding to the particular house on a particular spot, is the particular action that I have to take at a given moment, an action that will be determined by an inner decision at which I have arrived. In a great many cases, no imaginable issue of right or wrong is involved in the decision,—whether to buy this kind of cigarette or that. In many other cases, I shall simply follow the traditions of the society in which I have been brought up. But it may occur that, at certain points, I discard these traditions as not giving the correct answer to my problem, and look away to something deeper and, in my judgment, at that moment more convincing. What I am doing, consciously or unconsciously, is to go behind the traditions to my own idea of "the good life for man," to my own understanding of the way in which people ought to behave. Something like this must have underlain the action of German women who at the risk of their lives protected stranded American airmen who had had to bale out of their aircraft, knowing that their action was "unpatriotic" and, if discovered, would have most deadly con-

126

sequences for themselves. In any case, whatever exactly the nature of the action, I have acted, and I am therefore "responsible"; I have to accept as my own the consequences of the action, whether I have exactly foreseen what they would be or not.

A great many people today question whether there is any such thing as an absolute standard of right and wrong. Relativism in one or other of its forms is widely prevalent. Not very long ago, the issue seemed in the Western world to be comparatively simple. Right and wrong, it was supposed, are quite clearly defined. You know the difference. If you do what is wrong and are found out, then you must take the consequences, whether these take the form of parental punishment, or social disapproval, or the vengeance of the state through legal process. Now we are not sure that it is all quite so simple. After all, not everyone is agreed as to what is right and wrong. A capitalistic society is agreed as to the rightness and sacredness of property; the Marxist is convinced that private property is organised robbery. May there not be something to be said for both points of view? We have come to understand that views of right and wrong are to some extent at least socially conditioned; I think this is right or wrong, but that is just because I have been brought up that way and others around me feel the same; but members of another and alien society may have a different point of view. Some are prepared to carry this tolerance very far: "Well, if that's the way you feel, you'd better go on and do it; I feel differently, but that's probably just because of the way I was brought up."

There are at least five different sources from which this relativistic attitude draws support at the present time.

We may start with the anthropologists, whose business is the study of the different ways that men have learned of living together, under the extremely varied exigencies of different climates and regions of the earth. This is a fascinating study. The ingenuity of men in devising various forms of social order is almost beyond belief. And of course, the moment we begin to compare such forms of social order, we find that things which are permitted in one area are forbidden in another. Right and wrong seem to be related to the way in which particular groups of people have decided to live together. It is not necessary to look further than the question of whom you may or may not marry. In the West, marriage between

127

first cousins tends to be discouraged for eugenic reasons, but is not forbidden. In parts of Africa any marriage between cousins is regarded as incestuous. In the part of India which I know best, cousins related to you through your father are reckoned as your brothers and sisters, and marriage in this relationship would be regarded as incestuous; but if there is a girl cousin of suitable age related to you through your mother, you not merely may, you must marry her! Your personal inclinations have nothing to do with it.

We are indebted to the anthropologists for an endless store of enthrallingly interesting information. All the same, we have to keep a rather watchful eye upon them. Their business is to record and classify patterns of culture, to borrow the title of a deservedly famous book. But it is difficult for them to avoid the temptation to slip in every now and then a value judgment, a judgment of better and worse. For instance, when an eminent anthropologist points out that teen-age girls in the South Pacific who are not expected to observe sexual chastity are free from many of the strains and neuroses observable among American girls of the same age, there is at least an *implicit* judgment that the South Pacific way is better or more desirable. If we encounter such a judgment, we must at once challenge the anthropologist to stand and deliver; what does he mean by better, what are his criteria, his standards of value? Is he not implying that he knows what the good life for man is? But such a judgment belongs not to the craft of the anthropologist but to that of the moralist. We may find that the anthropologist has been playing at the science of ethics, with which he is very ill-qualified to deal.

The second source of relativism is in certain cases the sociologist. Here again we have gained enormously by his researches into the different levels of life within the same culture, the differences between a rural and an urban society, and the differences between different levels within the same urban complex. Here too we are confronted with most interesting varieties of ways of doing things and ways of looking at things, even within the society with which we are ourselves familiar.

But once again we have to keep our eyes open. It is not always clear that the sociologist makes the necessary distinction between *mores* and *morals*. But these are not the same thing, and a judgment

128

on one is not the same as a judgment on the other. Every society is governed by an incalculable number of unwritten rules controlling behaviour in all kinds of situations. It is this that makes it difficult to move from one society to another. British society and American society are remarkably similar in their main outlines. But one who moves from one country to the other finds himself continually perplexed and uncertain how to act; he is quite certain to fall into a number of social pitfalls by the way. If this should befall him, the judgment of the bystanders may well be, "This fellow doesn't know how to behave"; but that does not mean, "He is wicked"; it means, "He is uncivilised, he hasn't been taught how to behave in good society." Now even the simplest societies draw a quite clear distinction between the kind of judgment which means "That kind of thing is socially unacceptable here" and the judgment which says "That was wrong," in the sense of evil and nowhere to be permitted. This is well-known to anyone who has lived in India, and is familiar with the way in which the caste system works. If you are a member of a certain caste, there are certain things you may not do—you may not marry outside the caste, you may not marry outside certain narrow limits or inside certain other narrow limits within it; if you do, you will be thrown out of the caste. But other castes have quite different rules, which are in no way binding on you. There are other things, however, which are to be condemned whenever done and by members of any caste whatsoever. These are the kind of things that make the sun stand still in his course and the stars hide their light for shame. It is true that we do not all agree exactly as to what these terrible things are. But we must not confuse two types of judgment, the distinction between which is quite clear even to simple folk.

The third strand in our complex is the widespread unwillingness to exercise a "moralistic judgment." It is not easy to give an exact definition of what is meant by this common phrase. But perhaps what it means is something like this: "Most of our judgments on other people are made in the light of a mass of inherited traditions as to right and wrong, which have been accepted without looking very closely at them, and some of which may have been due to nothing more than the prejudices of our ancestors. We tend to apply this crude and probably out-of-date yardstick to people and situations of which we have only limited knowledge. And the issuing of

129

unfavourable judgments on other people tends to minister to our own sense of self-righteousness and superiority." With a great deal of this we shall find ourselves in hearty agreement. To exercise a judgment on any fellow creature is an exceedingly delicate operation. Any conscientious parent knows that dealing with the simplest matter of family discipline makes demands on human wisdom such as render him constantly aware of his own total incapacity to meet them. We shall merely enter at this point a caveat that the joyful rejection of *moralistic* judgments must not be allowed to exclude the possibility of genuinely *moral* judgment.

Closely allied to this last point is the now famous permissiveness of the psychiatrist. It is not the business of the psychiatrist to pass a moral judgment, still less a moral condemnation. He is there to understand and to help his patient to understand himself. In order to do this, he must maintain an attitude of calm, of sympathy, of neutrality. This is his job. This does not mean, as is sometimes unfairly supposed, that the psychiatrist himself has no moral standards. He may himself be deeply concerned with moral and religious problems. It may be part of his task to help the patient to pass a moral judgment on himself and his actions. But he must keep his own views most strictly in the background; he must impose nothing, otherwise he will be defeating his own chief purpose of giving the patient back his freedom as a man.

So we come finally to the mood of the existentialist. The existentialist is the man who has almost professionally rejected traditional morality. Morality can never be anything but a set of generalisations. But the business of a man is to decide and to act in this particular instant, which is unlike any that has ever existed before, and any that will ever exist again. Therefore it is an illusion to suppose that anything that has ever happened before can give him useful guidance. He must make his own morality as he goes along. He lives perpetually in the existential moment of decision. As will become clear later in the chapter, this is an attitude which we shall go a very long way to defend. The only question that arises at this point is whether the man who has made so complete a sweep of traditional morality and insists on having his own, which is valid for him and may not be valid for anyone else, may not become incapable of living in any society whatsoever, and may not end by

130

repudiating the principle from which this chapter started, the absolute reality of personal relationships, and their necessity for any human existence worthy the name.

All relativistic views in one way or another seem to imply a denial of any absolute sense of the words right and wrong. Things may be socially acceptable, or socially advantageous. They may appear right to me, and therefore I should probably follow them. But if something else seems right to someone else, he should have equal liberty to act as seems good to him. But that the word right should mean "right at all times for all people in all circumstances", and that wrong should mean "wrong for all people at all times and in all circumstances"—that is in many quarters most unacceptable doctrine today.

And yet, though we may live in a relativistic world, most of us do find it difficult to avoid the use of the words good and bad, right and wrong, in a sense which, if we analyse it, shows that we think that we know what these words really mean, and that we are using them in relation to an absolute standard of reference.

Many of us would find it hard to give a clear definition of what we mean by justice. It is interesting that we all have, by contrast, so immediate, clear, and definite a sense for injustice. This is true of the simplest people, as I have observed in India. The outcaste has very few rights, but he has some. If these are violated by some member of a higher caste, his whole being flames with the sense of having been wronged; he will throw up his hands to heaven and say, "He *ought* not to have done it"—or, rather, in the picturesque and vivid forms of his own language, he will probably put it as a question, "May he do such a thing?" Now he does not mean simply that he has been hurt and that his particular interests have been injured. Simple man as he is, he means that the world has been made in a certain way, that the man who has wronged him has gone against the order of the world, and that, if everyone acted in that way, the world just could not go on at all.*

We meet similar reactions in rather different spheres. At the crisis

---

*The simple man is unlikely to know that he is re-stating in his own words a fundamental principle of Indian thought, which goes right back to the Rig Veda (c. 1000 B.C.)— there is a *rta*, an order of the world, which not even the gods may violate.

of World War II, Mr. Churchill in one of his great orations, exhausting the rich resources of the English dictionary, reached the height of rhetorical fervour in describing Hitler as "that bad man." Mr. Churchill did not mean that at that particular moment of history the interests of Britain were being threatened by the strength of Germany, and that it would be inconvenient for Britain if Hitler were to win the war. He was talking in terms of values and value judgments. He meant that there are certain things of universal significance, some of which over the centuries have in a measure become incorporated in the life of Europe—respect for human life, for truth, for freedom—that all these things were being menaced by a dictator, that they could be lost, and that once lost, the recovery of them would be very difficult. The general view of mankind seems to be that at that moment Mr. Churchill was talking sense.

It is, of course, quite true that we all tend to spread a veil of moral rectitude over our own desires and feelings, that we speak of good and bad when what we really mean is what suits us or what meets with the general approval of the society in which we have been brought up. But that is not the whole story. Few of us can live very long without encountering situations in which demands are made upon us in terms quite different from those of self-interest or conformity. Very ordinary people on occasion are heard to make remarks such as, "I would rather die than do that," as, for instance, when invited to sign their name to a statement which they know to be false. This might be thought to be merely a rhetorical way of speaking—except for the fact that so many men and women in our lifetime have died rather than do what they thought to be evil. If "good" and "bad" have no more than a relative and social significance, this is no doubt a very ridiculous thing to do. But on the whole most people seem to be glad that there are men and women in the world who value something else even more highly than their most precious possession, their life.

This habit of choosing "death rather than dishonour" drives us to the question, which can no longer be evaded—when we speak in terms of right or wrong, responsibility and obligation, are we dealing simply with something that man has invented for his own convenience, or are we discovering something that is really there, as much a part of reality as carbon and oxygen? Some pages back we

132

spoke of "deeds that make the stars hide their light." This picturesque expression was deliberately chosen to draw attention in advance to the question that we now ask in plain prose. Are right and wrong just another example of the pathetic fallacy? The disappointed lover feels that the heavens are weeping in sympathy with his sorrow. Are right and wrong just ideas that we have generalised and imposed on the whole universe, though really they have no existence outside our own imaginations? Is the world made in a particular way, of which right and wrong are parts, or is it not? Is the man who dies rather than do what he believes to be evil acting more *really* than the man in an underground resistance movement who betrays his comrade in order to save his own life?

Clearly we cannot produce logical or demonstrative arguments in favour of either side of the case. All that can be done is to indicate certain possibilities; the rest must be decided "existentially" by personal experiment. And we have to start rather a long way back from the immediate question of whether I shall tell a lie today to suit my own convenience, or whether I shall tell the truth and shame the devil.

What first presents itself to man as reality (though philosophers regard this as a very naive attitude) is the visible world about him; he feels himself to be part of that world. Modern science has at many points confirmed that view. Man is a product of that mysterious process which we are generally agreed in calling evolution. Eighty years ago, scientists presented us with a terrifying picture of the process. Nature was red in tooth and claw, the whole of life was the struggle for existence, every man for himself and devil take the hindmost. The eminent English scientist T. H. Huxley, wishing to defend the ethical virtues of gentleness and mutual service, could find no way to do so except to say that in order to be truly human we must defend these things, though we know that they are contrary to the general tendency of nature and in the end will be swept away in the universal struggle. Today our biologists give us a rather different picture. They point out that co-operation is at least as much a law of the natural world as conflict. At a very low level of life, species begin to learn to organise themselves as groups for mutual protection and help. At quite an early stage of evolution the instinct of a mother to sacrifice herself for the sake of her young can be

133

observed. As we move upwards to the level of the higher animals, it is those species which have developed the greatest awareness, the greatest sensitiveness, the greatest capacity for fellowship and for suffering, which seem to have the best chance of survival in the world. On the animal level we would perhaps hesitate to describe these qualities as moral; what we call instinct plays a larger part in them than conscious and deliberate choice; but perhaps they are the natural material out of which those qualities which among men are known as moral have been developed.

We can go a step further than this. Students of my day learnt from Professor Pringle-Pattison always to think of man as "organic to the universe." This means that, while we can learn a great deal about man from his place in nature, we also have the right to use man to interpret the universe of which he is a part. There is a great deal in the universe that we do not understand. One thing we do know about it for certain is that it is the kind of universe that is capable of producing the kind of creature called man. We must not exaggerate our own importance in this rather large universe. But we are the only creatures of our kind that have come under our observation, and we are very different from any other creature that we know. We have this curious capacity to stand back from the world and ourselves and to ask questions. One of the odd things that the universe has done has been to produce folk called ethical philosophers, who do ask these questions about good and evil, obligation and responsibility. It may be, of course, that these are meaningless questions, just noises that have no more meaning for man than the endless calling of the cuckoo in May. It may be that they are questions that have a meaning, but to which no answer can be found. But we have no right to assume that this is so. We must keep in mind the third possibility—that we have another reality to deal with besides that which is the concern of the physicists and chemists, the reality of personal relationships, and that this world of reality has its "laws," just as there are discoverable "laws" in the world of physical observation.

If we are prepared to entertain this possibility, we shall not be in the least disturbed to find that so many different views as to the nature of this other kind of reality have been held among men. It has taken us an astonishingly long time to discover elementary facts about the visible world; it was only in the nineteenth century that we began really to harness the power of electricity that lay all about us in the world, only in the twentieth that we began to master the secrets of those atoms of which we are ourselves made up. The world of personal reality is a far more complex world than that of physical reality. It is not surprising if our progress in understanding it has been extremely slow and has been marked by many deviations from the straight path of discovery. And yet in both these worlds there is the possibility of events which mark epochs, of discoveries which once made never need to be made again. We might have expected that the fact of the circulation of the blood would have been among the first discoveries of medical science—after all the hearts of us all beat at the average rate of seventy a minute. In point of fact the discovery was not made until the patient observations of Harvey in the seventeenth century turned hypothesis into certainty. His initial discovery has had to be developed in endless directions, and there are many detailed problems still unsolved. But the initial discovery, once made, stood firm, and never had to be made again. It is not logically impossible that the same thing should happen in the other world of reality, the world of personal relations and of the obligations that they involve—that once for all the principles by which that world is governed should be set forth and made plain. The claim of Christians is that this is exactly what happened in Jesus of Nazareth.

It must be made clear that this is a far more tremendous claim than that put forward hypothetically in an earlier chapter—that Jesus is the real man, the one in whom the true nature of humanity can be seen. What is here being maintained is that in him the whole structure of the universe and its meaning can be seen. That is the significance of the words, "I am the way, the truth, and the life" (John 14:6). It makes little difference to our argument whether these are exact words of Jesus himself or, as some scholars hold, the interpretation put upon his words by the writer of the Gospel. This was at the least the manner in which his followers understood his significance for the world of men. The claim is not that he *spoke* the truth, though that also is true. It is that he *is* the truth. The Greek word *aletheia* is constantly used in the sense of "reality"; that sense is often to be found in the Fourth Gospel.

135

That is its meaning here. "Look at me, and you will see the essential structure of the universe, the way in which it works, the laws by which it is held together." Clearly this is a tremendous claim. But there is no logical self-contradiction involved in it, and we may ask at least that it should not be dismissed without serious consideration.

We may note at once that, if the inner reality of the personal world is to be presented to us at all, there are great advantages in this form of presentation. What we are here offered for study is not a doctrine, but a person and a life. Of a doctrine, we may feel that we have come to the end of understanding it. Knowledge of an inanimate object may be felt to be fairly complete. But no scientist whose concern is the study of living beings at however humble a level of life will ever maintain that he has touched more than the fringe of his subject. If reality is presented to us in the form of a personal life, we too may be sure that we shall never touch more than the fringe of the subject.

Secondly, there is remarkably little in the teaching of Jesus that is conditioned or limited by the time at which it was spoken. There is surprisingly little of direct precept or injunction, nothing that could really be included under the heading "moralism." He deals almost entirely in universals (not in abstract principles, which is a very different thing). It is instructive to draw the contrast in this respect between Jesus and Muhammad. Muhammad was also a religious teacher of genius and an inspired leader of men. But, in the Koran, he laid down detailed precepts for innumerable situations in life, and many of these bear the mark of Arabia in the seventh century. Doubtless they were of great value to those who first received them, but it is only with an effort of interpretation that they can be made applicable to the whole human race. For instance, the fast of Ramazan, which requires that no food or drink be taken from sunrise to sunset, can be observed though with some hardship in countries not too far removed from the equator. It becomes more difficult in more northerly climes, and would be almost impossible to observe on the Arctic circle, if the month of Ramazan happened to coincide with June.* There are

*As Muslims observe the lunar calendar, the month of Ramazan shifts from year to year, until it has completed the round of the seasons.

136

difficulties in the application of the principles of Jesus, but they are not difficulties of this kind.

Thirdly, the guidance given is couched in such general terms that the field is left wide open for personal experiment. The danger in any system of law is that it constricts individual freedom and tends to reduce men to a type. Of course it is possible to formulate even the Gospels in terms of law. But this is to violate their true nature. Jesus said that he came to make men free, and freedom is of the essence of a true following of the Gospels, as it is of any genuinely human existence.

If then we try to do what Jesus himself never did, and sum up his understanding of the nature of reality in brief abstract propositions, what shall we find to be, according to his judgment, the pillars on which the universe rests, the universals by which all personal relations are to be governed? Perhaps they can be reduced to no more than three—truth, justice, and mercy.

A whole book could be written about each of these. All that can be attempted here is to give a brief elucidation of the sense in which the terms are used; and this is important, as the reader is likely to become confused in following later arguments unless these meanings have been clearly grasped.

Truth does not mean merely speaking the truth, though this is an important element in it. In conformity with the sense of the word that was noted above, it involves primarily that inflexible realism which is not afraid to look every situation directly in the face and to understand it in the nakedness of its inner reality. But truth in this sense involves more than intellectual understanding; it also implies a particular kind of action. The New Testament several times uses the unusual expression "doing the truth." This must mean acting in complete sincerity in unconstrained relatedness to the realities of circumstance. Obviously to act in this way often requires great courage. It may result in getting crucified, and this is what actually happened to Jesus himself.

There are also two aspects to the meaning of justice. In the first place, it means recognising and respecting the individual value and freedom of every single human being. No human being may ever be regarded simply as an instrument for the forwarding of my purposes. Each individual is to be helped to the fulness of his own freedom and integrity. This conviction is not based on any abstract idea of equality—an idea which all too often breaks down in face of the manifest inequality of human beings—but on the conviction that each individual is personally and directly related to God. This comes out most impressively in what Jesus says about little children. His words and example have probably done more than anything else in history to humanise and lighten the lot of children in the world. But this teaching is not based on any sentimental ideas about the beauty and innocence of children—small children can in fact be little pests—but on something else: "See that ye despise not one of these little ones; for I say unto you, that in heaven their angels do always behold the face of my Father which is in heaven." The Semitic form of expression may be strange to us, the meaning is quite plain: every one of these little ones is present before God, and he is directly and personally concerned about each one of them. It is here that the Christian finds the basis for the idea of mutual responsibility and also for its unlimited character; we are responsible for one another because each one is the object of the care and concern of God, and it is to him that we are responsible for the way that we treat one another.

The other aspect of justice is the certainty that offences against it will meet with their due retribution. If there is a real and self-consistent structure of the universe, of which personal relations are a part, if the world is made in one particular way and no other, then what is "right" is that which is in accordance with that structure, and what is "wrong" is that which is contrary to that structure. We are well aware of this in the physical world. We have all become aware of a number of observed sequences, which for convenience we call the laws of nature. We know very well that these do not stand being argued with; if we disregard them, we do so at our own risk, and we know fairly accurately what the consequences will be. It is the conviction of Jesus that there is a certain moral structure of the world, which in some ways (though not of course in all) is rather like the physical structure. If you go against it, sooner or later you will pay the penalty, though the nature of that penalty may be as invisible as the "law" which you have transgressed. The life of the individual is so short that this cannot always become evident; we do seem to get away with a great deal

138

more than we deserve. But in the life of nations the slow working of these laws does seem to make itself more visible. States which come to value things more than people tend to become clumsy and unmanageable. Empires which indulge in cruelty and the oppression of the weak have within them the seeds of their own inevitable destruction. Hitler thought that he was settling the future of Europe for a thousand years; actually his rule lasted for little more than a third of one generation of human life.

Mercy is a general term for the principle that the best way of living is not always that of insisting on your own rights and defending yourself. The phrase "a pound of flesh" has become proverbial, and Shylock is the unpleasant type of the man who insists to the last limit on his rights. We do not like Shylock; but what he wanted is what we all instinctively want, and nothing is harder for us than to surrender a part of what we regard as our rights or to see them disregarded by someone who thinks that he can get away with the injustice. If all selves were nicely balanced and adjusted to one another, the world would be a very pleasant place to live in. But as a matter of hard fact aggressivity is a reality. So is weakness, and the almost ineradicable tendency of the strong to override the weak and to disregard their plaint. The Bible is full of the cry of the widow, the orphan, and the stranger, and the constant affirmation that God, concerned as he is about all men, is specially concerned about those who are not able to help themselves. But mercy is needed by the strong as well as by the weak. If we all got our deserts, there would be no living for any of us. We can see that that is a good world in which justice is tempered by mercy, and in which concern for the one who has done the wrong is sometimes stronger than the desire that the uttermost farthing which he is due to pay should be extracted from him.

It is evident that life lived on the principle that the rights of others are to be more carefully safeguarded than one's own is likely to involve suffering. It is not of course laid down that in every possible situation we must yield to every manifestation of aggressiveness—that might be bad for the aggressor. All the innumerable problems of discipline in the home and in the school and in society still remain to be worked out in detail—some of them will come before us in later stages of this study. Here we are concerned only with the principle and not with exceptions or modifications. If we accept the rule that, in general, we will not stand upon our rights and we will not defend ourselves, we are certain in this world of many clashing selves to suffer. It was so in the life of Jesus. Those who accept his principle do so in the conviction that suffering is not necessarily a bad thing, that it can be turned to creative purposes, and that it is in fact one of the most vivid elements in the freedom of a genuinely human existence.

This summary of what is found in the Gospels is not set out dogmatically for submissive acceptance. It is presented as one answer to the questions with which this chapter has been dealing, as to the nature of right and wrong, responsibility and obligation. Is this claim made by Jesus that he has, or is, the answer true or false? It cannot be shown to be either by purely logical demonstration. The same kind of evidence cannot be given in favour of it as can be given for a chemical or economic theorem. It is a different kind of truth that is being handled. In the end, perhaps (unless we start from the presupposition of an infallible divine revelation, which in this book we are not doing), the answer can be given only by personal experiment. Are there any facts known to us which this proposed scheme of truth does not cover? And what happens if we seriously set out to "do the truth," to live in the kind of way that is here suggested?

Clearly it is not going to be easy to live in that way or to work out in all situations the application of these principles to our own circumstances. We still find the need of working on three levels— the great general principles; certain broad rules which for convenience can be used to cover a large number of cases; and the immediate question, "What do I do now?" But, fortunately for us, we are not left solely to our own independent working out of the theorems. Jesus, after all, was not simply a teacher who announced high theoretical doctrines. He was a man, who also had to live in this world surrounded by a large variety of other selves and involved in most complex relations with them. How did he manage these problems of relationship? How did he succeed in combining relatedness with his own independence? How did he express, in personal dealings with all kinds of men and women, his own sense of unlimited obligation to all? To a large extent this is what the Gospels are about. Our next step will be to use them as a clue and, by considering the way in which one man handled these problems, perhaps to find guidance for our own steps as we try to find our own way about the complex world of relationships in society.

VI The Courteous Rebel

WE HAVE TO LIVE with other people; but other people are so difficult to live with. All the problems of "maladjusted" people are ultimately problems inside themselves; but in the great majority of cases the source of the trouble or one of the chief causes of it are relationships with other people that have gone wrong or have never been what they should be. What ought relationships with other people to be? And if they have gone wrong, how do we bring them back to where they ought to be?

The first point to bear in mind is that we do not begin life as individuals. As sociologists have rightly pointed out, if you begin with one you can never get as far as two. If you start with the idea of two entirely separate individuals, it is very difficult to understand how relationships between them can ever become possible. But in fact we do not start as individuals; we start as members of a group, usually a group of at least three members—two parents and a child. To begin with we are so completely members of that group, so identified with it, that there can hardly be any word as yet of any individual experience or point of view. In the West, we now tend to concentrate this experience in the tiny house, where the group consists only of parents and one or two children. Over the greater part of the world the pattern is still that of the joint family, with a splendid multiplicity of grandparents, aunts, and cousins in all sorts of degrees of relationship. This is a much more healthy way of living; a certain reduction in the intensity of feelings is compensated for by the far greater variety of relation-

142

ships that is being experienced all the time. But whatever the type of family, the primary task of the growing child is to become a self, an "I," to become emancipated from this mass of life and affection that clings around him. The dawn of individual self-consciousness and the problems that beset it is one of the major themes of child psychology. But the process of emancipation has to go on far beyond childhood, and perhaps in some of us is never completed.

If we like brief concise formulations, we may say that the process is that from the "given" to the "willed" community. The first community in which we live is one that we had no hand in choosing; it was just given to us by the accident that we were born into that particular family. We cannot live without other people and remain human; human life is just life in community. To grow up means growth in capacity to choose the community in which we live. Now it may quite well be that the people who make up the willed community are the same as those who make up the given community. We may well choose to live within our families because we find that we like the people there. But the two attitudes are completely different. Merely to acquiesce in a community because it happens to be there is a kind of slavery. To choose it as our own because we wish to live within it is a declaration of freedom.

The same point can be put rather more psychologically and in a different connection by saying that emancipation is synonymous with progress from the mother to the mate. There is nothing in the world about which we have less choice than our mother. In Western society, we are supposed to have some say in the choice of a mate. The exercise of this choice is one of the signs of development to maturity.

Because Jesus was a real person, we can trace in his experience the development of this personal freedom, both in his relationships with his family and in the wider field of the nation and of the race to which he belonged.

Concerning his assertion of freedom in relation to his family we have only a few hints, but these are very significant. On one occasion his family, agitated by the strange mission that he was engaged in and by the dangers that he might be bringing on

143

himself, came to fetch him home. His quiet comment was, "Whoever shall do the will of God, the same is my brother and sister and mother." There is no denial of the reality of the family relationship; there is an affirmation that its claims must not be made absolute; a man may have more important things to do (such as going to fight his country's battles) before which the claims of the family must for the time being at least recede into the background.

The same combination of loyalty and independence is to be found in the relations of Jesus with his mother. No student of the Gospels has ever doubted that there was a relationship of peculiar depth and tenderness between them. Mary is present at almost all the critical moments in the life of Jesus, and at the last she is found standing by the cross. But loyalty and the firm but gentle assertion of personal independence are not found to be incompatible. Mary has her sphere, the sphere of intimate personal relationships; but there is another sphere, that of his ministry, with which she has nothing to do. The words of Jesus, as they run in the traditional English translations, "Woman, what have I to do with thee?" sound much harsher than they do in the Greek; they are, nevertheless, a clear indication of the borders of the several spheres. This may have been a hard lesson for Mary to learn, as it has been for many other mothers; but it is one that mothers have to learn if sons are ever to grow up.

Of the relations between Jesus and his nation we have much fuller evidence, and the picture is much more complex.

First, we note that his life was lived in a quite definite historical situation. He was a Jew and never pretended to be anything else. He criticised his people but never tried to separate himself from them. He was conscious that he had a universal mission, but never doubted that this must be inaugurated in the place and in the situation in which he found himself. He works on the principle that we have already encountered—that the universal can best express itself in the individual, and that a drama worked out on a small and local stage may none the less be of significance to the entire human race.

Secondly, though Jesus is at certain points the foe of tradition, he never takes the view that tradition is a bad thing in itself. Here surely he is right.

Tradition in the life of a community is rather like habit in the life of an individual. If we had to think precisely of everything that we have to do and did it deliberately, we should be exhausted before half the day was through. It is said that if you try to walk down a flight of stairs calculating exactly where you will put your foot on each step, you are likely to land in a heap at the bottom with a broken leg; if you walk without thinking, you will arrive safely at journey's end. Happily we all learn by habit to do a great many things, even skilled operations like shaving with a cutthroat razor, almost without thinking about them. It is this economy of effort in routine affairs that makes it possible to concentrate our minds for part of the time on things that cannot be done with less than full attention. Similarly, in the life of any community, there are countless things that can be done without effort just because they are done the same way every day. The housewife about to lay the table does not have to stop to think where things should go except on very special occasions; they always go in the same place. In other countries they may do things differently; this may not even be the best way of doing them; but just the fact that it is the way we always do them here saves an enormous amount of time and thought and effort.

Tradition in the life of a people preserves for it the discoveries of the past and, if tradition is used in the right way, sets its energies free for new discoveries and new adventures of living. If every generation had to start out afresh to make every discovery that has ever been made, there could be no progress in knowledge or in anything else. We shall later defend our right to independence in relation to tradition; it is important not to overlook the point that such independence can be most profitably exercised within the framework of a general acceptance of tradition.

In general Jesus was loyal to the traditions of his people. And yet he was the perfect example of the courteous rebel. How this could be, we shall understand only if we distinguish three separate strands in his attitude to the past.

For one part of the traditions of the past he had nothing but enthusiastic acceptance. He read the Old Testament with inde-

145

pendence and with an imaginative mind. At certain points he criticised it as making concessions to the hardness of men's hearts. At many points he went beyond it in his own teaching. But for the most part he accepted its revelation of God as true. This God, the Creator of all things, righteous, patient, merciful, compassionate, as he is depicted in the pages of the prophets, was the God he knew himself in his own experience. This was the foundation of his teaching. This was reality on which he could build.

Many parts of the tradition he was prepared to accept without objection. Even though there might be no deep moral principle underlying certain precepts, equally there was no special point in disregarding them, and courtesy and a reasonable conformity might demand that they should be fulfilled. This comes out specially in the little episode of paying the Temple tax (Matt. 17:24–27). Jesus knew well that within a few years the Temple would be destroyed and that the religion of the spirit which he had come to bring in would need no such visible centre. But at the moment there was no point in starting controversy about the question; it was better that the tax should be paid.

There were other points, however, at which Jesus did come violently into conflict with the traditions of his people as interpreted by their leaders. The Jews were living under a system of legalism. Law, when it is true to itself, is as it were an expression in shorthand of the way in which people must learn to treat one another if they are to manage to live together. We keep the laws most of the time because we see that making life together possible is the principal purpose for which they exist. Law in this sense is an almost direct transcript from life. But legalism is the expression of something very different—the working out of first principles to cover all possible cases. This process, technically called casuistry, also has its uses, provided that it is kept within its proper limits. Among the Jews in the time of Jesus legalism had run riot, and the life of the people was controlled in every direction by innumerable regulations. Against all this Jesus, the champion of human freedom and of the fulness of human existence, was naturally in rebellion, and that on three grounds. First, because it set unnatural limits to the spontaneity of human freedom to live and to experiment. Secondly, because by making a virtue of the mere keeping of regulations, it obscured the real nature of the obligations between man and man and between man and God. Thirdly, because the application of legal rules without any regard for changed situations can result in positive cruelty. Jesus himself cites the possibility under Jewish law, as it was then understood, for a man to repudiate his duties to his parents under the excuse of a higher duty to God.

Jesus is a rebel, but he is always a courteous and constructive rebel. He is a revolutionary. Any attempt by either church or state to take his teachings seriously has always had most revolutionary consequences. But it is important to note the method that he follows and the kind of revolution that he is concerned to introduce. He never incites his followers to mass disobedience to the local authorities. He starts no campaign of defiance of the existing order. He will not countenance any kind of violence, knowing well that violence always leads to more violence and that high ideals can easily disappear in the stress of conflict. His method of revolution is both more subtle and more effective than that followed by most of the revolutionaries of this world.

In the first place, he called people back to the consideration of basic realities. He did not deny the validity of the ancient laws but showed that the real keeping of them depended much more upon motive than upon action. What matters is not so much the insulting word or the blow as the angry thought, the hatred, of which these are the outward expression. What matters is not so much the unchaste action as the lustful thoughts that have been allowed to dwell in the mind and to prepare it for the action. For these things God will bring men into judgment. The acute psychologist may at this point find in the teachings of Jesus a direct anticipation of one cardinal point in his own doctrines. Today we know well that a man's actions do not of themselves serve as an adequate criterion by which the man himself can be judged. So many of our actions are of the pattern of conditioned reflexes or are influenced by rationalisations of motives that we would prefer not to acknowledge to ourselves. We understand better perhaps than any earlier generation that men cannot be set right by the kind of discipline that regulates their actions, but

147

only by the cleansing and healing process that puts their thoughts and emotions in order.

Secondly, Jesus took the existing practices and filled them with new meaning. The central point of his controversy with the leaders of the Jews was the observance of the Sabbath day. This may seem to us rather trivial, and it takes imagination to realise that it was to the Jews a matter of tremendous significance. What was the controversy all about? It is important to note that Jesus did not deny the value of the Sabbath. He regularly attended the synagogue worship on the Sabbath day. He kept most of the rules by which it was safeguarded. But he did not allow his freedom of action to be limited by these rules, and defended himself by maintaining that his people were not keeping the day in the way that had been originally intended. He asked the radical question, What is the Sabbath for? The Jews kept it with reference to the past, to the ending of the work of creation. That meant that their attitude was primarily negative—the central point in the keeping of the Sabbath is the cessation of all work. This was defined in most detailed rules—that no fire must be lighted on the Sabbath day, that a man must not walk more than a certain number of paces, and so on. Jesus gave the day a forward-looking significance; it is a joyful anticipation of the end of all things, when all God's purposes in the world have been brought to a conclusion; then rest will really begin. But until that time comes, there is work to be done: "My Father worketh until now, and I work." The work that needs above all to be done is the restoration of human nature to its true and normal working; and therefore to heal on the Sabbath day, so far from being a violation of the holiness of the day, is the very best possible way of keeping it. Clearly the conflict on this point was in a sense only symbolic; what lent it its significance and its intensity was the fact that behind the clashing viewpoints lay differing understandings of the nature of reality, of man, and of God.

We have said that Jesus was always the courteous rebel. This may seem hard to square with the violence of his denunciations of the scribes and Pharisees, especially as these are recorded in Matthew's Gospel. These leaders are frequently referred to as hypocrites. This does not mean that they were consciously and de-

148

liberately insincere; probably the contrary is true—they were genuine, if hard, in their sincerity. But Jesus the realist is troubled by the way in which they have allowed their system to come between them and reality; as a result of loyal adherence to their system, they can no longer see things as they really are. The whole of the ministry of Jesus is filled with an urgency, an intensity, of trying to get men to see things in their stark reality. There was a political aspect to this. He could see with dreadful clearness the doom that his people were preparing for themselves, and that would certainly come upon them, if they did not change their ways. And yet the leaders who ought to have seen were apparently blind to the storms that were brewing. He was right. Exactly what he foresaw happened; the Jews rose in bitter rebellion against the Romans, the Romans came and burnt their city, and that was the end of the national existence of the Jews. But there was also a personal urgency, related to the mission with which he believed himself to have been entrusted. The violence of the language of Jesus is a measure of the unwillingness of those who have become enmeshed in a system to emerge from it and once again to look upon the world as it is. He is giving them their last chance, a chance which for the most part they will not take.

What all this adds up to is the probability that even the courteous rebel will get crucified. When a system is all-important, in church or state, it is likely that the man who criticises any part of it will be branded heretic or traitor, and those who burn or crucify him will congratulate themselves on their success as defenders of the *status quo*. From their own point of view they are quite right. We experience life as a whole. We can analyse it under different aspects—political, social, economic, religious, and so on. But in point of fact all these things hold together in one indivisible whole. It may well seem that, if one part is threatened, the whole will come toppling down. The part that is called in question may seem quite small and insignificant; but if this once begins, who is to say where it is to stop? "Stone dead hath no fellow."

And yet perhaps the most important people in history are the courteous rebels. They are the mature and creative people. Nowhere is the balanced maturity of Jesus more evident than in the crisis of the crucifixion. He is not the hot-tempered and impetuous

149

rebel. His is not the independence of the isolationist, of the man who dislikes his fellows and feels that he can get on better without them. Nor is this the independence of the Stoic, who retreats into his ivory tower and refuses to admit that the world and the suffering that it may cause can really touch him. Jesus lived in the midst of his people, and was convinced that everything he did was for their sake. His independence is made up of at least four factors—unqualified reverence for all that was good and true in the past; willingness to yield general obedience to the constituted order of society; respect and consideration for the feelings of others; but at the same time an uncompromising maintenance of his right to his own vision of reality, and of his right to criticise the existing order in the light of that vision.

It is unlikely that we shall attain to the maturity of Jesus. His was in some ways an exceptional path, and his life and death were charged with a fulness of meaning that perhaps does not necessarily attach to ours. Still, if we are to become genuinely human, the path that we must follow is the one that he has traced for us. This may seem a tall order, and we may well feel a little doubtful of our capacity to follow. But, as John Bunyan pithily remarked in *Pilgrim's Progress*, "The way's the way, and there an end."

In our study of Jesus in society and of his mature independence in relation to it, we passed rapidly over the question of the family, and gave most of our space to his attitude to the traditions and standards of society on the larger scale. Now that we are to consider the application to ourselves of the principles that we have discovered in the Gospels, we shall follow the reverse emphasis and shall give more space to the problems of dependence and independence in the family sphere. There are good reasons for doing this. Family experience is something that is available to us all, and every statement can be checked in the light of what we have ourselves passed through. All the problems involved in the relationships of human beings who have to live together are present in the family, in limited space and in peculiar intensity. And recent study has shown with particular clarity that our attitudes in the relationships of larger communities and societies are likely to bear the stamp of the kind of adjustment—or maladjustment—that has resulted from our experiences in the family. *The Child in the Family*

The human child in the first stages of its existence is totally dependent for its existence on the family. It is thrust into this miniature world with possibilities of love and hate, of rivalry and service, of self-assertion and self-giving, that are frightening in their intensity even in the most conventional and conservative of milieus. Fortunately, human nature is in general pretty tough and can endure a good deal of knocking about without taking serious harm. But many of the injuries that later reveal themselves can be traced back to relationships that have gone astray in these first stages of existence.

In this little world the parents move as omnipotent and all-knowing deities. It is not only that their physical presence is large and fills the child's horizon. The parents bring with them a strange aura of inherited tradition—ideas, prejudices, ways of doing things, half-thought-out, accepted without question, a queer jumble of shrewd practical sense and of absurdity. To all this the child also falls heir and absorbs it unconsciously through every pore. Every family has its own *mystique* of family living—of things that are done this way and not any other way, of things that are done and not done, of private jokes that no one outside the family can share, of special phrases and forms of speech. All these things are immensely valuable. They make every family different from any other family. They leave their impress on our way of looking at things and our way of doing things to the very end of our lives. All these trivial things make up the tradition of the family, its continuity and its unity. And yet, if we are ever to be real persons, it is essential that we should be completely emancipated in spirit from the family and all its traditions. The family is the chrysalis within which up to a certain point human personality can be formed; but personality cannot reach its fulness, any more than a caterpillar can become a butterfly, without the decisive transition of emergence from the chrysalis.

If all parents were wise and all children were sensible, this emergence from dependence into freedom should take place with very little difficulty, simply as the result of the natural process of growth and adjustment. But we are not all as perfect as we should like to be, and families are not always all that they should be. The process of physical birth often has about it a traumatic element; the rebirth of the child into the world of adult freedom can also take on a traumatic and even tragic quality, where parents pull too hard in one direction and the child of necessity has to pull too hard in the other.

For in much human love there is an element of possessiveness, often concealed under many layers of genuine devotion. Where this element exists, it is possible for parents to impose upon their children multiple forms of blackmail, each of which sets a barrier in the way of development to full and independent freedom.

The first and most obvious is the physical blackmail of mere strength and size. This is not to be identified simply with the fear of punishment, though this may be part of it. It is just the fact that, when the child is small, it can be picked up and put where it does not want to be. What is imposed upon it is the feeling of helplessness in the face of force too great for it to resist.

The second form is economic blackmail. Most adults have forgotten how acute this can be, and how bitter the restrictions that economic dependence can impose on freedom. This is far less felt among simple peoples and in the so-called working class, where financial independence arrives much earlier than in the so-called higher ranks of society. It is less felt in America, where children very early begin to earn their own spending money, than in Britain, where regular earning only begins at a later stage of existence. But such spending money does not really go very far. The parents can still exercise the threat of depriving the child of longed-for pleasures or even of cutting off the resources that will make possible a much desired career.

The third form of blackmail is moral. The child at first accepts implicitly and without criticism the standards of conduct that are currently approved in the family and in the society of which it forms part. These standards are regarded as sacrosanct and reinforced by sanctions which are sometimes all the more terrifying for their vagueness. Hints may be dropped of divine displeasure if certain rules are broken or certain taboos infringed. Signs of disapproval, without a single word spoken, can be very daunting to a child. The suggestion or the threat of the withdrawal of love if a child continues to be "naughty," and the horrifying idea of exclusion from the warmth and fellowship of the world of love which accompanies it, can exercise a far stronger tyranny upon the child mind than any direct and immediate punishment.

The last form of blackmail is the emotional. We have already 4 noted the harm that can be done when emotion is imported into family situations where it does not belong and emotional demands are made upon the child that it cannot meet. Here we are dealing with a slightly different problem. The child or the younger person can be faced with the situation in which the exercise of freedom becomes identified with guilt—the guilt of hurting or injuring the parents whose love has made the home, and to love and honour whom is evidently the first duty of the child. It is natural that a father should hope that his only son will follow him in his profession. It is equally natural that the son should have other ideas about his future. How easily a mother can slip in a phrase such as, "Of course you must choose for yourself; but it will break your father's heart if you go off on your own like this." How often it happens that a young man is driven by the fear of guilt to accept for life a profession for which he knows himself to be wholly unsuited. In Western society marriages are no longer arranged by the parents, as they were until a comparatively recent date. But a father can still say, "You must make up your own mind; but it will break your mother's heart if you marry that girl." It may seem noble to surrender the impulse of the heart for the sake of a mother's feelings; but equally it may be the very worst thing that a young man could possibly do.

To become a real person is a costly business, and part of the price that has to be paid is that of emancipation, at whatever cost, from all these forms of blackmail, or to put it in other terms, from every trace of childish dependence on the family and its traditions. The cost may be very high. In some cases freedom can be attained only by literal separation from the family and a completely fresh start elsewhere. It is no less true that a genuinely fresh start has to be made even when the evolution proceeds perfectly peacefully within the bosom of the family. The affection that a young man or woman can offer to parents and others of the older generation is wholly different from the emotional relationship of a dependent child to those on whom it is emotionally dependent. One form of affection cannot really coexist with the other. The adult relationship is a fine and precious thing and can become permanent as the earlier dependent affection never can or should be. But if it is to come into existence, there is a point of no return to be passed. The dependent child must cease to exist in order that the free independent adult may come into being.

In theory parents want their children to grow up. In practice it is not always by any means easy for the children to escape from the world of blackmail.

From the first two forms of blackmail the escape is comparatively easy. By the end of adolescence children are as big as their parents, and physical control of the old type is no longer possible. In early manhood or womanhood economic independence has generally been secured. It is with the other two that the difficulties may become menacingly great.

It is never easy to break free from moral ideas or prejudices that have been absorbed in early childhood, and are reinforced by all kinds of associations on the deeper levels of consciousness. They may acquire the compulsive force of taboos as these are felt in primitive society. This is familiar to anyone brought up in an atmosphere in which the use of alcohol is unknown and strongly condemned. The first drink is an experience of intense moral confusion. It is not only the fear of the moral disapproval of others that is involved, though this may also be a factor, if I take to drinking while still living in a mainly prohibitionist society. The real conflict is interior. If I have instinctively and emotionally accepted since childhood the view that all drinking is wrong, even though I may have reasoned myself out of this attitude the emotional associations may still be there and may produce a very uncomfortable and unwelcome feeling of guilt every time I transgress the law which governed my childhood.

Still more difficult is emancipation from the emotional tyranny that parents can impose. On general principles it is wrong to hurt people's feelings. All the more must it seem wrong to hurt those of whose love and devotion to their children there can be no doubt. But we have said that the emancipation must be won at whatever cost; and sometimes the cost may be precisely that of wounding, knowingly and deliberately, those whom at almost any cost one would wish not to wound. It may happen that parents are making demands which they have no right to make. Then woe betide the child who accedes to those demands. It may be that parents are setting their feelings astride the child's path to freedom. Then it is their fault and no one else's if those feelings have to be hurt. They may try to imprison children within feelings of guilt over disobedience to the parental will. But if it is the parental will that is itself at fault, then no guilt can be involved in disobedience. This is hard doctrine. But freedom cannot be easily won and cannot be easily maintained. In human society, as we have made it, the way to adult manhood is almost necessarily hard and steep.

If this hard way is not taken, there are two other possibilities of adjustment.

The first is that of mere acquiescence in things as they are, mere acceptance of tradition and its requirements. The rebel will no longer asserts itself. Peace and harmony have been restored, and there is nothing left except to live happily ever after. Unquestionably this solution can be accompanied by a good deal of peace and happiness. But such a surrender so frequently results in continuing emotional immaturity that the sympathetic observer may be inclined to think, and with good reason, that the supposed solution is in reality no solution at all.

The second possibility is that of outward conformity accompanied by inner rebellion. It is hard to imagine any situation more favourable to the production or development of neurosis. The rebellion never expresses itself in act, though it may sometimes find its way out in explosions of apparently pointless rage. It feeds on its own inner resentments and discontents; and the apparently peaceful outward adjustment merely masks the reality of unresolved tensions.

The way of freedom is the only way to maturity and to real mental health.

It must not be supposed that all parents are exercising all the forms of blackmail listed above, or that all relationships between parents and children are of this traumatic type. The art of being a parent is an exceedingly difficult one. The marvel is not that some make a mess of it but that so many, in spite of the difficulties, manage to bring it off so astonishingly well. But our analysis of possible situations may have served to indicate that there are certain ways in which parents, if they have a right understanding of the problem, can immensely help their children in their difficult problem of growing up.

The abandonment of every attempt to exercise discipline is not one of these ways. All recent research has emphasised the truth that children need a stable framework within which to grow. What is set up by the parents may not be the best possible framework, but even an imperfect structure is better than none. This need continues through adolescence; just because these years of growth are accompanied by so much inner stress, a stable order within which to live is needed in this period almost more than at any other time. No parent can ever hope to find the perfect balance between authority and liberty within the home; it is possible to accept the fact that both in due proportion are necessary.

There appear to be four main ways in which parents can positively help their children forward to a mature and independent existence.

The first is a steady refusal of any pretence of omniscience. The child starts by imagining that its parents know everything. It is bound to be a shock when first this idea of their omniscience becomes untenable; something in the child's universe that seemed stable and assured has suddenly become shifting and uncertain. The parents can help a great deal to mitigate the shock, if from the start they accept and make plain to the children the evident fact of their own ignorance of a great many things and their willingness to learn even from their own children. The fatal attitude is that of, "We thought all these things out a long time ago; why cannot you accept the findings of our wisdom?" If it is possible to make the children feel from a very early age that they are engaged with their parents in a fellowship of learning, many points of possible strain and tension can be avoided.

Secondly, it helps immensely if parents can make it plain that they expect obedience to the law of the home because they themselves are obedient to the law. This can quite well be worked out in independence of any system of religious belief, provided that there is genuine acceptance of the validity of certain moral principles; but it is at this point that Christian faith presents itself as the most creative of all factors in family life. Christian parents believe that the world has been made in one particular way and no other and that happiness is to be found in acceptance of that way. They know that their own understanding of that way is imperfect, and that their best efforts to live according to it fall very far short of what they themselves would desire. But if the law of Christ is accepted as the law of the home and the parents regard themselves as equally subject with their children to that law, then family order and discipline are to a large extent freed from that arbitrariness and capriciousness which are likely to characterise them if they are dependent on nothing but the impulses, the whims, and the prejudices of the parents. It may be that in time the children will come to have a different understanding of the law of the world and to reject that to which their parents were attached. It is unlikely that they will look back with anything but gratitude if they have been brought up in the atmosphere of fellowship in obedience to a law which does not derive its authority from men's ideas.

It follows upon this that parents must at all times be prepared to admit themselves in the wrong. I recall the profound impression made upon my mind in early childhood, when a grown-up member of the family apologised to me for what was in itself only a trifling act of discourtesy. This was something that I had supposed could never happen. The idea that even a child has rights, which grown-ups must not infringe, and which in certain circumstances it may assert against the grown-ups, was quite new. But the principle, once introduced, lays the foundation for a self-respect and independence which must in the end produce a peaceful revolution in family relationships.

Fourthly, it must be made clear as early as possible that honest criticism involves neither guilt nor disloyalty. Family post-mortems on every conceivable subject are not to be encouraged, and at times decisions have to be taken over the heads of the children. But it is characteristic of adult friendship that it can thrive on very considerable differences of opinion, and even of principle. There is no reason why the same should not be true at a much earlier stage and between the generations.

When these and similar precautions are observed, it is surprising how quickly a new kind of fellowship can take the place of tension. It is certain that there will be periods of tension within the family; these generally begin with the onset of adolescence but may, of course, appear much earlier. But recent and very careful research suggests that not later than at the age of fourteen or fifteen, the adolescent begins to discover that it is quite a good idea to have parents, and is prepared to enter into a new relationship with them that is marked by appreciation and genuine affection combined with firm insistence that they must recognise that he is no longer a child. This is not regression to infantile dependence; it is a willed and chosen fellowship, accepted because at that stage it satisfies in the right way the unfailing human need for fellowship and does not prejudice the independence which the growing personality requires.

The new attitude is likely to combine general loyalty with a considerable amount of detachment. The growing boy or girl may find much to commend in the life of the home—its order, its security, its sense of mutual responsibility. But at the same time there is likely to be disagreement on a great many subjects—it would be a sad thing if the generations found no subjects on which to disagree—tempered by a willingness to discuss the differences rationally and without heat. There will probably be a desire to change certain things, though this cannot always be achieved; the education of parents by their children, though highly important, is a slower and more difficult process than the education of children by their parents. There are likely to be moments of exasperation. Certain family traditions and taboos may be regarded as rather absurd and irritating and yet be accepted without rancour as one of the necessary conditions of fellowship. In the home in which I grew up, tobacco was prohibited in the dining room and drawing room—the very words speak of a more spacious and now vanished age; it would have been boorish discourtesy on the part of the young men of the family to attempt to overthrow a rule which the parents had a perfect right to establish in their own home. No human relationships are ever perfectly easy. But if there are on both sides courtesy and humour, tolerance and a willingness for quiet self-criticism, this stage of existence can be wonderfully stimulating to both parents and children and can make a contribution of the highest importance to the development of a sane, balanced, adult, independent personal existence.

It has to be recognised with regret that there are many families in which these ideal conditions do not exist. What is to be done when young people are growing up in a situation that tends to thwart rather than to promote the development of their freedom? The word that is often used in this connection is "adaptation," and with good reason, since, if people cannot be taken right out of an unfavourable situation, they must learn to live with it and within it. But adaptation must never be understood in the sense either of acquiescence or of approval. If a situation is wrong, it is wrong, and there must be no pretence. It is evident to anyone with experience of the problems of young people today that what a great many of them need is to be taught how to rebel. Rebellion, whether of the violent kind that wants to break everything up or of the sullen kind that ungraciously submits, is useless and harmful. What is required is to learn how to be the courteous and constructive rebel after the pattern of Jesus Christ. To see that a situation is wrong and yet to be prepared to live with it and to suffer under it; very gently and courteously to detach oneself from its emotional control; very gently and courteously to affirm one's own personality and independence; to repudiate all false ideas of guilt; to recognise the righteousness and necessity of rebellion; and yet to retain real affection for those who, perhaps unconsciously, have done and are doing the wrong—these are hard lessons to learn. But there is no other road to the recovery of growth and mental balance when these have been threatened or impaired by an unfavourable emotional situation.

At this point there is a natural transition from the problems of the home and of the family to the parallel problems that arise in the relationships between the individual and the larger society by which he is surrounded.

Maladjustment is one of the major problems of the society in which we live. It is often taken as almost axiomatic that the aim

159

of education, and of that kind of re-education which is the task of the psychiatrist, is to make people socially adapted. In so far as a society is good rather than bad, just rather than unjust, this is good and reasonable; but it leaves a major question unanswered. Is it good that people should be adapted to a society if that society itself is inhuman or is based on a refusal to recognise certain essential human values? If a man cannot escape from the society in which he lives, then he must learn to live within it and to that extent must learn to adapt himself to it. But if this simply means that he accepts its standards and values as just and right and true, or at least unalterable, he may have committed the inner treachery of the abandonment of that right to an independent moral judgment which is part of the equipment of every adult citizen. If he lives in a state of smouldering and ineffective resentment, he will almost certainly make himself ill. Are we not here once again confronted by the truth that, in many situations, the only healthy and adult attitude is that of the courteous and constructive rebel? If so, how should this principle work itself out in practice?

As in the family, so in the larger world of the community and the nation we are heirs to an extraordinary jumble of ideas, traditions, and so-called principles; the myths and traditions of our nation, glorified and exalted in time of war to an almost hysterical patriotism; the *mores* of the particular stratum of society to which we belong; the taboos and prejudices of a particular social group. All these things are impressed upon the conscious and less than conscious levels of our being by the kind of education we have received in school, through the daily papers, by the kind of conversations we heard in early life, by the unspoken attitudes and criticisms of those with whom we are brought into contact. And all this tends to be uncritically accepted and taken into ourselves; it becomes part of us as we become part of the society in which we have lived. If we have to carry the weight of all this all our lives, what hope is there of any genuinely personal existence?

It is clear once again that the road to maturity is the gradual emancipation of ourselves, intellectually and emotionally, from our own past. It goes without saying that this is an extremely difficult task. Our freedom is much more limited than we imagine. We are far more made up of prejudice and preconception than we suppose. We shall never succeed in setting ourselves entirely free. But to recognise our presuppositions and to be able to criticise them, to recognise our prejudices and to allow for them, even to make fun of them—these are essential steps in growth. To say that this process will never in any one of us be complete is merely to affirm that maturity is something of which we can never affirm that we have finally attained it; it is something towards which we tend throughout a long life, and growth into which is a process to which there need never be an end. If this is true, it makes the process of living much more interesting than is sometimes supposed.

We must start by recognising that what we are in the larger world is to a great extent conditioned by what we have become in the small world of the family. It is no longer true, as it was in the days of Gilbert and Sullivan, that every child that's born alive is either a little liberal or else a little conservative. But though words have changed, realities have not; and two basic attitudes towards authority run through the whole of human life. To express them, for the sake of clarity, in a rather extreme form, there is the attitude which regards authority as an evil thing, to be rejected whenever possible and to be disregarded whenever it is safe to do so; there is the other reaction which thinks of authority as that power with which it is well to be on good terms, even though the price to be paid is conformity with everything that authority recommends or demands. We all tend in one direction or the other. In cases in which one tendency or the other is strongly marked, we are likely to find at one end the revolutionary, and at the other the die-hard. Both would seem to be types of adolescent "fixation."

The revolutionary is inclined to think that everything is so bad that any change is certain to be for the better. The first condition for the bringing of a new world into existence is the total destruction of the old. A study of history does not afford very much encouragement to those who adopt this point of view. The French Revolution certainly constituted a memorable challenge to inherited privilege, and has left a permanent mark on human history. But the Terror was followed by the empire of Napoleon, Napoleon by the restoration of the Bourbons, by the Holy Alliance, and by the period of reaction under Metternich. The Russian Revolution of

1917 kindled high hopes in many hearts around the world; but the brief period of promise was followed by the dreary tyranny of Stalin and by a new colonialism that is perhaps in every way worse than the old. Hate plays rather too large a part among the motives of the revolutionary, and hate is not a good basis for any kind of constructive action. Rebellion without courtesy is not a good remedy for any ill.

It is probable that the strongest motive in the make-up of the die-hard, though one of which he may himself be unconscious, is fear. He has identified himself with the *status quo*, with the authority of the past. If any criticism is permitted, will not the whole structure be endangered? If change begins, have we any assurance of the point at which change will stop? This attitude is perfectly exemplified in the religious conviction known as fundamentalism (in contrast to intelligent conservatism). The Bible has been accepted on authority as perfect and inerrant. If any criticism is permitted, will anything of its authority be left unharmed? If the Bible can be shown to be untrue in any point, will not the whole structure built up on its inerrancy collapse? The die-hard attitude of one hundred per cent or nothing is immensely strong, but it is also dangerously brittle. From his own point of view, the die-hard is quite right; if the structure begins to crack, who shall say how far the cracks will go? But fear also is no sound basis for constructive action. Courtesy is no excuse for the refusal to rebel when rebellion is indicated as the right and necessary course to follow.

It may be hoped that there is a more adult attitude to be found between these two forms of adolescent immaturity. We must honestly recognise that hate and fear are present in each one of us and play perhaps a far greater part than we know in determining our point of view and in controlling our actions. But the business of growing up is almost identical with the process of working these two out of our system as far as we possibly can, of becoming aware of their operation, of allowing for them, of emerging from their dominion and allowing something better to take their place. In this process the Christian has two advantages. In the first place he has in the life of Jesus the perfect picture of what has to be done and how it has to be done. In the second place, he has been promised a Holy Spirit, who is sent precisely for the purpose of

162

helping us to grow up. (The word "grown up" occurs much more often in the New Testament than is generally recognised, because it is obscured in most translations.) "God has not given us a spirit of timidity," we are told in II Timothy 1:7, "but a spirit of power and love and common-sense" ("self-control," says the Revised Standard Version for the last of the three positive qualities; this is too negative; "proportion" is an almost exact rendering of the Greek word). If there is anywhere a better brief definition of balanced maturity, I have not encountered it.

What, then, are likely to be the attitudes of the man who is growing up to the society in which he finds himself?

In the first place, it is to be hoped, though it can by no means be assumed, that he will find it possible to accord general approval to the principles on which it is based. Freedom and responsibility are not mere meaningless noises; they have a meaning, though it is not always easy to separate the intellectual and the emotional factors in our apprehension of that meaning. Most Americans would probably affirm that they believe in democracy. They might have some difficulty in defining exactly what they mean. But to say that we cannot define an idea exactly does not mean that we have no notion of it at all, and to say that our thinking is to some extent muddled does not imply that our thinking bears no relation at all to reality. Most Western men are convinced that life is better, in the sense of more genuinely human, when the individual has to take some responsibility for the kind of society in which he lives than when he is no more than a robot, blindly obeying unseen and uncontrollable forces. Up to this point, it is to be hoped that most of us can approve of the society into which we were born and in which we have to live.

When we scrutinise our society a little more closely, we shall find that a great deal of what happens in it is determined by custom, habit, tradition, and even by taboo. Such things must exist, otherwise there would be no possibility of a common existence of men in society at all. To most of these traditions the adult man is prepared to accord a detached and humorous tolerance. This may not be the very best way of doing things; but all this is of little importance in itself, and we may as well cheerfully accept it as the framework within which we have to live. The greatest misfortune that has ever befallen the male sex is the invention of trousers. It is impossible for a man to look anything but ridiculous if he encases his shapely legs in two long shapeless tubes, and is compelled by the demand of fashion to keep in those tubes two creases which nature never intended to be there. But unless the Western world is sensible enough to go back to the costume of George Washington, we had better make the best of our misfortunes and accept as cheerfully as we can the ungainly garments in which we are compelled to live. The wise man recognises that other peoples have different ways of doing things and have a right to their own way of doing them. The Englishman assumes that in all civilised countries, traffic moves on the left-hand side of the road. As he moves about the world, he is pained to discover how few civilised countries there are left. But if he wishes to survive, it is as well for him to recognise, as soon as he crosses the twenty-one miles of the English Channel, that these queer foreigners have a right to their own misguided way of doing things.

But we are not likely to go very far in the dispassionate consideration of our society, before we come to things that strike us as definitely wrong. All human societies are so imperfect, so immature, that this is bound to happen to us unless we resolutely wear the blinkers of the die-hard. Every society is marred by betrayals of its own principles, or by failure to apprehend certain principles on which the development of genuinely human existence depends. Let us not be too afraid of the word "wrong."* When the Victorian reformers said that it was *wrong* that little boys should be sent up chimneys to clean them at the danger of their lives, they did not mean that this was socially undesirable or that it was liable to produce maladjusted persons; they meant that there are certain values that are intrinsic in human personality and that, if a society flouts or disregards these, it does so at its own peril—it will in the end pay the penalty for folly and injustice. It is the great advantage of the free society that criticism is not immediately regarded as treason, and that sharp and even violent criticism is

*We shall come later to the question of "absolute" right and wrong; all that is pleaded for here is a provisional acceptance of the fact that the words can have some meaning, in advance of a clear definition of what that meaning may be.

recognised as being perfectly compatible with general approval of the society and loyalty to the principles for which it stands. If we look at things calmly as they are, we must criticise. If we wish to grow up and to continue growing up into maturity, we are bound to be rebels to the end of our days. The question is simply this— shall we be futile rebels, or destructive rebels, or shall we learn the difficult art of being courteous and constructive rebels?

There are at least six ways in which sane, balanced, and constructive rebellion can express itself.

The first is patient endurance of the wrong, and suffering through it. "Let us endure an hour and see injustice done," writes the poet. There are situations in which there is no other course open to us; there is no means by which feeling and judgment can immediately be translated into action. But this does not mean mere acquiescence in the evil; it means willingness to endure suffering as a positive and constructive contribution to the situation, and patient expectancy of the moment at which action may be possible. Perhaps much in this field can be learned from the development of Lincoln's attitude towards slavery, and from the sage and prudent timing of all his actions in this regard.

The second is a steady effort to change the minds of other men about that which we have seen to be evil, but of which they think otherwise. This is always a delicate operation, and it is here more than elsewhere that the courtesy of the courteous rebel must be called into play. We cannot help people to change their minds or to abandon their prejudices unless we approach them with respect. To combine the passion of the crusader with the patience of the saint is, however, never easy for undisciplined human nature. But history makes it plain, and the philosopher A. N. Whitehead has worked it out in his book *Adventures of Ideas*, that great and widespread changes in general human attitudes do take place and that the major factor in change is not so much the thunderous oratory of the leaders as the quiet, patient witness of the simple individuals who have themselves become convinced that change is necessary and must come.

The third measure is combination with other like-minded individuals to bring about changes in the law by which society is governed. Laws do not of themselves make men righteous; but a better law may serve as a great barrier against evils that an inferior law has made possible. Here too patience, wisdom, and constant self-criticism are needed. We none of us act from perfectly pure motives. Self-interest plays a part where we least suspect it, and there is in all of us a tendency to identify our own interest with the interests of society or nation. If we are to act at all, we must act with others equally impelled by mixed motives, some of which may not be the same as our own. We may have to accept compromises on the principle that half a loaf is better than no bread. We may find that excellent projects, when put into execution, disappoint expectation; and that the results of action, in the infinitely complex interactions of men upon one another in society, are different from what we had expected. All these difficulties must be taken into account. They need not deter the adult man from having ideals and from working for their at least partial realisation in the society in which he lives.

Fourthly, it is to be recognised that in local society it is desirable that each of us should at certain points maintain his independence in relation to the habits and customs of his neighbours. If we have learned to respect the individuality of others, we have a right to claim that they should respect ours. In a society in which it is customary to buy a new car every year, it may take a certain amount of courage to drive an old car. But if we have better ways of spending our money, who has a right to control the freedom of our decision? The neighbours may look down their noses; but if we set them up as our judges, we have exchanged our freedom for a servitude which can know no end. There is no need to flaunt our independence; we must, however, have the courage and the confidence in ourselves to maintain quietly but firmly our freedom in relation to standards which may be valid for others but which we can see no reason to accept as valid for ourselves.

There are more important questions than the purchase of new cars. The organisation of society may at certain points raise in acute form the issue of "right" and "wrong," and the mature man may find it necessary to take his stand on the side of what he judges to be right against his own interests and against the common judgment of the society in which he lives. The consequences may be decidedly unpleasant. In a multi-racial society, where relations between the various races are bad, the individual who ventures to cross the line of segregation that society has laid down is liable to find himself denounced as a traitor, ostracised by those of his own kind, perhaps even treated with violence. But maturity must find expression in action on the basis of what we believe to be right, at whatever cost to ourselves. Of course, the action must be taken quietly and unobtrusively, not defiantly and in such a way as to draw the maximum of attention to ourselves. It must be defended courteously and gently, with respect for the opinions of those who take up a different position and find themselves led to act in other ways. But, if we let other people's consciences be our judges, we make ourselves dependent on them, and by so doing we make it impossible for ourselves ever to grow beyond the position of adolescent dependence.

There remains, lastly, the possibility of martyrdom. A man may be by birth a member of a society, of which he finds that basically he cannot approve, because it is founded on principles that seem to him to deny the worth of humanity and to make impossible a genuinely human existence. If the law tells him to do what he believes to be wrong, his conscience may tell him quietly and firmly to disobey. This was the situation in which tens of thousands of good men found themselves in Hitler's Germany, over such matters as the persecution of Jews or the policy of eliminating the mentally and physically unfit by action of the state. It is good that we should ask ourselves what we would do if we chanced to find ourselves in such a situation and could not escape from it by emigration to a better and a freer world.

It is as well to remind ourselves at this point that the vocation of martyrdom is a perilous one. The martyr complex is a well known form of human aberration. All kinds of strands may combine in it—the desire for an otherwise unobtainable prominence, an unhealthy interest in suffering for its own sake, the pleasure that some people take in the feeling of being unjustly persecuted. Bernard Shaw, with the penetration of genius, presented a number of these attitudes in the first act of *Androcles and the Lion*. But that is not the whole story.

Real martyrs are not at all like that. The first thing that we notice about them is that they disliked very much indeed the idea of being martyrs. This comes out, for instance, in the story of Savonarola, the Florentine martyr of the fifteenth century, or in that of Bishop Hugh Latimer, burned at the stake in the reign of Queen Mary in England, who wrote from his imprisonment, "I am so afeard I could creep into a mouse-hole." In general at the time of their death martyrs are tranquil and confident. But here too the Gospels tell the whole story of humanity; Gethsemane comes before Calvary, and it is in Gethsemane that the battle has to be won. The real martyr has to work his way through black depths of darkness before he comes out into the light. But we do not need to go so far back in history. We now have accessible many records of those who died in Hitler's Germany. Letters written by those who knew they were about to die, some of them quite simple people, reveal not neurotic tension or hysterical exaltation, but in most cases a calm, gentle, balanced simplicity, a sense of the worthwhileness both of living and of dying, such as might well be envied by those of us who most regard ourselves as integrated and well-balanced personalities.

But even this is not the last word. Even in his death the martyr must remain the courteous rebel. His attitude must be free from self-pity, from railing, or from arrogant self-righteousness. He must understand the motives of those who are killing him. If he is a Christian, he must imitate his Lord and pray for them. His concern must be not with himself, but with that cause of truth and right-eousness and humanity for which he believes himself to stand.

This may seem to be setting a rather high standard for poor frail humanity. But it is a standard to which a great many very ordinary people have attained, and it is through them that the human race really lives. And if we suppose that attaining to a genuinely human existence is an easy task, we have not even begun to learn the lessons that apparently we were put into the world to learn.

VII Real People in a Real World

on facing reality

Much mental disorder, if not all, can be recognised as consisting in one way or another in a flight from reality or a refusal to accept reality. This negative attitude to reality can take on a great many different forms, and it varies very much in intensity from individual to individual. At one extreme are the pathetic cases of those who have withdrawn so far from ordinary reality that they are no longer accessible to the friendly approaches of human speech and companionship, and live their lives in a world which those by whom they are surrounded cannot penetrate, and which appears unrelated to the world as less afflicted people see it. At the other end of the scale is the unwillingness to face unpleasant facts or duties from which all of us on occasion suffer. There are situations in which we would rather not know the truth, in case the truth should prove uncongenial. Many people will write a letter rather than face an interview which may prove to be painful. Almost all of us put at the bottom of the pile of letters to be answered that one to which we know that it will be most difficult to compose the answer. But the only way to live a really human life is to face reality exactly as it is, without anxiety, without postponement, and without condonation of its harsher aspects; and this is a lesson which we do not find it easy to learn.

We are not born with the art of seeing things just as they are. This is something that we have to learn toilfully and with the certainty that in this life we shall never get to the end of learning. We project something of ourselves on to all that we see and experience, and our likes and dislikes, our hopes and fears, affect our apprehension of that which we encounter. The child does not at first focus its parents as individuals. They are part of a group of emotional forces, of immense power, moving in unpredictable orbits. Their ideas and their behests determine the world in which the child moves. The recognition that these apparent gods are really no more than individuals very much like the child itself may come as a considerable emotional shock. When a young man marries, all too often he is not really marrying a girl but taking to his bosom the projection on to another of his own highly imaginative picture of what young love can be. He may wake up one morning to discover that the reality is very different from his dream. If the passion of love can distort, so can the passions of hate and prejudice; at a later stage we shall consider those "stereotypes," those fixed patterns and ideas which make it impossible for those who accept them to see a Jew or a Negro, for instance, otherwise than through the distorting medium of the fixed idea.

This element of projection is present in all our contacts with the outside world and with other people. We shall never be able completely to get rid of it. Part of our training for life must be a steady self-discipline in the attempt to get rid of preconceived ideas and theories and to look at the world about us with the clear eyes of an uncompromising realism.

The Christian has a word to describe the state of living in a world of illusion. That word is idolatry. In the Greek tradition the word *eidola* is used of the wraiths, the shades of the dead, which lack the good red blood of life. When Odysseus meets them in his descent into the lower world recorded in the eleventh book of the *Odyssey*, the loudest sound that they can make is a flittermouse shriek. In the Greek translation of the Old Testament this word is taken over to represent the Hebrew word for the false gods of the heathen; the complaint of the prophet against these gods is that they can in reality do nothing, whether good or evil; they are as powerless as the ghosts of the dead. John at the end of his first Epistle urges his readers to keep themselves from idols. It was not likely that these readers would fall back into the worship of Apollo and Artemis and the other gods of their non-Christian neighbours; it was all too likely that they, like ourselves, might fall back into the twilight

170

world of illusion, that they might accept a counterfeit as though it was the real thing. It is the aim of the apostle to recall them to the living God, and to that stern acceptance of the realities of the world which should be the distinguishing mark of the Christian.

It must be recognised that this is not the view of the Christian faith which is taken by many of its critics. Religion, in its Christian form or in any other, is regarded by many people as simply a form of escapism. Karl Marx held the view that religion is the opiate of the people, a means of blinding folk to the possibilities of this world by holding out to them the delusive prospects of comfort and relief in another and non-existent world. Many who are not Marxists would go so far at least with Karl Marx as to feel that the effect of religion is much more to withdraw people, through the indulgence of their fancies and desires, from the conflicts of the real world than to strengthen them to face reality. We need not be surprised if the objection is found to contain a certain element of truth. John Calvin once used the remarkable expression that the heart of man is the great idol factory; it has an astonishing capacity for taking that which in itself is objectively true and so twisting it to its own service that it ceases to be really true. It is not to be wondered at if man can take religion, and even the Christian religion, and turn what ought to be the shining armour of the warrior into a comfortable protection against the rain. But if we were right in our judgment in earlier chapters on the forthright realism of Jesus, it is clear that escapism has nothing to do with the Gospel. If there are forms of religion that are escapist, the Christian is pledged to do his utmost to see to their disappearance. At the same time, he would do well to exercise a rather austere self-examination in order to make sure that his own heart has not been engaged in the business of idol-making against which Calvin warned us.

Paul the apostle lived in an idolatrous world, and he has identified for us two features that seem invariably to reproduce themselves in the twilight world in which idolatry lives. Several times he has drawn up for us lists of aberrations from the central line of genuinely human existence. More than half of the items in these lists are concerned with those things which make impossible the fellowship of human beings in ordered society—envy, faction, wrangling, animosity, and so forth. Rather less than half cover the various forms of man's inability to control himself and his own natural instincts and desires. The two marks of the world of the idols are cruelty and inordinate sexual indulgence. Even in what might be regarded as civilised times Carthage had its great image of the god Moloch, with outstretched hands on which were to be placed the first-born infants of the faithful, in order to be precipitated into the raging fires of the bloodthirsty god below. In Paul's day the great temple of Artemis at Ephesus was surrounded by the houses of the dedicated prostitutes, just as certain great temples of the gods in India are surrounded to this day. The idols of the Western world are not quite so crude and so obvious as those of other and earlier cultures; he would be a bold man who would affirm that the West is no longer under the sway of idol-worship.

These characteristic defects of human nature singled out by Paul, cruelty and uncontrolled sexual indulgence, clearly have one feature in common. Each would be impossible if every human being accorded to every other the respect due to personal existences with an intrinsic value of their own. If I regard other beings simply as means that may be used to my own advantage or as instruments that may be used to contribute to my pleasure, they have ceased to be real people, existing in their own right; they have become part of my dream of power or of delight. It is here that we touch one of our deepest problems in living. It is hard for us to be aware of other people in the full three-dimensional reality of their own existence; they tend to be for us merely figures that move in our own minds and thoughts, and we claim or expect the right to manipulate them at our will. This limits us to a one-way traffic of experience; it makes impossible the deep reciprocity of genuinely personal experience.

Both the Christian Church and the psychiatric profession labour under the imputation of taking an undue and morbid interest in sex and its aberrations. In both cases there may be certain grounds for the criticism, but in neither is it entirely justified. Both the pastor and the psychiatrist have occasion to be perturbed by the astonishingly high proportion of the problems presented to him in which a sexual factor is evidently present. Each, if he is to do his job competently, must make his reckoning with this inescapable fact, must be prepared to understand and to sympathise, and must have

172

some idea of the kind of guidance that should be given in the very varying cases that are committed to his care. *Sex*

The constant presence of this factor in human problems should not occasion any surprise. The reproductive instinct is probably, next to the instinct of self-preservation, the strongest of all the motives by which human nature is swayed. We have difficulty enough in preventing the one instinct from transforming itself into that aggression against the rights of others that leads to war. It is not to be wondered at that bewildered human nature experiences difficulty in finding the right method of handling this other powerful instinct and guiding it into orderly and creative channels. There is the further point that the apparatus and mechanism of reproduction are so central in the human organism, so important and so sensitive, that any severe emotional shock, any intense inner strain, anything that tends at any point to hinder the harmonious growth of the person towards maturity, is likely to be registered in this region and to manifest itself in some dislocation of its working, in some disorganisation of its relationship to the many other factors that make up a harmoniously balanced human being.

The general attitude of Christian faith towards sex is extremely simple and positive. In the earliest chapters of the Bible it is affirmed that God created human beings male and female and that he had a good purpose in so creating them. This sets the tone for the attitude that is maintained throughout the Bible. The relationships of sex and marriage are taken for granted with a practical and almost earthy directness. Indeed the unvarnished language of the Bible is liable at certain points to shock the refined feelings of our own supposedly more emancipated day. The story of Judah's transgressions in Genesis 38 fulfils all the canons of brilliant and dramatic narrative; but if read aloud in church today it might considerably startle a contemporary congregation. This frank and natural attitude towards sex is to be found as much in the Gospels as in the Old Testament. Jesus quotes with approval the words of Genesis on the creation of man as male and female, and on God's purpose as fulfilled in the union of the two and the procreation of children. He recognises the possibility of vocations other than marriage when for one reason or another celibacy is necessary or desirable. He indicates the limits of the marriage obligation—in

173

the heavenly kingdom they neither marry nor are given in marriage, but are as the angels in heaven. But no reader of the Gospels is likely to be surprised to find Jesus present at a wedding feast and apparently perfectly at home at it; if his Gospel is not a gospel for such situations as this, it is in his eyes no gospel at all.

It is often asserted that an unhealthy element of asceticism entered into the Christian Church with Paul. This can hardly be maintained, when everything on the subject that is contained in his extant epistles is brought together. It is by no means certain that he himself was a celibate. The evidence of I Corinthians is at least as consistent, perhaps more consistent, with the view that he had been married as a Jew and that he had not availed himself of the permission to marry again that he accords in certain circumstances to Christian converts. In view of the time of persecution and distress that he sees lowering over the Church, he does advise the Christians that it may be better for them to refrain from marriage; yet at the same time he gives them highly practical counsel regarding the marriage relationship and the mutual loyalty and respect by which it is to be controlled. And it must never be forgotten that in the Epistle to the Ephesians, which, if not actually from the pen of the apostle is a wonderful summary of his doctrine written by a near disciple, marriage is presented as a sacred symbol of the relationship between Christ and the Church; such words could never have been written by one who regarded sex as in itself unclean or marriage as no more than a concession to human weakness. Is there, in fact, any other passage in the literature of the world in which so sublime a view of marriage is set before us?

It is true that there has been an ascetic strain in Christian history. It would not be difficult to collect a number of passages from Augustine and Jerome and others of the Fathers of the Church supporting the view that human sexuality is simply a result of the fall of man, and that any use of this human quality in thought or act is to be eschewed by those who would be truly Christian. Such ideas, however, have nothing whatever to do with the Gospel tradition, or with those lines of Christian thinking that have been directly derived from the Gospel. They have crept in from that pessimistic strain of oriental and Hellenistic thought, which regarded matter, and of course the human body with it, as evil, and

174

therefore brought together under one sweeping condemnation everything that tended towards physical pleasure as binding the spirit ever more firmly in the imprisonment of the body. This created a certain climate or atmosphere of opinion. At the same time, the infant Christian communities, by reaction against the extremely lax standards prevalent in the non-Christian societies by which they were surrounded, tended towards a rather rigid moralism, in the categories of which "sins of the flesh" came to be bracketed with murder and apostasy as the worst of sins. Exactly the same phenomenon can be observed in the growing Christian communities in the non-Christian countries of Asia and Africa, and for exactly the same reasons. A natural and healthy reaction against ancient traditions and indulgences which are felt to be evil produces a certain timidity in the face of that which by Christian standards should be accepted as natural and right.

The joyful and whole-hearted acceptance of sex which is characteristic of the Gospel is not, however, unthinking or indiscriminate; it works along the lines of certain clearly intelligible principles.

The first principle is that sex in Christian thought is associated with the creative activity of God—he made them male and female—and with man's capacity to participate, on his own level and derivatively, in that creative activity.

It is at this point that a bridge could perhaps be built between Christian thought and one of the most discussed and criticised aspects of the Freudian psychology. The *libido*, to use the Freudian term, is sometimes understood in the narrow sense of the purely sexual urge, an unfortunate narrowing to one particular region of personality of what, taken in a wider and more general sense, is a fruitful concept. The *libido* should surely be taken in the wider sense of that total creative impulse, the impulse that makes a man want to express himself, in some way to reproduce himself in something outside himself. Sex, no doubt, is an important part of this creative impulse, but surely should not be regarded as constituting the whole. Allied to it, but not identical, is the impulse which finds its outlet in artistic creation, and also that impulse of the self to go out from the self which is expressed in certain forms of religious feeling and activity. The connection between the various forms of the one central creative impulse is evident in the close association

175

between sexual tension and artistic production in the lives of a number of the greatest writers and artists, of the details of whose inner lives we have evidence; and also in the alarmingly close relationship between religious emotion and sexual excitement that has proved a disturbing problem in times of religious revival. On the other hand this inner kinship between different forms of creativity accounts for the possibility of what has come to be known by the not very satisfactory term "sublimation," the transference of the creative impulse from one channel to another, and its satisfaction in a medium other than that to which it was originally directed. This can work in a variety of different directions. On one side, women of the highest artistic sensibility and talent have found that for a number of years the care of a home and the upbringing of a family have provided full emotional satisfaction; for the time being the special artistic impulse slumbers, perhaps to awake again when family responsibilities have been fulfilled. In another direction, those who for one reason or another have been denied the natural satisfaction of the sexual instinct have found happiness and release in artistic production or in self-forgetful service of others.

The best Christian thought considers sex in this context of the wholeness of human personality and thus understands it always in terms of its creative function. In the great majority of cases this creativity finds its natural expression in the procreation and the care of children; it is not by accident that in the marriage services of the historic Churches, this is put first in the exposition of the privileges and duties of marriage. But it would be incorrect to limit the creativity of sex to this one aspect of marriage alone; otherwise it would find no expression in the married life of those who would like to have children but for one reason or another do not succeed in producing them. But those who are happily married are all the time creating one another; in continual reciprocity of life and affection shared, each is being fashioned into something different from what he or she could ever have been in solitude. And both are engaged all the time in creating that mysterious entity—a home. Rudyard Kipling, in his autobiography *Something of Myself*, made the extremely acute remark that the house never lies. People separated from their background can put on a successful act and make themselves out to be different from what they really are; the home

176

gives them away. A house has an indefinable atmosphere, revealing what kind of people they are that live in it. A sensitive visitor, immediately on entrance, can classify a house by its position on the spectrum of possibilities. It will stand somewhere on the semicircle between prim and uncomfortable precision at one end, through comfortable and congenial confusion, to squalid disorder at the other. And from the house certain inferences can be made as to the kind of people that live in it.

It is the principle of creativity that has led the Christian consciousness at all times to disapprove of certain manifestations of the sexual impulse in which the creative impulse either is not present at all, or in which it can never find more than a very imperfect outlet. The most obvious examples are homosexuality and masturbation. It is probable that neither of these activities is as harmful as popular estimation has supposed, or as we have been given to understand by the slightly hysterical denunciations of Christian moralists. But each falls below the level of genuinely human activity. To take the extreme case, if all males were at the same time to enjoy the pleasures of sexual stimulation and to avoid the burdens of family life by taking to homosexual practices, the human race would come to an end in a single generation. No one familiar with Latin literature of the period of the Empire will for a moment regard this as a purely imaginary bogey. Masturbation involves the completely uncreative use of something which was given for a creative purpose. To exaggerate the wrongfulness of such acts may defeat itself by producing a state of nervous tension in which the impulse which it is intended to control may acquire compulsive power, and the last state is worse than the first. To pretend that such things do not matter or are not wrong is to fail to recognise that, though the way to a genuinely human existence is hard and toilful, to find that way is an obligation that rests on the human race and the human individual.

In the second place, Christian realism has always associated sex (2) with the principle of the responsibility of human beings for one another. If we have recognised the principle that human existence is not human until it is personal and that personal existence is different from every other kind of existence, we are bound to admit that we are all responsible for one another all the time. No other personal being may be regarded as a means to my profit or pleasure. And what we do to one another may have permanent effects for good and evil. The Christian view of sex is simply one application of this principle. Just because the sex relationship is so intimate and should be so profoundly personal, in this region more than any other the principle of responsibility should be operative. It is for this reason that the Christian tradition maintains that sexual intercourse should be the expression of one thing and one thing only—the acceptance by two persons of permanent and unshakable responsibility for one another's well-being and happiness. It must be stressed that, on this view, the acceptance of mutual responsibility is primary and that the expression of this responsibility in sexual relationships is secondary. If the principle is regarded as sound, certain convictions as to what is and what is not permissible in sexual relationships will inevitably follow.

There is no doubt that the Christian view is at present extremely unpopular. Perhaps it always has been. Two factors may perhaps help to account for its special unpopularity in our own day.

The first is the markedly adolescent attitude towards sex which persists in many grown men and women in the Western world of today. Adolescence is an age of irresponsibility, in which responsibility is disliked and evaded. The adolescent tends to be the centre of his own world; he has not yet fully discovered the reality of other people and the significance of mutual responsibility for personal existence. At this stage it is not unnatural to suppose that casual sexual intimacies can be divorced from responsibility, that they are not important and have no lasting consequences. Quite apart from any questions of moral judgment, pastoral experience suggests that this simply is not true—that in many casual contacts of this kind one party or the other gets badly hurt, whether the affair "comes to light" or not. But that is not the important point. Such an attitude towards sex, and the conduct which is the natural expression of it, tends to keep those who hold this view permanently in a state of adolescent underdevelopment, and to interpose an unnecessary obstacle in the way of development towards a responsible and fully personal existence.

The other difficulty finds expression in such well-known phrases as "Sexual Behaviour in the Human Male," and "Sexual Behaviour in the Human Female." Such phrases suggest that sexual activity is primarily an activity of the individual, a means by which certain of his innate impulses and desires can find expression. It is not, of course, to be suggested that such phrases bear no relation at all to the realities of human nature; we have already fully recognised the role of sex as part of the creative endowment of the individual and as one instrument for his individual self-expression. But unless we are to forget the difference between the human and the merely animal, it is a cardinal error to forget that in sexual behaviour "the other" is as important as "the self." The very heart and centre of the sexual drive in the adult human person is not the expression of the self but the search for the other—that other to which the self can wholly commit itself and in which it can find the satisfaction and rest that is denied to it in its isolation. This must not be regarded as simply the poetic expression of an ideal; it is basic to a right understanding of the problem of the relationship between male and female and of the possible solutions to that problem. The purely human quality of living has only been very gradually attained; the gains are seen to be highly precarious, and the human can very easily slip back to the level of the animal from which it has so painfully emerged. Constant vigilance and effort are needed if the gains are to be conserved. To treat the animal factor as central and the personal as marginal or optional is at once to distort the perspectives. It is only if the personal is steadily and firmly kept in the centre of the picture that the right perspective can be maintained and the ideal of truly human existence can become the object of directed and intelligent striving.

The Christian ideal, then, can be expressed quite simply in a single sentence. It is that of perfect chastity for man and woman inside the bond of marriage and outside of it. Chastity has unfortunately come to be used of abstinence from all sexual relationships, but this is not its proper use. It means simply that respect for oneself and for all others which finds its outward expression in self-discipline, self-control, moderation, and responsible action at all times. The Christian view, in this as in so many things, is not a theory; it is based on the example and practice of the Master. Nothing in the records of his life is more remarkable than the fact that he was able to enter into relations of friendship with so many

179

women and yet that, among all the slanders that circulated about him and about the circumstances of his own birth, not one word was ever spoken to question the perfect integrity of his friendships with the women who were his friends.

Voices will not be lacking to maintain that this ideal is in the first place undesirable, and that, if it were desirable, it would be impossible of achievement. *Sex denial is not harmful.*

No evidence has yet been produced by anyone to show that perfect chastity, based on self-respect and a sense of responsibility, ever did any harm to anyone. To wish one thing and to say "No" to the wish is something that we all have to do in innumerable connections every day of our lives. Of course there are other forms of chastity. That which is based on a Manichean dislike of the physical, and of our incarnation in extremely material bodies, is likely to be strained and morbid. A chastity based on fear of sex or on a puritanical prudishness is undesirable, and may be even positively harmful. But, in all such cases, it is not the chastity which does the harm but the potentially pathological factor which underlies it.

In judging of the practicability of the ideal, the pastor has an advantage over the psychiatrist in that so much of his time is spent with "healthy" and "normal" people, these terms being used of course in a comparative and not in an absolute sense. Even the pastor does spend a great deal of time in ministering to the mentally and the spiritually disturbed, but that is not the whole of his profession. If he is engaged in serious and intimate personal work, he is likely to number among his friends some people who at an early age have acquired knowledge of the "facts of life" with unconcealed interest but without the smallest trace of prurience, who have passed through the stormy days of adolescence with only minimal disturbance of their tranquillity and without irregularity of conduct, who at a suitable age have fallen in love once, profoundly and for ever, have entered into the experiences of married life with humour, a sense of adventure, and mutual tolerance, and have produced bouncing and eminently satisfactory families. The fact is unquestionable; perhaps unfortunately, the pastoral relationship even more than the relation of doctor and patient makes it impossible to violate the confidence of friends by giving further details. If such cases are less common than we might wish, the reason may be

180

sought in that lack of emotional equilibrium which is marked in most Western societies today and appears to be a symptom of some deep and as yet only imperfectly diagnosed sickness of society.

At least four factors can be identified as making life more difficult and complicated than it need be for young people who are on the way from childhood to adult and responsible manhood.

The first is the lack of proper instruction about the human body and the way it works, and as to the relationship, as far as this can be put into words, between the physical and the emotional aspects of human growth. With the emphasis on the physical that shouts at us from advertisements and magazines and from the popular press, it might be supposed that all young people have all the information that they could possibly need about their own physical make up and all its operations. Experience shows that this is far from being the case. Anyone concerned with the pastoral care of the young becomes aware from time to time of astonishing gaps in the knowledge even of well-educated young people and of the way in which the gaps tend to be balanced by equally astonishing pieces of incorrect information. This puts the younger generation in the west at a disadvantage as compared with their coequals in simpler societies, where life is lived much more in public, everything is known, and a great deal is discussed in public which on many levels of Western society would be hidden behind veils of reticence and restraint. Nothing could be worse for young people than a restless and unsatisfied curiosity, a sense that there are things which ought to be known but which have somehow remained concealed. Nothing could be more important than the provision of the right kind of education in this field of knowledge.

It is perhaps not merely the imagination of older people which suggests that in the last forty years or so there has been a marked decline in the respect felt for and shown to persons as persons. Various reasons can be suggested for this decline, if it is a reality. Two world wars have made human life cheap and have perhaps shaken the belief in the fundamental worth of human personality as such. The prevailing view of man regards him as primarily the product of biological evolution, and this has pushed into the background the older view which took it for granted that the important thing about him was that he was an immortal soul. Almost every-

181

where in the Western world there has been a reaction against the primness and rigidity of social conventions inherited from a supposedly more puritanical era. Naturally the change is most to be observed among younger people, who to a large extent are unaware of any other possible standards. It would be unfair to suggest that young people of the present day are wickeder than their parents and grandparents; they may or may not be—there is no reliable evidence on the basis of which an objective judgment can be formed. What does disturb older people is that so many of the young do not seem to have got beyond the point of regarding one another as animated bodies, contacts between which can afford certain forms of pleasure and mutual stimulation. Where there is no clear sense of personal worth and dignity, there is little room for the development of a deep sense of responsibility for persons as persons. And where this is lacking, there is no adequate foundation for personal and adult living or for the development of love on a genuinely personal level.

Not everyone recognises how recent and how revolutionary are the views and habits that generally prevail among us with regard to marriage and the choice of a partner. It seems to us self-evident that in so very intimate and personal a matter the decision should be made by those most directly concerned, and that the all-important thing is that two young people should be "in love". This romantic view is hardly more than three hundred years old in the West. It is almost unknown in the simpler societies of Asia and Africa. In India, even among Christians, it is almost universally the custom that marriages are arranged by the parents and not by the parties; even today it is no rare event for a college student to be suddenly summoned home to marry a girl whom he has never seen and whom he will not really see until after the marriage ceremony is over. People of education and of modern outlook who defend the ancient custom will maintain that parents who sincerely love their children and carefully consider their character and temperament are much more likely to make a wise choice than young people who are likely to be carried away by the passing excitements of a moment; in support of their case they can point to a large number of highly successful unions in which arranged companionship has passed into deep and abiding affection. The Westerner may criticise the disregard of personal choice involved in the system; he should note one positive and favourable result of it—no one, either boy or girl, in such a society need waste much time in anxiety as to the possibilities of getting married. The boy knows quite well that a marriage will be arranged for him in the early dawn of manhood. The girl knows that she may not draw first prize in the lottery but that at least she will get someone, and she may know long before the date of the marriage who that someone is to be. In such societies, the existence of bachelors and spinsters seems to be due only to the infiltration of Western ideas of independence. There are advantages and drawbacks in every system. We pay the price for our greater freedom, for our greater respect for personal choice, in the cloud of anxiety by which the subject of sex and marriage seems to be surrounded in the minds of many younger people in the West today.

The picture of marriage presented to us in the modern novel is hardly engaging. I know of hardly any modern novels, other than the not very serious books of Angela Thirkell, in which happy and successful marriage is taken for granted as the regular thing. And yet getting married tends to present itself, especially to the girl, as the supremely important object in life. For this the attitude of our society is largely to blame. The vocation of the nun is accepted and respected. The mere spinster tends to be the butt of the not very interesting jokes of not very interesting people. This is most unfair. There are perhaps few families which have not somewhere the universal and invaluable aunt who, having for one reason or another failed to get married, spends the rest of her life adding to the happiness of other people. Nevertheless the lot of the unmarried woman tends to be lonesome and dreary; and since, in our society the initiative is left in the hands of the male, this discouraging prospect tends to produce in the mind of the woman anxiety as to whether she will succeed in sufficiently attracting the attention of the possible male partner. It is not surprising if girls tend to spend more time than is good for them discussing the problems of sex and concentrating on the means by which a successful marriage can be brought within their reach. For the boy the problem is less acute. Yet sexual potency has come to be so glorified as the essential element in virility that quite a number of young men spend more time than is good for them wondering whether they will be able to come

183

up to the standard that is expected of them. In both cases, it is the element of anxiety in the looking forward that is harmful and tends to complicate emotionally the purely physical urges that are a natural and necessary part of growing up.

Finally, there is the further fact, also a highly revolutionary fact, that the age of marriage among us is so much higher than it used to be in the West, and so much higher than it is in other types of society. In many parts of Asia, except in the highly educated classes where a more Western pattern has taken shape, a boy can count on being married at the age of sixteen, a girl shortly after the end of her fourteenth year. Mr. Gandhi was married at fourteen, and as he emphatically stated in his autobiography, that meant married and not engaged. Where such traditions prevail, there is only a short gap, perhaps no gap at all, between the attainment of puberty and the beginning of married life. I do not think that anyone who has lived in a society where such early marriage is the rule would grudge to our young people the years of study and fun and fellowship which we have interposed between the beginning of adolescence and marriage. In countries where early marriage is the rule the vast majority of women are illiterate; and where intelligent companionship between men and women is the exception rather than the rule, the purely physical tends to loom rather too large in the marriage relationship. Emotional maturity comes more slowly than physical maturity; perhaps the fulness of happiness in a genuinely personal marriage is more likely to be attained when both parties have had time to attain to a measure of emotional maturity before they have been brought together in the marriage bond. In this, as in other matters, it is possible to see advantages in both systems and on both sides of the argument.

But we in the West have to live with our Western system. It is only common sense to recognise that it has created new problems; it interposes a long period in which young people are no longer boys and girls, yet in which they are expected to remain unmarried and are not encouraged to take up the full responsibilities of adults. The New Testament lays down quite clearly one standard of conduct. Natural impulse points very plainly to another. Society tolerates a good deal that by the standards of the New Testament is intolerable. A number of psychologists, philosophers, and novelists

184

regard the New Testament view of personal existence and responsibility as out of date, if not positively harmful, and give advice which points in a very different direction. It is not to be wondered at that this is a major field of conflict and confusion in the modern world.

It must, however, be insisted that in this conflict and confusion there is nothing that must of necessity be regarded as pathological. The conflict between inclination and judgment is something that meets us on every level of human existence, and no one was ever any the worse for allowing judgment to win the day, provided that the conflict took place in the clear light of day and on the level of conscious thought. Inclination may well say that another little drink wouldn't do us any harm; judgment may reply that the last drink had better be the last, and that it is time to go home. Judgment is probably right; and if judgment wins the day, it will probably be the better for all concerned. The decision may be mildly painful, but it is hardly traumatic. The situation is rather different if what presents itself as judgment is really the stirring of an old guilt complex on the subject of drink inherited from generations of pussy-foot ancestors. But the ability to say "No" is not necessarily the manifestation of any complex of any kind at all. And this is as true in the sphere of sex as on all other levels of human life. Conscious and deliberate refusal moves in entirely different categories of being from that suppression or repression of impulses which may be harmful in its consequences.

If we may once again look to the Gospel for at least hypothetical guidance in this matter, it may be permissible to suggest four lines along which the delicate problem of sexual development in relation to the general development of personality can be handled.

It would be a good thing if the Churches could all recover the free and unembarrassed manner in which the subject is dealt with in the Bible. There has been far more progress in this matter than is supposed by some of those who are not directly familiar with the life of the Churches, but there is still a good way to go before the Christian level of liberty is attained. This would not, of course, mean a great deal of discussion of the subject or the ventilation of it on every possible occasion. Nothing is more wearisome than the discourses of the valetudinarian, who is always expounding to others the symptom of his various diseases. Endless talk about sex is usually a sign of adolescent immaturity, or of the failing strength of middle age rather than of vigorous and normal health.

Such an attitude should make possible the proper instruction of all young people in the subject. It is often maintained that the right people to give such instruction are the parents. Perhaps this conclusion has been reached without due consideration of the difficulties involved. Not all parents find it easy to speak without embarrassment of a matter in which the most tender intimacies of their own personal life are involved; and the first requisite is that embarrassment should be entirely excluded from any discussion of the subject. And children, almost without exception, feel it indelicate to enquire, even in thought, into the sexual relationships that may exist between their parents. It seems most likely that the entirely impartial atmosphere of the classroom is that in which biological instruction as to the functions of the body and its reproductive functions can best be given. The subject is in itself so enthrallingly interesting that, if rightly taught, it is likely of itself to blow away any prurient interest that may already have taken root in the minds of the learners. If this basis of scientific instruction has once been given, it is not difficult for a minister, or indeed for any older friend, to follow it up with the development of those aspects of personal respect and responsibility which are the main theme of this chapter.

But how is respect for people as people, for the value of personal existence as such, to be recovered and to be inculcated? That is perhaps the major problem of our sick society. The natural instinct of adolescence is towards hero-worship. Of this a certain use can be made. But it is a two-edged weapon. In the first place, the instinct rarely lasts beyond adolescence. In the second, what in itself is natural and healthy can easily find its perversion in the cult of the superman. And what we need is respect for personality even in its less admirable and attractive manifestations. A friend who is now occupying a situation of considerable prominence once told me that when he was a boy his father had only once beaten him, and that was for mimicking people who spoke with the peculiar accent of the uneducated Londoner. The particular method of

186

inculcating truth may not be advisable in every case; but the principle was sound, and in this case at least the lesson of respect for persons as such, whatever their station in life, had never been forgotten.

There is no doubt at all as to the school in which respect for persons as persons can best be learnt and taught. The Churches could do more than they are doing. Teachers have excellent opportunities, provided that classes are not too large. But it is still the family and the home that is the incomparable school of personal relationships. No special method or syllabus is required; everything depends simply on the way in which parents treat their own children. It is not enough that they should treat them with affection; it is not enough that they should give them wise and firm directions. It is required of parents that they respect their children. Each child needs to be studied, to be treated even from a very early age as a real person different from every other, with his own need for living room in which he can expand according to his own nature; with his own rights as an individual, that must not be infringed even by those who have natural authority over him. This demand may seem to add yet a further dimension of difficulty to the already formidable task of being a parent; but with the admixture of a little humour it may not prove so difficult after all. It is only when we ourselves are treated with respect that we come to understand what it means to respect the personality of others.

Next comes the general problem of self-discipline. The sex instinct tends to be violent and disorderly; it does not very easily come under control. But it is a great mistake to isolate this problem from the general problem of acquiring an ordered and disciplined personality. If young people have never learned self-control in such matters as order and punctuality, it is unlikely that they will be successful in an area where considerably greater resolution is required. Both the word and the idea "discipline" are extremely unpopular among the young; this is natural, but perhaps may be in part accounted for by the very negative way in which the idea is usually presented. No one is likely to be inspired by the idea of not doing something which is pleasant in itself merely because older people happen to regard it as wrong. On the other hand, the capacity of young people for imposing discipline on themselves, if interest or ambition is engaged, is almost unlimited. They will deny themselves all kinds of pleasures for weeks on end in order to save up enough money to make some desired purchase. They will submit themselves cheerfully to the slavery imposed by the football or basketball coach, if this is the price that has to be paid for winning or holding a coveted place on the team. If young people as a whole are not much interested in the ideal of self-control in the field of sex, this may be because it has never been presented to them in the form of a positive ideal, to which their deep-rooted impulse to grow up will respond.

The Christian attitude to sex is that it is good for a man to be master in his own house; that he should be able on all occasions to say a reasoned "Yes" or "No" to impulses, and that he should no longer be at the mercy of what Shakespeare pungently called "the expense of spirit in a waste of shame." Without this self-mastery no adult or responsible life is possible. If this concept can be expressed in terms of a religious ideal, or related to it, the power of its appeal is naturally enormously increased. But, even where the religious factor is absent, the ideal of adult and responsible manhood can be expressed in terms which make not the smallest appeal to fear, but demand only courage, resolution, and a willingness to grow up.

It is clear that such a statement of the case will make no appeal at all to those who think in terms of "sexual behaviour" and of sex activity merely as a form of self-expression. It will make only a limited appeal to those who have not accepted the basic principles of respect for persons and of the permanent linking of all sexual activity to mutual responsibility. It might be hoped, however, that when these positive principles had been accepted and supported by good will and a readiness to learn the art of self-discipline, particularly when all these are backed up by a religious ideal, the problems of the individual would be at an end. Experience shows that this is not so. Even when all these favourable factors are present, morbid sexual thoughts and fancies may continue to haunt the mind with obsessive persistence; adolescent habits may show unexpected resistance to the desire to be rid of them; the urge to actions which reason would condemn may take on compulsive power. What has gone wrong?

In almost every such case, it may be taken as certain that some other and hidden factor is at work. In the complicated mechanism of human emotion, it can easily happen that two streams can, as it were, combine and flow along a single channel. The impulse of sex is strong enough in itself. If some other stream has been diverted into the channel along which it flows and so has reinforced its current, it is hardly to be wondered at if the impulse proves almost irresistible. This is a commonplace both of the psychiatrist and of the pastor. Each, confronted by any serious disorganisation of the sexual mechanism, will at once ask himself whether this is the disease, or whether it is the surface manifestation of something that lies far deeper in the personality. In the great majority of cases, this preliminary estimate of the situation is proved by later investigation to be correct. Advice on the immediate problem may be useful; but it is almost certain that it will not be permanent in its effects, unless successful steps have been taken to identify the hidden factor which lies behind the disturbance, and which must be dealt with before the sexual dislocation can be repaired. The number of hidden factors which may operate in this way is very large. But three stand out above all others, both by their frequency and by their significance. The names of these three great enemies of the human race are fear, frustration, and resentment; to the consideration of these we must now turn.

VIII _Levit. to ch 7_ The Three Great Enemies

AMONG ALL THE ENEMIES of the human race perhaps the worst are fear, frustration, and resentment, and the greatest of these is fear. Perhaps it is for this reason that the words "Fear not" echo with almost monotonous iteration in every part of the Bible from its beginning to its end.*

Not every form of fear is harmful. Like pain, fear seems to have a creative part to play in the ordering of the world. Fear conveys the instinctive warning of danger; this results in that reflex and immediate action by which the danger is avoided and survival is made possible. In the evolutionary process it has perhaps contributed to the speed of the ostrich, who scorneth the horse and his rider, and to the grace of the gazelle. If we were not provided with it, it hardly seems likely that we should be able to survive at all in so dangerous a world as ours.

But there is another form of fear which has quite different effects. It leads either to confused and mistaken activity, such as impels the threatened animal to run directly towards the danger instead of away from it. Or it results in paralysis of action; the rabbit, fixed by the weasel's stare, remains rooted to the ground; it cannot for the life of it run. For a name for this second kind of fear we are indebted to the Greeks, who called it panic. They meant by the word first that strange terror that falls on man in

---

*The first occurrence is in Genesis 15:1; the last in Revelation 1:17. A German friend, with characteristic thoroughness, has worked out the figure for me—the words occur ninety-nine times in the Bible.

190

lonely and savage places, terror that a man cannot account for and that is unrelated to any specific cause for fear. Then the word can be used of that equally strange terror that makes a crowd of brave men run at full speed, why they know not, from what they know not, in a self-abandonment of which, once the cold fit has passed, they will be mortally ashamed.

A great many of the fears of childhood are of the panic dimension. Foolish adults sometimes speak of the trivial sorrows and fears of childhood. The child is small, so the argument seems to run, therefore its experiences must also be small. To speak or think in this way betokens a singular insensitiveness. As a matter of plain fact, no later experiences of sorrow or fear are so acutely felt as those of early childhood. The reason for this is obvious. One of the advantages of growing up is that we come to know our world so much better, and have yardsticks by which to measure its realities. We begin to know the proportions and the limits of things and to be aware of the healing properties of time. Not so the child. To it the world is still almost wholly unknown, the nature of the creatures that move in it uncertain, and the consequences of action unpredictable. Everything tends to take on the dimensions of the absolute and the eternal; the situation of distress feels as though it would never pass away. Many of the panics of childhood are related precisely to that which is unknown and invisible, to that which is always just over the brow of the hill or just round the corner. If only it could be induced to come to our side of the hill, to come into sight round the corner, it might be possible to deal with it; but it tends to remain obstinately out of sight, and therefore charged with an indefinite and illimitable power of menace.

Between the ages of three and six, panic is one of the natural reactions of a child to both things and persons. A considerable part of the process of growing up is the business of growing away from panic, so that it manifests itself ever more rarely in our reactions to the situations with which we have to deal. It is unlikely that this process is ever complete. Most of us carry about somewhere inside us a frightened child, whose presence we are fortunately able most of the time to conceal. It is probable that almost all of us could be reduced again to the childish level by the extremity of pain or of menace—records of experience under the Hitler regime suggest all too painfully this possibility. Sometimes in nightmares we revert to childhood and recover for a brief space the bitterness of earlier experiences which on the conscious level we may entirely have forgotten.

This killing kind of fear may take on many forms, and be related to many different things. There is the haunting fear of failure, of being laughed at, of being despised and written off as useless, of being excluded from society or from a group in which membership is greatly desired. Guilt, real or imaginary, is one of the major sources of panic. There are the strange dark fears associated with things or persons that for some reason have become symbolic of something else, such as the kindly and harmless chimney sweep of the days when there were chimneys. Every sensible person fears pain; but for some the threshold of pain is much lower than for others, and for them the fear of pain may become a haunting agony; though in such cases what is feared may be not so much the pain itself as the inability to bear it as it ought to be borne. There is the fear of being afraid, or at least of being seen to be afraid. But as in childhood, the worst fears are those to which no precise name can be given and which do not appear to be related to any identifiable object; those fears which dwell like a grey shadow on the very borders of the conscious mind and seem always ready to start out in living and terrifying form.

Fear, in its panic form, has gravely harmful effects on the working of the human system.

In the first place, it appears to slow down or to inhibit the process of development towards emotional maturity. If infantile or adolescent traits persist in otherwise grown up people, there is a strong probability that panic has somewhere been at work. This is not difficult to understand. If some part of the inner being is still living on the level of the panic-struck child, this is bound to show itself in some disharmony of development. Only if the source of panic can be identified and the individual released from the tyranny that it can exercise is it possible to set him once again on the path of growth to maturity.

Secondly, when fear only rarely rises to the level of crisis but persists like a dull and unvarying pain in the mind, it has much the same effects on the human mechanism as are exercised on the mechanism of a car by driving it with the brake hard on. The human mechanism will continue to work, but it seems to be paying a disproportionately high price for what is being produced. It works under conditions of strain and tension and pays in exhaustion for work that does not seem to demand any very considerable effort. This condition is often incorrectly described. A man is spoken of as highly-strung or as taking too much out of himself. He may be on the way to a nervous breakdown, and this, if it arrives, is likely to be attributed to the hard work that he has done or to the heavy responsibility that he has been carrying. It might be truer to say that the man has simply been hag-ridden by fear; he has been driving with the brakes on, and eventually the mechanism will stand it no longer. Very few men have ever been driven into a nervous breakdown by overwork. It is usually the other way round; when fear has built up a certain amount of nervous tension, a man becomes unable to stop working, not because he really has work that he must do but because of the restlessness that is born of fear.

This may be illustrated from a sphere which has already provided us with an illustration in another connection—the art of preaching. If a man has something to say and a moderately well-developed capacity for saying it, the tiredness which he feels on coming down from the pulpit should be akin to the pleasantly relaxed tiredness of the athlete in good training who has just run a mile and not to the nervous exhaustion which is the result of strain. If what he feels is exhaustion, one of the causes for which we shall certainly look is our old enemy—fear; not the fear of the Lord, but the panic fear that makes a man less than he really is. Once again this fear can take many forms. The preacher may be afraid of what his congregation is thinking of him, or rather of what he imagines they may be thinking of him, since their thoughts are probably far kinder than he imagines. He may be afraid that he will not be able to keep it up and that next Sunday's sermon will show a decline on the one before. If, as happens to even the greatest preachers, he comes down the pulpit stairs knowing that he has preached a thoroughly bad sermon, he may conclude that he will never be able to preach again. He may be anxiously comparing himself with other preachers, perhaps with his own assistant.

The fear may be so acute as to produce a kind of mental paralysis, and even physical nausea, before the moment comes for entering the pupit—though for some more fortunate people the black cloud is dissipated the moment that they begin to speak.

I have taken my illustration from a field that is specially familiar to me. Others could supplement this from the experiences of actors, concert pianists, or even professional boxers in the day or the hour before their appearance on the stage. It is a little too much to say that all "nerves" are fears; it can hardly be doubted that fear, unanalysable fear, panic, plays a large part in almost every form of nervous tension.

Sometimes fear is related not to one particular activity or sphere of responsibility but to the whole of life. It then takes on the grey forms of anxiety and worry, a general feeling that things are likely to go wrong and a sense of inability to cope with the disasters that may befall.

In many cases, perhaps in all, such worry can be analysed into a displacement of the human individual in relation to space and time. Space and time are the two lines, the co-ordinates, on which we have to live out our lives. At every instant these two intersect at one point and no other, the here and now in which we are, and in which alone at that moment we are presented with the opportunities of experience and action. If we remain firmly placed in that one moment of actuality, it is possible to look either forward or backward in time and out upon the whole universe without a trace of anxiety or tension. The writing of a book involves extensive planning into the future. Even the business of taking a holiday involves the consideration of alternatives and decisions as to actions which may still lie months ahead. Provided that the relationship between present and future is kept perfectly clear—I think of these things now, and I shall do them when the time comes—imaginary voyages into the future are a delightful occupation. Nothing gets done in them, but the exercise of the imagination is in itself a pleasurable thing.

Anxiety sets in only when the sense of the "here and now" becomes confused with the "there and then." If people are worrying about a relative who is lying sick in some distant place, not infrequently what the anxiety is really saying, though often this is not recognised, is something like, "I ought to be doing something about it, and I can't because I am here and she is there; I ought to be there and I am not." When a student lies in bed worrying about the examination that lies three weeks ahead of him, he is probably trying to answer the examination questions, with the slight inconvenience that the paper of questions is not yet in his hands. It hardly needs to be said that a robust realism does not exclude the possibility of regret for the past, of intense sympathy in the present, and of careful planning for the future. But in none of these need there be any trace of worry. The realistic question asked by the "here and now" is, "Can I at this moment do anything about it?" If the answer is "Yes," then whatever needs to be done should be done promptly and without delay. If, as is much more often the case, the answer is "No," the student had much better turn over and go to sleep; the business man had much better wait for the arrival of the morning paper to tell him what the markets have really been doing overnight.

Fear is a very terrible enemy. What is to be done about him? If people are afraid, as so many of us are, it is not the slightest use saying to them, "Don't be afraid" unless it is possible to support the injunction with such solid reasons as can really eject the enemy. If we are afraid, we are afraid, and this is the first fact that has to be taken seriously. To say to a Jew in Hitler's Germany, "Don't be afraid" must have seemed the bitterest cynicism. The favourite trick of the mentally well-balanced is to say to the mentally sick, "Just pull yourself together, and you'll be all right." There could hardly be any stronger ground for bringing in a verdict of justifiable homicide. If the sick man could pull himself together, he would not be ill; to tell him to do the very thing that he cannot do will only goad him to infuriation or increase the already heavy weight of his despair. We must have better remedies than what Tennyson called "vacant chaff well meant for grain."

The first step is to make sure that fear is clearly identified as fear.

It has the capacity to disguise itself under all kinds of fancy names. The minister who has difficulty with his sermons is likely to speak of his conscience; it is such a tremendous responsibility to stand up before a congregation to preach the word of God. It is. But responsibility in itself never caused anyone the loss of five minutes' sleep; the fear of responsibility has reduced a great many people to nervous wrecks. Oddly enough, one of the disguises under which fear hides itself is courage. During the late war a high-ranking officer who was suffering from mental strain was sent to see a psychiatrist. The psychiatrist told him, "The real fact is that you are afraid to go back to the front." The officer, a man of lionlike courage in the field, was naturally furious. For all that it is quite likely that the psychiatrist was right. To be afraid, honestly to admit that you are afraid, and to go on quietly with whatever has to be done is the adult and reasonable attitude. To refuse to admit that you are afraid and to compensate for fear by an exaggeration of courage may win you the Victoria Cross, but is one of those forms of overcompensation that are not to be encouraged; it is all too liable suddenly to give way.

If the presence of fear has been honestly admitted, the next thing is to find out, if possible, just what the fear is afraid of. Here the variety of possible answers is so great that a whole book would be required to describe them all, and the possible ways of dealing with them. The fear may be identified as no more than a survival from infancy, which, once recognised as such, and looked at in the light of day, ceases to trouble. Fear of authority can often be traced to the threatening presence of the father figure, from whom the grown man has never been emotionally set free. The anxious student may be measuring himself against his own past achievement, and wondering whether he can keep it up. The anxious minister may be comparing himself with an impossibly high ideal of what he imagines that he ought to be. In that case, what he needs is to be put back inside his own skin, and to learn to be content with a ministry of less than superhuman proportions.

It must not, however, be supposed that when all imaginary or pathological fears have been dealt with the task is at an end. We live in a dangerous and menacing world, and many are the occasions on which we feel the need of a courage greater than we possess. We are all afraid of cancer, and with good reason. No doubt the element of the unknown and the difficulty in many cases of either cure or alleviation have inflated the natural fear to the level of

196

panic. But no one who has ever had to help a woman who has just been told by the doctor that she has cancer is likely to underestimate the difficulty of the task. The courage with which human beings do face their troubles and afflictions is a source of continual astonishment to the pastor who shares them; but there are moments in which courage seems to ooze out through the fingertips, leaving nothing but a bleak and surging ocean of dismay. Even then, there is much that can be done. Dangers directly faced lose something of their power to appal. It is possible, in face of the sudden menace of dangerous or painful illness, to point out the advances in modern methods of treatment, the alleviations of pain that are now possible. But fear is an enemy whom it is very hard to exorcise, and before whom the spells of the charmer are often uttered in vain.

It is in such circumstances that the "Fear not" of the Bible may seem to have a power that merely human consolations often lack. The words were often spoken in situations of apparently desperate need. They ring out with confidence when the children of Israel are caught almost literally between the devil and the deep sea, with the pursuing hosts of Pharaoh behind and the Red Sea in front. They recur at almost every grave crisis of national or of individual life. It was a Jesus who knew quite well that he was going to be crucified who said to his friends, "Fear not, little flock, it is your father's good pleasure to give you the kingdom." Sometimes as here he uses the familiar Old Testament form, "Fear not"; but often he phrases the thought in the more positive expression, "Be of good cheer; take heart; cheer up."

One of the most characteristic of the words of Jesus, and the one that the modern world finds it hardest to take seriously or literally, is the command not to worry: "Take no anxious thought for the morrow." In modern terms, this means exactly, "Don't worry." Obviously, in the light of the rest of the New Testament, this cannot be intended to inculcate a happy-go-lucky, irresponsible attitude to life. When some enthusiastic Christians, confident that the Second Coming of Christ was just round the corner, had given up the fulfillment of the ordinary duties and tasks of life, Paul very soon brought them to their senses with the dry admonition, "If any man will not work, neither shall he eat." Christian faith demands a serious and responsible attitude to life; but it also takes seriously the fact of God.

Mental health depends upon a willingness to live in the "here and now." As we have said, that is the only time in which we can experience and in which we can act. But it is also the only time and place in which we can meet God, because only then and there are we really ourselves. It may well be that, when we meet God, he will tell us that we are in a place in which we have no business to be and that we must get out of it as soon as possible. That does not alter the fact that we are where we are and nowhere else. When the prophet Elijah, in a very uncharacteristic fit of depression, had left his work and his witness and had fled into the desert, the Lord did meet him at the mount of Horeb, pointed out very plainly that he had no business to be there, and sent him back at once to take up again the work that his timidity had for the moment interrupted. To live in the "here and now," as and where we are, means to live one day at a time and to leave the future in the hands of God. This does not, of course, exclude the possibility of careful planning. It does exclude the possibility of worry, and to the Christian worry is sin. Again, this attitude is not based on a facile optimism. It simply accepts realistically the unknownness of the future. There are innumerable factors that are beyond our control, innumerable possibilities that we cannot foresee. If we began to attempt to foresee them all, we should never be able to do anything at all. The Christian simply recognises that these things are not beyond the control or the foreknowledge of God, and that they can all be safely left in his hands.

The argument that Jesus advances in favour of this trustful confidence is the faithfulness of God as it is seen in nature. This world is no automatic and self-working machine; it is God who every day causes the sun to rise upon the evil and the good alike and gives his rain without distinction to the just and to the unjust. But there is a more intimate note as well. He marks the falling of the sparrows; and man is worth many sparrows. The affirmation of the Gospel is that God is personally and directly interested in every human individual. All the resources of his wisdom and his power are at the disposal of those who care to call upon him. This does not mean, of course, that any special protection is available to the Christian; he is as likely as any other man to be run down by a reckless driver after dark. What is promised to him is that he will never be overwhelmed by a sense of the vastness and the meaninglessness of life; that his life will be lived out as the development of a personal destiny in relation to another who cares and who does not permit that anyone who has trusted in him shall live in vain. No promise is given that he will be exempt from the very worst of sufferings, from hate or calumny or injustice or physical disease. It is promised that, if suffering comes, strength will at the same time be given to bear the suffering, and that what might otherwise appear to be senseless suffering will begin to take on a shape of meaning in relation to the pattern of the whole. Even death will be transformed into the last and most exciting adventure.

This view rests not on the words of a sage remote from the trials and conflicts of ordinary men, but on the witness of a man who was on his way to be crucified and yet affirmed that he had overcome the world; not on the dreams of a visionary, but on the stark realistic outlook of the most uncompromising realist the world has yet seen. Jesus never for a moment encouraged his followers to think that life would be easy. The violent contrast between his principles and those that are generally accepted in the world made it certain that to the end of time his followers would find themselves in conflict with the society around them. Jesus tells them quite plainly that this will be so. It is sometimes harder to send others out to suffer than to accept suffering for oneself. Jesus does not fail at either point; he goes without hesitation to meet his own death, and he sends his followers out in the certain expectation that some at least among them will have to face times no less hard than he. If the Church has sometimes looked more like a hospital for sick souls than a training camp for heroes, the fault cannot be laid at the door of its founder. He was in the habit of looking at things as they were and of telling the truth. If he was able both to tell his followers of the trials and sufferings that would come upon them and also to encourage them not to be afraid, this was only because of his unshakable confidence that the world is made in one particular way and not in another, that God is always on the side of what is right and true, that no one will be led into trials harsher than, with the help of the grace of God, he will be able to bear, and that nothing of all these sufferings will be wasted or will be in vain.

This belief in the presence and the providence of a loving God has proved of such value, century after century, in giving human beings confidence and peace, it has shown itself of such immense therapeutic power in cases of mental illness, that some might judge it better that, even if the belief rests on an illusion, humanity should be left in possession of such a precious illusion rather than that it should be disillusioned. Such would seem to have been the view of, for instance, Alfred Adler, who did not himself believe in the existence of such a God. He wrote: "From the point of view of Individual Psychology, the conception of the Godhead and its enormous importance for mankind can be understood, recognised and prized. It personifies man's feeling for what is good and perfect."* *believe every bogus –*

A psychologist may well regard himself as justified in accepting the utility of ideas without regard to their objective truth. For the Christian this is impossible. The first thing that he has learned from Jesus is to be done with the illusions, with the idols, and to hold only to that which is ultimately and objectively true. If the belief in a good and loving God corresponds to the truth, it will certainly be useful in the development of a genuinely human existence. But the converse argument does not hold. The fact that something is useful is not necessarily an argument in favour of its truth. The Christian can take his stand on the Christian belief in God only if he is convinced that on this, as on so many other subjects, Jesus talked sense and that in so far as such propositions can be verified at all these can be verified in relation to the total picture of the universe and of man's life which they present, and in relation to the total experiment of attempting to live in the light which they provide. If incontrovertible evidence were to be produced on the other side, the belief in a God of love, however comforting and however therapeutically valuable, must inexorably be given up.

Our second great enemy is frustration.

*Quoted in Lewis Way: *Alfred Adler: An Introduction to his Psychology* (Pelican Books, 1956), p. 52.

It must first be recognised that limitation, which is not readily distinguishable from frustration, is a necessary and inevitable part of our lot, as creatures endowed with sense, intellect, and imagination, fated to live for a number of years weighed down by a very material body, in the midst of material objects that always present a measure of resistance to the purposes that we would put into execution through them. Here, published on the very day on which this chapter was first written, are two sentences which vividly portray the nature of such limitation, and the kind of human conflicts to which it can give rise: "Vere, passionate, imaginative and highly strung, thirsts instinctively for some mode of experience in which his own nature can fulfil itself in rapture. The problem of his life will always be to reconcile this thirst with the cramping limitations of the human lot."* That is always the problem for all of us. We live in a world where high aims and aspirations are likely to be foiled by the recalcitrance of the raw materials, human and non-human, of which our lives are made up, in a world in which matter is never perfectly capable of receiving the forms that imagination would impose upon it.

The master of the plastic arts wrestles with the problem of imaginative expression in visible form, and by means of materials that are recalcitrant and never perfectly responsive to his will. We may learn from him both what the problem is, and how the wise man will set himself to deal with it. The artist always knows that something in his vision will certainly escape him in the process of recording it. "Heard melodies are sweet, but those unheard Are sweeter." The painter knows that he will never be able really to catch the gleam of early light upon the waters or the flashing hues of the peacock's tail. If the creative impulse in him is not very strong, he may give up the struggle and be content to paint in imagination pictures far more splendid than his hands could ever achieve. If he is a real creator, he will wrestle with his vision, make the best of the materials that he has to hand without complaining of their inadequacy, and will come as near as he can to a perfection that he still knows to be forever unattainable. This is both the glory and the agony of the artist. In order to be able to

*Lord David Cecil, in *The Sunday Times*, Aug. 26, 1956, p. 5.

create at all, he must accept the limitations of his art, of his materials, of the real and the possible. It is in vigorous and healthy conflict between the unlimited ideal and the limited possibilities that the work of art is born. Once again the parallel between life and art is relevant. The material in which we have to work—the situations and the contacts of everyday life—is no less recalcitrant than that of the artist. Wise men do not complain of their tools or of their materials but set to work to create something within the limits of the possible. *accept & work within limitations. feel he all to*

There are two ways of dealing with frustration that are harmful or at least dangerous.

The first is to avoid facing the reality of the frustrations by remaining always in the world of the imagination. The man of little ability but overweening ambition can give a good account of himself in this way; he has never done anything very important, but he certainly would have done so if circumstances had been a little different from what they are—if only he had been given a chance, if only his parents had sent him to a different school, if only he had not suffered from a particular illness at a particular time. All too often the enumeration of the "if onlies" holds him back from the real though moderate achievement that might be his if only he would move out of the world of imagination into that of the hard and less glowing realities. What holds him back is perhaps fear of the loss of self-respect if actual performance falls below the level of achievement of which he has always believed himself to be capable.

The other method is to bulldoze through obstacles by an intense and exhausting application of the will. Some of those who have been born with such a handicap as very small stature or a weak voice have been known to attain to fame as dictators or as great orators, through such rigorous self-dedication to a single object as has enabled them to overcome the defect. The danger in such overcompensation is that the one desired object may be attained only through the sacrifice of many other desirable things and qualities and that such achievement may in the end prove to be dangerously brittle. There is the further truth that for one Demosthenes, who made good in spite of his weak voice, there must have been ten who have died worn out and heartbroken in an attempt which from the beginning offered very little hope of being successful.

The first lesson in the art of dealing with frustration is the simple and realistic one of accepting ourselves just as we are, and the situation in which we find ourselves just as it is. What, like the artist handling refractory materials, we may be able to make out of this unpromising self and these unpromising circumstances is another question. But we make many of our frustrations for ourselves by our failure in this elementary realism.

The baby crying in his cradle may be our first object lesson. What he is probably trying to say is that there is something that he wants very much and that he must have it now and without delay. The hard lesson that he has to learn is that there are some things that he will never be able to have; and that others he will be able to have, but only if he is prepared to wait for them in their appointed time. Baby may be stretching out his arms to clasp the round bright moon. He may stretch them out till dooms-day, but the moon will never come to his embrace. He may want his bottle very much, and he may want it quickly. If he is lucky, his crying may attract the attention of those inexplicable grown-ups and soften their hard hearts so that they give him what he wants; but it is equally possible that they will conclude that there is no reason for interrupting routine and that baby had better learn to wait until the regular hour. If so, he had much better learn resignation and go to sleep. What he wants will come if he is willing to wait. Even the least cynical observer of human conduct must conclude with regret that the majority of the human species has never learned these two elementary lessons of renunciation and patience. If they had, our life would be less marked than it is by the principles of grab and snatch, and there would be less resemblance than there is between our contemporaries and that prodigal son who demanded his inheritance on the instant without the willingness to wait for the day on which it would legitimately be due.

Because we have not learned these two lessons, we create a great many frustrations for ourselves.

A girl makes up her mind to go on the stage and beats fruitlessly on the closed doors of the theatrical world. She is likely to complain of the wickedness of agents and managers and the lack of opportunity for talent. She suffers agonies of frustration and near despair. The trouble may really lie simply in her lack of ability in the dramatic art. If she is willing to recognise this and to make terms with reality, it is likely that the frustration will disappear, and that she will find happiness and contentment in some other, perhaps less glamorous, career.

A young man has ambitions in the political world. He is frustrated by his lack of success. It may be that he has the necessary gifts but has made an error of calculation on the time scale and therefore is subject to frustration. He has failed to reckon with the necessity of long and concentrated study, of patient service in the not very interesting jobs that have to be done in the lower echelons of the political world by the vast majority of those whose aim it is to rise higher. If he can make up his mind to long patience, it is quite possible that success will come to him in the end—and to wait patiently when the necessity for patience has been recognised involves no frustration at all.

But this is not the end of the matter. There are certain frustrations which we are all likely to encounter and which are not easy to deal with. Most of us are one day going to grow old. The advance of medical science makes it certain that an ever increasing proportion of human beings will live to a ripe old age, and old age is bound to be accompanied by some frustrations which death alone can cure. In the sober words of the historian Edward Gibbon, who by his own confession was less sensible of pain than of pleasure, "I must reluctantly observe that two causes, the abbreviation of time and the failure of hope, will always tinge with a browner shade the evening of life." It is well that we should learn in time how these problems are to be dealt with.

Accident or sudden ill-health may suddenly reduce our field of activity within very narrow limits. The success of psychiatry in certain areas has been so great that there has perhaps been a tendency for an optimistic public to believe that there is nothing in this field that cannot be cured; and some psychiatrists have perhaps held out hopes that they cannot fulfil. But this is not so. The mysterious psyche of which we still know so little can suffer permanent injury no less than the body. If a limb of the body has been amputated, no one expects it to grow again. If something similar has happened to the inner self, it is hardly possible to hope for perfect cure. In a field which is so beset by uncertainties, and in which there is so very little that can be regarded as established scientific knowledge, it is necessary to speak with due caution. But there is reason to think that in certain cases, though by no means in all, homosexuality may be the result of some such grave and early injuries, and in such cases it is hardly possible to hope for the full restoration of normal emotional development. In other cases, the needed help has come too late; mental health has been restored, but the precious years, in which a career could have been planned or emotional fulfilment sought, have passed and cannot be given back. There is a reality of permanent and irreparable loss.

This does not mean that nothing can be done. It is important, however, that the difficulty and the seriousness of the problem should be recognised. Where limitations of achievement and of hope are unavoidable, the first lesson that has to be learned is that we must live within the limits of that which is possible for us. What this means has been vividly illustrated for our generation by the experience of the countless men and women who have had to live for years as prisoners of war or in concentration camps. In such circumstances three types of reaction can be sharply distinguished. There are the escapists—those whose passion to break out from captivity never lets them rest and leads to an almost frenzied recklessness in the effort to escape. (These must not be confused with such sober and methodical plotters as are depicted in *The Wooden Horse* and other sagas of escape from prison camps in the period of World War II.) There are those who cannot adapt themselves to the hard circumstances of captivity, sink into melancholy, and end up in one form or another of physical or mental disease. There are yet others who make up their minds to make literally the best of what is bound to be at least a troublesome, and at worst can be a tragic, experience. It is astonishing how much men of this type can pass through, and emerge to all appearances mentally and emotionally unscathed. Their doctrine can be summed up epigrammatically in the advice: "If you have to live in a cell eight feet by eight, mark out on the floor an area six feet by six and live within it; you will then always have the feeling of free space around you; you will be living within your possibilities and with a margin to spare."

This is the first lesson, but it is only the first. It is the negative side of the matter. The second, and the harder lesson, involves the willingness to recognise that frustration itself can be the opportunity for creative achievement.

No man in history can ever have been more hemmed in by the realities of frustration than Jesus of Nazareth. He was born into the midst of an oppressed and subject people. The religion of Israel had had its great days; but in his time it had become so ossified that it seemed well-nigh impossible for the leaders of the people even to understand the language that he was speaking. We have already commented on the obtuseness of the disciples and their failure to discern the way in which their master was trying to lead them. It is deeply moving to see what Jesus makes of all this.

He firmly rejects two possibilities of evading the frustrations that were open to him. He might have set himself at the head of a Jewish nationalistic movement of revolt. Forty years later such a revolt did break out. The Jews were ill-led, divided, and unskilled in the military arts; yet with all these drawbacks they held out for three years against all the power of Rome, and the ferocity of their resistance was such as almost to shake the stability of the entire Roman world. It is interesting to speculate on what the consequences might have been if the unique insight and powers of leadership possessed by Jesus had been dedicated to the cause of violence and not to that of peace. The other possibility that was open to him was that of turning from the stubborn Jewry of Palestine to the open world of the Gentiles. The Jews outside Palestine were far more accessible to new ideas than the traditionalists of the old country; many among the thoughtful Gentiles were seeking a more living truth than that which they knew. The story of the Acts of the Apostles makes plain to us the richness and the variety of the opportunity that lay before Jesus in the Gentile world, if he had wished to take it. These two possibilities were ever before him and both he deliberately rejected. He had a task to perform; it was clear to him that it could be performed only in

206

Jerusalem, and only at the cost of his life. So he accepts the situation with all its limitations and its problems as the raw material that has been given him. Like the artist, who takes the materials that he has at hand without complaining that they are no better and makes out of them the matchless creation of his skill—shows his skill perhaps most wonderfully, when his materials are most inadequate—Jesus takes this particular stretch of space and time and uses it as the material out of which he will create the fabric of a perfect human life. Frustration is used by him as the opportunity for a particular form of creative activity; even the bitter criticisms of his foes are transformed by him into the exquisite parables of the lost sheep, the lost coin, and the lost son.

Something of this kind is within the reach of us all, if we are prepared to learn certain rather hard lessons. There is no frustration which, if calmly and imaginatively accepted, cannot be turned to creative use; no rind so bitter that it cannot be found to conceal sweet fruit within. When effort and self-sacrifice are devoted to the overcoming of some physical defect or handicap, the effort is in many cases visible to the world and is regarded as admirable. Even the enemies of Franklin Roosevelt could not withhold their admiration from the dogged courage and self-discipline that brought the career of a statesman within the reach of a man so terribly paralysed by the ravages of poliomyelitis. When the handicap is inward and invisible, the conflict is precisely the same, but is lonelier and therefore harder. The man or woman who accepts some irremediable loss, such as the permanent frustration of the hope of marriage and parenthood, and makes a career and a character in spite of it, is likely to have little recognition other than the inner voice of conscience; yet some who have no idea of the price that has been paid may be aware of some special strength or sweetness of character, for which they can find no ready explanation.

The third and the most deadly of the three great enemies is resentment. This is the most toxic of all the ills that can assail the human spirit. In many cases it is possible to see the venom that it distils and to trace its harmful effects on every part of the inner constitution of man. And just in proportion to its deadliness, this sickness is difficult to cure. In the gigantic tragedy of *King Lear*, Shakespeare has shown us, without sparing a single stroke,

207

just what havoc resentment can wreak in the mind and heart of man. It is true that Lear is to a very large extent responsible for his own misfortunes. When he says, "I am a very foolish, fond old man," he is speaking the exact truth. But this does not alter the fact that he has been abominably treated by his daughters, all the more abominably that their offence has been committed against a trusting though rather foolish affection. There are many Lears in the world, though not many of them have found a Shakespeare to sing their tragedy.

Clean wounds heal quickly; the festering wound never heals. The festering wound is the symbol of that injury which has been met with resentful indignation. It will not do to say, as foolish comforters say, "Think how trivial all this will look in a thousand years." Some wounds are healed by time but not all. Fifty years later, the injury caused by an unjust schoolmaster or an unkind parent may be felt just as keenly as on the day on which it was inflicted; the wound burns and smarts whenever recollection is turned back to it. There is no reason to suppose that, if life could be continued for a thousand years, the situation would be any different at the end of that time from what it is after the lapse of fifty years. If such wounds are to be healed, some healer more potent than time must be discovered.

Patient discussion of the facts may help to alleviate the ill. It may be possible to show that there was no real injury at all, or that, if there was, it was purely accidental. Perhaps the real injury was far less serious than inflamed feelings have suggested. But this is not always so. After all, parents do inflict the most dreadful injuries on their children; sometimes by thoughtless severity; sometimes by an unwise solicitude that makes it impossible for the child to have any independent existence of its own; more often through such capriciousness as reveals the lack of any settled principle in the minds of the parents and makes it impossible for them to provide that stable, ordered universe within which alone a child can feel secure and grow. In many cases there was no deliberate intention on the part of the parents; but the one who has been injured has reason on his side if he cries out, "But they ought to have known; after all they have been children themselves." It is always the injuries caused by those nearest to us, by those on whose trustworthiness we feel that we should be able to count, that cause the deepest agony and the most implacable resentment. More than two thousand years have not dulled the force of the words of the Psalm: "For it was not an enemy that reproached me; then I could have borne it; neither was it he that hated me that did magnify himself against me; then I could have hid myself from him. But it was thou, a man mine equal, my guide and my acquaintance. We took sweet counsel together, and walked unto the house of God in company." It is not surprising that Christian tradition has regarded these words as a prophecy of the betrayal of Jesus of Nazareth by Judas Iscariot, the man whom at the moment of the betrayal Jesus addressed as "Friend."

Such injury, inflicted within the inner circle of those who should be worthy of love and trust, can produce the most devastating effects. It may result in a permanent feeling of being rejected, of being unloved and unlovable. It may project itself outwards in a universal distrust, an unwillingness to repose confidence in any human being. This is a situation with which both psychiatrist and pastor are familiar, and one with which it is most difficult to deal. The one who desires to help lies under the same judgment of total untrustworthiness as the whole of the rest of humanity. In such a situation, where can a remedy be found?

When I read technical books on psychology, there is one word for which I always look in the index and rarely find. It is the word "forgiveness." There is no other word in the English language which expresses exactly the same idea; even "pardon" has a different ring and slightly different connotations. If the absence of the word implies also an absence of this central idea from contemporary psychological thought, this may indicate a lacuna the filling of which would be greatly to the advantage of both psychological thought and psychiatric practice.

The willingness to forgive* does not involve treating the original offence and the resulting injury as though they were unimportant, still less pretending that they have never happened. It does not involve finding excuses for everything, and pretending that the

*In Chapter IV, we considered the passive, the value of the assurance of *having been forgiven*. Here we take up the active, the duty and the possibility of forgiving others.

one who has done the wrong was not really in the wrong. The correct term for this approach is "condonation," at times a legitimate method of procedure but one which has nothing to do with forgiveness. Forgiveness is sternly and ruthlessly realistic. It starts from an unemotional and factual consideration of just what has happened, of the consequences that have flowed from it, and of the responsibilities of those concerned. Being akin to justice, it makes full allowance for ignorance and inexperience, for the strength of temptation and the confusion of human motives. But being realistic, it insists on treating responsible beings as responsible and will not palter with any attempt to assist them in evading their responsibilities. When every allowance has been made, when every legitimate excuse has been accepted, the verdict still may be, "This was wrong; they knew, or if they had thought for a moment, they would have known that it was wrong; and still they did it." We need not at this point read a very moralistic sense into the word "wrong." It need mean no more than such aggression against the integrity of a human being as has made that human being less efficient in the task of being a human being than he otherwise would have been. The word can mean more than this; it can hardly mean less, and in this connection the minimum meaning will serve. Now when this is the situation, when the unfavourable judgment has been passed, it has to be recognised that resentment is a natural, almost inevitable, and in part even justifiable human reaction. Yet as long as resentment lasts, nothing can be done to improve the situation; the harm both outward and inward continues to work.

It is at this point that forgiveness can and does work miracles. It operates entirely in the world of personal relationships and recreates a situation that has gone most grievously awry. Resentment rejects the wrongdoer; it would annihilate him if it could. Since in the majority of cases this is not possible, it may solve the problem by annihilating him from consciousness; for me he no longer exists; or, if he exists, it is only as a symbol of the cruelty and perfidy of the human race and not as a genuinely human creature. Forgiveness exactly reverses this process. It recognises the wrongdoer as a person. He has done wrong, and about this there is to be no pretence. But that is not the whole truth about him. He is still of infinite value as a person, since every person is unique and irreplaceable by any

210

other. Since he has so greatly injured himself by doing wrong, he is in special need of help, and help that can be rendered only by the one to whom he has done the wrong. Only the hair of the dog that he has bitten can heal him! Forgiveness can spring only from a self-forgetfulness that is more concerned about another's well-being than about its own, and that longs for the renewal of fellowship even when fellowship has been flouted and destroyed by the wilful aggression of another.

If resentment is the most toxic of all the ills that flesh is heir to, forgiveness, the act of forgiving, the willingness to forgive, is the most potent, the most rapid, the most efficacious in its working of all known remedies. Cases are on record of those who have gone to bed one night still weighed down by the burden of resentment, though eager to be delivered from it, and have woken up the next morning to find that the burden is gone, and that they are looking out on the world with new eyes.

In certain cases mere human reasonableness may lead to the abandonment of resentment. But this appears to be somewhat uncommon. The more usual attitude is to say, "That was unforgivable, and I can never forgive it." No one who has ever had occasion to forgive a really grievous wrong is likely to doubt that forgiveness is an extremely costly medicine, or that most men find it difficult to make up their minds to pay the necessary price.

Here, more than at any other point, the Christian Gospel proves its enormous therapeutic power. It is based on the belief that forgiveness is at the very heart of the universe; in a unique way it shows men and women how to forgive and helps them to do it.

There is, first, the example and the teaching of Jesus himself. No one in recorded history has ever had better grounds for resentment; in rejection by those who ought to have welcomed him; in desertion by his disciples; in betrayal by his friend; in the pettiness and corruption of so-called human justice; in the fickleness and beastliness of a crowd; in the abominable heartlessness of religious men who would mock a crucified prisoner. Yet for all this his first recorded word from the cross is "Father, forgive them, for they know not what they do." Nothing in the whole of human history is more important than this; it is here revealed once for all that there is no situation so desperate that forgiveness cannot reach it. But Jesus

211

made no secret of his demand that other men must be prepared to do what he was willing to do himself; on nothing is he more insistent than on the duty of men to forgive one another, however great the wrong, and even though forgiveness should be needed until seventy times seven.

Yet for most men it is neither the example nor the words of Jesus that makes forgiveness possible; it is the discovery that through him they have themselves been forgiven.

Most of us have a fairly good opinion of ourselves, and would be prepared to echo the words of Hamlet, "I am myself indifferent honest." There come, however, moments of self-knowledge, particularly in the light of what Jesus was and did, in which the next part of Hamlet's speech seems painfully appropriate: "I am myself indifferent honest; but yet I could accuse me of such things that it were better my mother had not borne me; I am very proud, revengeful, ambitious, with more offences at my beck than I have thoughts to put them in, imagination to give them shape, or time to act them in. What should such fellows as I do crawling between heaven and earth? We are arrant knaves all; believe none of us."

For in fact we are not very pleasant people. God has given us a wonderful earth full of beautiful things. It seems to be man's pleasure to turn it into a desert. He has given us nimble brains and skilful hands, and we create the awful pullulations of our giant cities, where the air is polluted with the smoke of our chimneys and the ground littered with the mess we make. We use our inventiveness for our own mutual destruction. Behind all these things must lie grasping, ungenerous, ungrateful hearts. For the most part we wash our hands of these things and say that we are not responsible; but at moments the recognition comes that, though we have not done these things, we are akin to those who do them. It is not what we have done that matters, but the kind of people that we are. A young friend once came to see me with the words, "I feel that I would like to say that I am sorry." To my somewhat astonished question, "What for?" he replied, "Just for being myself." If God is in the least like what Jesus affirmed him to be, that is exactly what we all need—to be forgiven just for being ourselves, for what we have made of ourselves in this beautiful world.

The most astonishing experience in life is the realisation that such as we are, without desert and without expiation, without fee and without compensation, we have been accepted by God in Jesus Christ. Forgiveness is always creative; it brings into being a totally new situation; it is hardly an exaggeration to say that it brings into being a new world. But those who without any deserving of their own have received this miraculous gift of God's forgiveness can hardly refuse to forgive their fellow men. However great the offence, it cannot be more than trivial in comparison with the immense weight of those offences against God for which the Christian knows that he has received forgiveness. It is never easy to forgive others, if they have done us really grievous wrong. In the light of the cross of Christ, and the assurance of God's forgiveness that this has brought us, the forgiveness of man by man can no longer be thought impossible. The aim of the life and death of Christ was to reconcile man to God. A secondary result of it has been to make possible the reconciliation of man with man.

— or self justification / guilt

IX The Way to Freedom

THE CHILD'S IDEA OF FREEDOM is that it means "being able to do whatever I like," without having to obey other people's commands or to pay attention to other people's interests. "I am monarch of all I survey" was written first of Alexander Selkirk, the original of Robinson Crusoe, and no doubt this is a description of an almost perfect form of liberty; on the other hand life in solitude on a desert island is not the pleasantest or most human form of existence, and not one that most of us would readily choose. In any case, even if we would wish to choose it, we do not as a matter of fact live on desert islands and, if we are to be free at all, we have to find our freedom in a very different setting.

Children are not the only ones who have cherished this kind of ideal of freedom. The Stoics under the Roman Empire thought that the free man was one who had constructed within himself an ivory tower into which he could retreat in order to be entirely free of any human contact, and the key to which he would not surrender even to the wife of his bosom. Any deep human affection, any form of dependence on others, they held, was a form of slavery to which the wise man should not be subject. Those Stoics of the first century A.D., who asserted their independence and were prepared to resist the Roman emperors even unto death, have left to us admirable examples of heroism and constancy; but they do strike us as rather cold and inhuman. Perhaps if men have to live under an irresponsible tyranny, this is the only kind of liberty they can hope for or achieve. But it seems to be a rather melancholy kind of freedom.

And does it really correspond to the idea of freedom, when we think out accurately what that word means?

It would seem that real human freedom is almost exactly the opposite of what the child or the Stoic imagines it to be. It is freedom in the fellowship of other human beings. We have to live in society. To be free means to be able to enter into all kinds of human relationships with all kinds of people and to remain ourselves in all of them. Just because the free man is always himself, he has something original and valuable to contribute to every such relationship, and at the same time he can be himself enriched by everything of wisdom and experience that others have to offer. It is clear that such a life of unconstrained and multiple relationships would be endlessly enjoyable and rewarding; we must not be surprised if it is somewhat difficult to achieve, and if it is obtainable only at a rather high price in this austere world, in which nothing that is worth having can be had unless a just price has been paid for it.

That this is a correct account of human freedom becomes probable the moment we think of the way in which nature and circumstances cause us actually to live. This is an individualistic age; we think of ourselves as individuals, and perhaps that is the starting point of all our thinking about freedom, as about almost every other subject. But we do not in reality start as individuals. Society comes before the individual. As we have already noted, the child begins life as the centre of a complex set of relationships, and in a state of almost complete emotional dependence on human beings other than itself. The emergence of the individual is a slow and difficult process. Quite a long time passes before the growing child begins to speak of itself as "I." A much longer period elapses before it has reached the level of individuality in the full sense of the term, and is able to make a stand and to take decisions of its own in full emotional independence of parents and older people.

But the aim of this long process of education into individuality is not that the child should emerge into proud isolation from all other human beings; it is simply that it should exchange one set of relationships for another. The old dependence must absolutely disappear if we are ever to attain to maturity; we have considered some of the difficulties that stand in the way of that liberation. But what follows is the possibility of genuinely human and personal relation-

ships, freely chosen for their value, or at the worst freely accepted if
they cannot be avoided. Such relationships can stand at any point
on the scale, between the total and permanent self-commitment of
a happy marriage, and the chance association of a brief encounter
with friendly people on a railway journey.

In even the simplest society human relationships will be found to
be of three types—superiority, equality, and inferiority; or, to put it
a little more formally, authority, equality, and subordination. There
can also be certain combinations of the types. Parents are necessarily superior to their children—in age, in experience, in authority.
Children are equal to one another in the relationship children-
parents; but unequal among themselves in the relationship between
younger and older children. Even when we grow up, we are likely
to find ourselves accompanied all through our lives by all these
situations, separately or in combination, at home, in our work, and
in our responsibilities as citizens. A great many men who are about
half the way up the line of authority in their jobs could make their
own the remark of the centurion in the Gospel, "I am a man under
authority, having soldiers under me." Equality is the rule in relationships of true friendship and colleagueship. The family and
fatherhood make demands for the wise exercise of authority. The
happy man is at home in all these forms of relationship, and can use
them all as fields for the exercise and the enjoyment of his freedom.

It is no surprise to find that all three types of relationship are to be
found in that life to which we turn back from time to time for
indications as to the nature of a genuinely human existence. In the
one fragment which is preserved to us from the early years of the
life of Jesus, we read that he went down to Nazareth, and was subject to his parents. There is no suggestion that he found this subordination and the long years of occupation in the carpenter's shop
irksome. In his association with his disciples he deliberately puts
them on an equality with himself: "I have not called you servants,
but I have called you friends." But, at the same time, there is the
unmistakable note of authority: "I say unto you." He makes tremendous demands of those who will follow him and expects that his
commands will be obeyed, though he always respects the personal
integrity of those to whom he issues the commands; there is no
attempt to coerce them, only a recognition of their right to go away,

216

if they desire to do so. "Ye call me master and lord, and ye say well; for so I am." But he will not exercise that coercive jurisdiction, which is the mark of the rulers among the Gentiles, and which makes impossible the fulness of freedom among their subjects. And, paradoxically, he chooses for himself a situation of inferiority among those whom he commands and whom he has promoted to be his equals—"I am among you as he that serveth"—and lays this down as the principle that is to govern the new society which he is bringing into being. In all three relationships he is perfectly at ease, and in each one of them holds himself with the poise and balance which are the marks of the man who is truly free.

We all have to live in one way or another in this cluster of relationships. The mastery of each of them is for most people a lesson that has to be learned by patient application, rather than something that comes spontaneously and by nature. The exercise of authority can be marred by arrogance and intolerance of the imperfections of others; the equality of friendship by self-assertion, by suspicion that the other is taking advantage of the friendship, or by anxiety lest the friendship be transferred elsewhere; the relationship of subordination by undue submissiveness, a renunciation of personal integrity which may well be balanced by inner resentment. It sometimes seems that one who is bad at one relationship is equally bad at all; and this raises the question whether in a great many instances of the failure or imperfection of human relationships there may not be one single underlying cause. If such a possibility can be entertained, it may be suggested that the underlying cause in each case is the individual's uncertainty as to his own value, as to his capacity to cope with the situations with which he has to deal, in a word, as to his own ability to live.

This may seem at first paradoxical. It may seem strange to attempt to account in the same way for the overstrictness of the martinet and for the agonised uncertainty of the man who cannot make up his mind about anything. Is not the one as much due to overconfidence as the other to lack of confidence? And yet appearances may be deceptive, and the difference in manifestation conceal an identity of cause. Human nature has to be held in some kind of equilibrium if it is to continue to work at all. If there is a "down," there is almost certain to be a balancing "up." Arrogance, boastfulness, fault-finding, harsh criticism of others, and the tendency to show off, are almost always signs of an inner sense of uncertainty or insecurity, a compensation by way of exaggeration for the feeling of some inner defect. If a child has a tendency to show off, the natural reaction of older people or of older children is to snub the child, to suppress it, or to cause it some kind of humiliation. What is often needed is exactly the contrary—encouragement and help towards the recovery or the attainment of the missing self-confidence. If successful steps can be taken to bring the uncomfortable "down" a little way up, the unpleasantly compensating "up" is likely to begin without effort to find its way down.

It is not difficult to recognise in this feeling of uncertainty about personal value that which is commonly known as the "inferiority complex" or the "inferiority sense." Among those who dabble in psychology there is no term which is more commonly used. It has passed into popular parlance, and it is so useful that it is unlikely that we shall ever be able to dispense with it. But if we are to use the term at all, it is desirable that we should attempt to fix its meaning a little more accurately than is generally done.

What is wrong with inferiority? Obviously there is nothing inherently painful about it. We are all inferior in innumerable respects to innumerable people, but we seem to be able to accept the fact on the whole very calmly. I cannot sing like Caruso or play the fiddle like Kreisler; this may be regrettable, but I have never lost a moment's sleep because of it. What is wrong with being small? I am taller than two of my brothers, and shorter than one of them. My father was not as tall as any of his sons. On the whole I am inclined to think that he was proud of the fact rather than discontented about it. It is clear that inferiority only takes on the dimensions of a "complex" if it is felt for some reason to be intolerable inferiority. "I am small, and I don't like it. I want to be large, and I want to be large now." "Simpson can drive a golf ball two hundred yards, and I can drive it only a hundred and seventy. I am as good as he is. I ought to be able to drive as far as he can." As always, the dangerous word "ought" puts up for us its little red flag. Yet once again, we note that constant source of human discomfort and loss of equilibrium, the refusal to accept reality, the unwillingness calmly to

218

accept things as they are, and then to see what, if anything, can be done about them.

There is a whole rich variety of ways in which the situation or the feeling of intolerable inferiority can be brought about; and a whole rich variety of ineffective ways of dealing with the painful situation.

When, in Wonderland, Alice was reduced to the height of three inches, she complained bitterly of feeling unpleasantly small. The caterpillar, sitting calmly smoking his hookah, drew himself up to his full height (which was exactly three inches) and affirmed that three inches was an excellent height to be. The wise caterpillar could never suffer from such painful inferiority feelings as were afflicting poor Alice at that moment. But it is very far from being the case that most us have as yet attained to the wisdom of the caterpillar.

Among the chief architects of "inferiority complexes" are older brothers and sisters and their friends. It is irritating to children to be expected constantly to look after children three or four years their juniors, to have these youngsters endlessly tagging along behind, never quite able to keep the pace and never quite able to take part in the games that their elders enjoy. It is endlessly thwarting to the younger children to be perpetually engaged in the fruitless attempt to keep up, to be given all the time the feeling of not being wanted, to be constantly excluded from things that promise to be interesting on the ground that "you are too young," to be all the time set at hurdles that are too high for them and then derided for failing to clear them. Such a situation, if it continues for any length of time, can result in a permanent sense of indignation against the fact of being small, and in a loss of self-confidence for which later it may be extremely difficult to find a remedy.*

Parents can produce a sense of inferiority in the intellectual and moral realms through the very excess of their affection and by making demands that a child cannot meet. Nothing has done greater harm in recent years than the emphasis on success. The impression left on the child's mind is that he must at all costs be a success. He

*This is not to be confused with *jealousy*, another not uncommon phenomenon among children, arising when affection appears to have been diverted from one child to another, or where there is a feeling that affection has been unfairly divided between them.

is required to do well in his studies, to make good at games, to show powers of leadership, to be popular with his fellows, and all the rest of it. Parents who impress upon their children this ideal of success might justify themselves by saying that it is right to hold out a high ideal before children and to encourage natural ambition; they might fail to realise that, by doing this in the wrong way, they may convert what ought to be regarded as very satisfactory achievement into dismal failure. A boy has been told that it is expected of him that he shall not be lower than fifth or sixth in his class. To be seventh or eighth in a class of twenty represents more than average achievement; but if it is measured against the higher demand, it is miserable and humiliating failure. In countless cases of "inferiority complex," it can be noted that the sufferer, instead of measuring himself upwards from the level of the minimum possible achievement, is measuring himself downwards from some imaginary standard that he supposes must be attained, and therefore is perpetually haunted by a sense of inadequacy and failure for which there is no rational justification. His mark is always reckoned in the "minus" of failure, and not in the "plus" of positive, though perhaps limited, achievement. If the imposed standard is that of perfection, naturally there can never be anything but failure and the bitter and tormenting feeling of having failed to come up to expectation.

Sometimes the sufferer himself is at the bottom of his own troubles. He has formed a mental image of what he "ought to be" (once again we note the tyranny of this misplaced "ought"). This picture of himself is a little larger than life-size, a little more "perfect," a little more effective than he is at the time capable of being. Once formed, the larger-than-life self sits on his back like an old man of the sea, draining away the lifeblood that ought to go to strengthen the real self, always critical, always finding fault, always mocking. Life presents itself as a series of hurdles, each higher and more menacing than the last. Sometimes such a man achieves that which he demands of himself, but usually at the price of terrible strain and effort. If he fails, he has not come short of other people's expectation of him, but of his own expectation of himself. He has let himself down not in their eyes, but in his own; and from that unfavourable judgment there is no escape. He is the man who is always inadequate, incompetent, unsuccessful. He may manage to conceal this from others; from their point of view he may even be a man who has won more than average success. From himself there can be no concealment; the standard he has attained is not the standard that he had set himself. And no measure of success can ease the anxiety, since this success may have been due to no more than luck. The next hurdle is likely to be even higher and more exacting, and there is hardly any possibility that it will be cleared. In serious cases this restless dissatisfaction with the self may be not far short of despair.

A slightly different form of the same disease is that sense of insignificance, of not mattering, that the pressures of life in the West seem to impose on many men of the present day. We live in mass societies. It is not just that there are so many of us—even when numbers are great the individual still remains an individual. It is that the forces that control the life of man seem to have moved so far away from him, and that so much in his life is determined by decisions that he himself has had no share in making. We live under democratic systems. But how much influence is exercised by the vote of the ordinary man? Does it really matter very much whether he votes or not? A slight change in the economic system, which is far beyond the limits of any influence that he can exercise and which he cannot understand, may throw him out of work and destroy the sense of security which he has been occupied for many years in painfully building up. But industry will get on equally well without him. Does it seriously matter whether he exists or not? Studies made in Britain during the worst period of the depression of the 1930s showed that what hit the unemployed man hardest was not the weariness of having nothing to do or the poverty that accompanied that tragic situation. It was the sense of not being wanted, of not counting any more. It is this that saps a man's manhood and makes him feel that he is less than a man.

In that form, this profound doubt as to the value of human existence perhaps most strongly affects the "little man," the man who has no great stake in the life of his country and who feels himself to be very much the plaything of the forces that operate in the industrialised and welfare state. But in a slightly different form it affects a very different class of society, the intelligentsia. Not long ago, a highly intelligent Swiss student said to the writer, "When I

221

look into myself, what I encounter is nothingness." Perhaps the same answer would be given by a great many students in all the countries of the West today. The anxiety that underlies the answer is not simply doubt as to whether anything worth while can be achieved in a civilisation threatened by the atom bomb, or the philosophical question as to whether the life of mankind as a whole has any meaning. It is the pressing personal question posed to the individual by the individual as to his own value. Have I really any significance? Does it really matter to anyone whether I live or not? Can anyone suggest any convincing reason why I should make the necessary effort to continue to live? It seems that, in some cases, the most faithful love of parents or wife or friends fails to give a convincing answer, to penetrate to that very deep level of personality in which the uncertainty dwells, or to still the haunting anxiety.

Comparatively few people are completely free, always and all the time, from such feelings of inferiority, of insignificance or frustration. If we all gave way to them, we should probably end by being paralysed and incapable of any action at all. As most of us have to go on living, and earning our living, it becomes desirable to find forms of compensation by which human nature can be held in some kind of balance, even though the balance may be somewhat precarious. These compensations are almost as numerous as the individuals who devise them; but there are certain classic types which it may be useful briefly to enumerate.

The most typical form of all is the Cinderella story, the pattern in which the myths of suppressed people or suppressed classes almost invariably tend to form themselves. The two elder sisters are rejected, and the despised and neglected younger sister wins the charming prince. This is what ought to happen. If it does not happen in the real world, we will call in the delightful world of fancy to put things right. Very few of us are so well satisfied with our position in life as not from time to time to do a little Cinderella dreaming. Such fancies are natural in childhood; when kept within reasonable limits, they do very little harm in adult life. There is, however, a certain danger. This arises, if we begin to suppose that the kind of things that happen quite naturally in the fancy world are likely to happen to us in the much more prosaic world of three dimensions. Mr. Micawber, who lived perpetually in the expectation of something turning up, was a not unattractive but not very effective person. Those who go chasing Cinderella possibilities are liable to miss the less exciting realities that do come their way. Harriet Smith in Jane Austen's *Emma* allowed herself to be persuaded by Emma to reject the marriage proposals of an entirely suitable young farmer in the hope of attracting the affections of an apparently superior, but as events proved wholly unwilling, suitor. Miss Austen's satire is gentle, but it is penetrating because we can recognise so much of her characters in ourselves.

Myths and fairy stories are very revealing. The Cinderella type is not the only type. Probably Jack the Giant-killer was also numbered among our early friends. In such tales it is not difficult to detect the traces of suppressed hostility and the desire for vengeance. The giant is the impersonation of oppression and evil; therefore it is good that he should be killed. This is what we would do if we were able. Such stories, too, do little harm, if they are kept in the realm of fantasy. But they are not always kept within the limits of fantasy, and terrible things may happen if they cross the borderline from the world of imagination to that of reality. Juvenile delinquents are capable of terrible crimes of violence. Apparently irrational cruelty seems often to be the desperate expression of a desperately felt need for significance, in the face of surroundings or of a society that seems to have condemned the individual permanently to a state of insignificance.

A much less dangerous form of compensation for feelings of inferiority is the adoption of the pose of the good boy, the virtuous man—the besetting temptation of younger sons. If the eldest son, as is often the case, is characterised by vigour and independence and is in consequence frequently in trouble as a result of his insubordination to the general law of the family, it is very likely that the second son will take up the exactly contrary attitude of virtuous conformity to what is expected of him. Virtue in such a connection has no very exalted meaning; it is not chosen for its own sake and is not followed with disinterested self-abandonment. It means little more than avoidance of anything that is likely to be disapproved. The younger son knows that he will not be able to assure himself of his own significance through strength, courage, enterprise, or adventurousness; the glow of superiority engendered by the sense of his own virtue and the approval that it evokes may serve as a very satisfactory compensation for feelings of inferiority that may have been called into existence by the sense of his own ineffectiveness. In the ancient story of the Book of Genesis, Esau the elder son is the hardy man, the bold hunter who goes on his own way and can easily find himself on the wrong side of the law. Jacob is the quiet man who stays at home, is obedient, and is the favourite of his mother. Jacob is not a very attractive character; but in the ancient tale he is abundantly rewarded; he manages to make his own both the birthright and the blessing that should by law and custom have been inherited by the elder brother. It is by no means always the case that virtue is its own reward. But it is doubtful whether virtue of this kind will ever rise above being that which Milton said that he could not praise—"a fugitive and cloistered virtue"; and unfortunately this is what a great many people confuse with Christian conduct.

The fourth form of compensation affects not one individual but a mass of individuals. Modern man is lonely, and oppressed by a sense of his insignificance. If he can be caught up with a great many others in some great movement, in the companionship of that movement he can forget his loneliness and, in a sense of the greatness of the purpose for which the movement strives, he can be eased of the painful feeling of his own insignificance. The greatest example of this in modern times is the success of the Nazi movement in Germany. It has often been remarked that Adolf Hitler was the apotheosis of the "little man" on the stage of history, just as Charlie Chaplin was the apotheosis of the "little man" on the silver screen. His success in lifting Germany from the depths of collapse in 1933 to a position of world dominance in 1942 was astounding. He inspired the young men of Germany with self-confidence, courage, devotion, and willingness to sacrifice everything cheerfully to a cause. This success is all the more deserving of close study in that it comes very close to what we shall later put forward as the true solution to the problem of modern man, a caricature that comes so close to the original as hardly to be distinguishable from it without careful observation.

There are, however, three points at which the Nazi solution can be seen to be defective, and incapable of serving as a permanent and satisfactory solution of the problem. In the first place, the aim of the movement was such that it could not possibly be raised to the level of a universal principle. It was based on the conviction, earlier expressed in the philosophy of Friedrich Nietzsche, that some are naturally born to rule and that others are naturally born to obey. Hitler's aim was simply the glorification of the German people, at whatever cost to the life, the liberty, and the fortunes of others. This aim, as history has shown, contained within itself the seeds of its own destruction. Secondly, the individual was not so much liberated into a genuine fulness of existence as relieved of those responsibilities without the exercise of which a fully personal existence is impossible. Thirdly, there was little room for concern for the destiny of the individual as such. Deification of the state, the people, was carried to such a point that the individual seemed to exist for no other purpose than that of the immolation of himself on the altar of the survival of the people, and of finding therein the most glorious fulfilment of human destiny.

These, and the other possible forms of compensation, are all to be classed as evasions and not as solutions of the problem of man's uncertainty as to his own value. They may serve as anodynes. While they are in operation, the sense of inferiority or of insignificance may be less acutely felt. But if for a moment the drug ceases to operate, the old distress returns in full force; it is clear that it has not been really dealt with. Through compensation, the human entity can be maintained in some kind of equilibrium at a considerable expenditure of effort. But no more is needed than some new failure, some new humiliation, for the equilibrium to be shown up as no more than precarious; this is not that assured balance of the man with both feet firmly planted on the ground, without which genuinely human and confident living is impossible.

The common weakness of all these forms of compensation is that to some extent they live in the world of fantasy, of the refusal of the stark realities of the world. Satisfactory solutions can be found only in the acceptances of the realities, and perhaps in the discovery of certain aspects of reality which the sense of inferiority tends to conceal.

The first lesson in realism that has to be learned is that of the reality of time as the dimension in which growth is possible. Time will proceed at his own equable pace, and nothing in the world will induce him to change it. Human growth can take place only in its own leisurely fashion, and no means has yet been discovered by which it can be speeded up.

This is obvious, and yet it is a lesson that we all find it extremely difficult to learn, especially in these days in which the external pace of life has been so much quickened. As usual, our admirable Shakespeare has something very much to the point to tell us. Rosalind in *As You Like It* expounds the different speeds at which time seems to move. He "trots with a young maid between the contract of her marriage and the day it is solemnised," gallops "with a thief to the gallows, for though he go as softly as foot can fall, he thinks him too soon there," and stays "with lawyers in the vacation, for they sleep between term and term and then they perceive not how time moves." And yet in reality he moves at the same pace for them all, and they deceive themselves if they think otherwise. Human beings do not all grow at exactly the same rate, either physically or emotionally; but the same stages have to be passed through by all, and roughly the same span of time has to be covered by all before maturity is reached.

Almost all of us suffer from impatience. This means that we are unwilling to accept time as he is, and to recognise the length of time that is required for growth. We want achievement of some kind here and now; we leap upwards in the attempt to seize it, and fall back into bitter frustration, because we cannot have it; whereas, if we were willing to wait until the appointed time, we might well find it quite easily within our grasp. This is obvious in relation to the frustrations of the child who feels himself inferior to older and larger children. If a boy is four years old and is afflicted with a rather dominant and unsympathetic brother aged seven, the difference between them is immense, and may be painfully felt at every moment. Ten years later, the younger is rapidly catching up, and may already be taller than his brother. When yet another ten years have passed, and one is twenty-seven and the other twenty-four, the difference is so small as now to be insignificant. "I am small, and I want to be big, now and straight away," says the child; and that way lies the beginning of what may prove very harmful and frustrating discontent. If the child can learn to say, "I am small now; but it is

226

only a question of waiting, and then I shall be big," he is adjusted to the flow of time, and can let time do his appointed work without interruption by human fuss and fret. The illustration from physical growth has been given because it is so obvious and measurable by the eye. But the same principle is applicable to other and less immediately evident forms of growth. If we are so fortunate as to retain the capacity for learning from life and a ready interest in other people, sympathy, wisdom, and understanding can go on increasing to the very end of our days, and the later years of life may prove themselves to be richer, more interesting, and more effective than the earlier years of apparently more exciting achievement.

It has been remarked that, though time moves at the same speed for us all, we do not all grow at exactly the same rate. This means that each of us has to learn his own adjustment to the stream of time. Each has his own ladder to climb. The speed at which others may be climbing their own particular ladder is an irrelevant consideration. It is impossible and perhaps undesirable completely to eliminate the element of competition from life. The provision of statistical averages as to the age at which children begin to walk and to talk is certainly a help to inexperienced parents as giving them guidance as to what their children "ought" to be doing at a certain age, and how they stand in relationship to the observed average of what other children are like at that age. But more than almost anything else it is comparison with others supposedly more successful than ourselves that keeps alive in us the sense of inferiority. The preacher who draws only moderate audiences looks anxiously and perhaps enviously at his colleague who draws the crowds. The nervous tension which results is not likely to help him to do his job better than in the past. In any case, what is his criterion of success? Is the ability to draw crowds the only thing that matters in a religious ministry? Jesus of Nazareth ended up with only a handful of followers, and in the crisis most of those forsook him and fled. The preacher would do far better to give all his attention to climbing his own particular ladder, without sidelong glances to see how others are getting on in the operation of climbing theirs.

Similar to, but distinct from, this comparison of oneself with others is the habit of comparing one's achievement with the expectations about it that others may be supposed to have formed. The

judgment of others is certainly not to be despised. Very few authors can write a book which will not be the better for the criticisms of candid friends. But such appreciation of the help that the critic can give is, emotionally, quite different from that fear of the judgment of others, that subservience, which are the mark of the sense of inferiority. A child knows that his parents expect of him a certain level of accomplishment; he is miserably anxious for fear that he may not be able to come up to expectation, and miserably humiliated if he has actually failed to do so. An author is unduly sensitive to the reception accorded by the public to his work; what he is doing is in fact to substitute the popular judgment for his own as to the value of that work, and enslaving himself to that perhaps uninstructed popular judgment. Some quite good poets have never published a poem, for fear of what the critics might say about their work. Some eminent scholars have never published a book, because all their lives they have been haunted by the fear that they might not get everything just right, and that life would no longer be worth living if the critics caught them out in a single mistake.*
It is not good that we should be slaves of the opinions or judgments of others. It is necessary to learn to say quite firmly, "They are they, and I am I. They are entitled to their opinion, and I to mine, and, if our opinions differ, so much the worse for them." If a sense of inferiority has been deeply rooted in the mind, it is extremely difficult to make this declaration of independence. But there is no other way to recovery; for the statement "I am I, and they are they" is one of the simple formulae in which the nature of mental health can be summarised.

Nothing is more therapeutic for those troubled by deep inner uncertainties than membership in a living group small enough for the individual to feel that there he is appreciated at his true worth, and that his opinion and his voice count for something. The terrifying thing about mass society is its anonymity; the individual seems to be reduced to a number, and hardly anything seems to be changed if one number takes the place of another. It has to be taken

*Very different was the bluff statement of a famous economic historian: "That's the way it looks to me, and I shall publish. If I am right, some American woman will dig up the evidence; and if I am wrong, I will change it in the next edition."

as fairly certain that this tendency will increase. Populations increase; cities grow larger and larger. If life on this planet is to be made possible at all for so large a population, it has more and more to be subjected to organisation. The welfare state takes over ever increasing responsibility for the citizen, provides orange juice for his infancy, free education to an ever higher level, free care in sickness and insurance against unemployment and old age, and finally a grant in order that he may be decently buried. All this means that, from the point of view of genuinely human existence, ever increasing importance attaches to the smaller voluntary groups and societies within the mass, within which it is possible for a man really to breathe and to stretch himself. Lodges, clubs, and fraternities all help to meet this need; but many of them are limited in their effectiveness by the triviality of the aims with which they are concerned and the consequent superficiality of the relations established between their members. We draw much nearer to reality when the smaller group or fellowship is concerned with something really important like politics or religion. If there were no other reason for the existence of Churches, their ability at least in a measure to meet the human need for a sense of significance would be sufficient reason for keeping them in being. And, if the Churches were what their founder intended them to be, there would never again be occasion for anyone to be friendless or to suffer from feelings of inferiority, valuelessness, or isolation.

A good deal of study has recently been made of the size at which such groups do their best work in the way of creating freedom and responsibility. If the fellowship is too small, it becomes a clique; if it is too large, it falls back into the anonymity of the mass. In Britain the trade unions seem to have reached the conclusion that a membership of eighty is the maximum which should be permitted; beyond that the effectiveness of the group is in inverse ratio to its size. This is a point to which the Churches also might well direct their attention. The mass Church is a typical phenomenon of the mass society and may well suffer from the same defects. There is much to be said for the policy of one bishop in the United States who will not allow any church to be built in his diocese to seat more than four hundred people.

But even in such a group the feelings of inferiority and insignificance may persist. For many people, the only thing that helps is the tranquil, undemanding, utterly reliable affection of a friend. This is what the family ought to supply. Our tragedy is that so often it fails to supply it. Behind the familiar phenomenon of the "inferiority complex," again and again we find the story of a love that failed—of parents who did not want children; of parents too busy to be bothered with their children; of parents who made too heavy demands on their children either for achievement or for a responsive affection. Love that is demanding can wear out its object; and all too much of what passes for love in the modern world is the love of the vampire that drains its victims of their lifeblood. Real love is never demanding; it is patient and prepared to wait; it gives without demanding repayment. It is calm and tolerant, undismayed by the worst that it discovers in human nature, always hopeful of a better future. This is the kind of interest, to call it prudently by this less emotional term, that either psychiatrist or pastor can take in one who needs their help; but it is also the service that can be rendered by a quite unprofessional friend. The important thing is that it should be made clear that the love is unconditional and unchangeable; the one who is loved has not earned the love by anything that he has done; he cannot lose it by any demerit. He is loved simply because he is himself; as himself he is of immense value and importance. This value and this importance, and the love that is based on a recognition of them, cannot be ended by anything short of his death.

There is no greater privilege in life than to be allowed to give such love to one who stands in need of it. But even such love may not prove to be the perfect remedy. We are all human, and our affections, like the tides, have their ebb and flow. Even the best of friends have their misunderstandings. It may happen that we judge some action too harshly, through ignorance of motives or of the circumstances that underlie it. It may be that a friend still fears the effect that some disclosure of imperfection or unworthiness may have on the best-tried friendship. And when all has been said and done, there are those among us who still remain mysteriously alone; there seem to be depths in them that not even the most devoted and patient of human friendship can plumb, a profound unrest that the most reliable of human affection cannot lay to sleep. Then the only medicine that can take effect is assurance of the unalterable love of the everlasting God.

Most religions have some general and diffused idea of the benevolence of God. In the Gospels, Jesus substitutes for this general idea a very precise and definite one by assuring us that each one of us is the object of the particular, definite, and detailed love of God. With oriental hyperbole he tells us that the very hairs of our head are all numbered, and that not a sparrow falls to the ground without our Father who is in heaven. He is everywhere present; if we take the wings of the morning and abide in the uttermost parts of the sea, we shall find that he is there before us, and that we cannot pass beyond the reach of his care. There are depths in us that no human friend can reach, secrets which no human friend can share. But there is no depth that he cannot reach, and no secret of which he is unaware. His love is entirely unsentimental. It extenuates no fault, and yet is merciful and compassionate. It takes account of the unspoken aspiration, the good intent that was not achieved, the plan that went astray. It is independent and unconditional; above all, it can never fail or come to an end.

If all this is true, no man need ever doubt his worth or his significance. That worth is not derived from anything that he has done, but simply from the fact that he is the object of the unchanging interest and concern of God. Man did not create that worth, and he cannot destroy it. Whether he is aware of it or not, God's interest in him and concern for his welfare remains unchanged.

For those who believe that this or something like it is the truth, certain consequences necessarily follow.

The first and most obvious is that what is true of me must also be true of all other men. If my value as a man is derived from the concern of God for me, that concern assures to every other existing human individual a value similar to my own. But in that case the value of each human personality is ultimately independent of attractiveness, capacity, or usefulness. It is intrinsic and inalienable. The inequality of men is much more evident than their equality; the principle that all men are equal can be rationally maintained only in the light of a common relationship to a God who is concerned for all alike. From this may follow certain de-

231

ductions as to the principles that must govern all relationships between men and men.

There can be no despised individuals and no excluded classes.
There can be no place for the idea either of supermen, or of
naturally inferior races. We may find occasion to deplore the character that certain people have built up for themselves by folly and
excess; that does not alter our estimate of their ultimate value as
human beings. Inevitably we shall find social relations with certain
classes of people easier than with others, but that must be reckoned
a defect in us rather than a sign of superiority.

No human being may be used by another simply as an instrument for the fulfilment of his own purposes. The greatest evil
that industrialism has fallen into has been its tendency to use men
simply as instruments, as animated machines. We are all in danger
of doing the same thing in our immediate relationships with others.
A love which is demanding may very easily be concerned far more
with its own pleasurable feeling than with the real advantage of
the one who is loved, and then it falls into the peril of becoming
the vampire kind of love. We may seek the approval of our fellows
not because we respect them, but as a means of propping up our
own uncertain confidence in ourselves, or in the light of the financial and social advantage that may accrue to us from their approval.
In all such cases, the other human being is the instrument of our
purpose, and not in himself a centre of independent human interest.

It is only when a man has reasonable confidence in his own
worth, and an unforced respect for the worth of others, that he is
capable of entering into genuinely personal relationships.

As long as a man is suffering from the sense of inferiority or
inner uncertainty, the centre of interest is in himself, and it is
difficult for him to go out from himself in order really to meet
the other. We are familiar with this problem in a slightly different
setting. If we are suffering from so elementary an ill as toothache,
the pain draws all our attention to itself and makes itself for the
time being the centre of our world to such an extent that it is
difficult for us to be fully aware of anything outside ourselves. If a
man is suffering from the continuous gnawing pain of uncertainty,
the effect of it is in much the same way to draw his attention
inwards on himself. If he meets others, he is inclined to be

232

thinking all the time of the impression that he may be making on them; this robs him of his spontaneity and makes him constrained, inclined to show off or to act. Or he may be thinking of the advantages that may accrue to him from this meeting; then he is not genuinely interested in the other as a person, he is interested in him only as a means to a purpose to the fulfilment of which he may be able to contribute.

When a man has attained to reasonable self-confidence, to an assurance of intrinsic value which is not dependent on the opinions or estimates of other people, he has no longer any need to be anxiously concerned about himself. He is free to go out from himself, to explore this wonderful world, which is so full of beautiful and enchanting things, and so surprisingly full of delightful and interesting and admirable people. When he meets others, he can be interested in them for their own sakes. Because he is himself free from painful self-consciousness, he is able to spread confidence around him and to help others to be their natural selves. Because he is no longer particularly interested in himself, he is able to delight in the success of others without regarding it as a robbery carried out at his expense. If his attention is drawn to the defects or the failures of others, he can look upon them with patience, with humour and with compassion. Free two-way traffic between persons then becomes possible, and this is the source of endless enrichment for all concerned.

This is true human freedom, a freedom that can never be taken away. Such freedom is never exercised at the expense of any other man. The free man is at all times ready to be serviceable to all his fellow men.

X Perfect Freedom

What kind of a world would make man happy?

"IT HAS ALWAYS SEEMED TO ME that man has some sixth sense, or some faculty apart from sense, that must be satisfied before he can be completely happy." Rather surprisingly, the speaker is the Prince in Dr. Johnson's *Rasselas*. He has been brought up in the Happy Valley, which is rather like a preview of the welfare state as the secularised socialist imagines it; and yet he is not happy. Already, as a cloud like a man's hand, the suspicion has arisen that in the perfect welfare state man will be intolerably bored. He needs more than food and clothes and warmth and organisation. Like Cleopatra, he has immortal longings, and it goes ill with him if these are disregarded or denied. Whatever answer we may be led in the end to give to it, we cannot forever refuse to consider the question of God, and of the possible relation between God and man.

The term "sixth sense" is not altogether a happy one, if used of man's capacity to imagine himself in relationship to a transcendent and invisible world. It might suggest that the religious sphere is one particular sphere, separate from others and concerned with only one set of phenomena. In that case, a man who had no religious sense could be normal in every other respect, just as a man who is colour-blind may enjoy the perfect functioning of all his other senses. But that is not what is meant by religion. If it has any reality at all, it must be the experience that underlies, affects, and colours all other experiences. It was suggested in the last chapter that the nature of man's freedom is to be sought in

234

What are not those with 6th sense.

the richness and the variety of the relationships into which he can enter. If God exists, and if it is possible for man to enter into relationship with him, clearly that relationship is basic and far more important than any other. "O Lord, thou hast made us for thyself, and our hearts are restless, until they find rest in thee," wrote Augustine. If that is true, it is only when his potential relationship with God becomes a reality that man enters upon a genuinely human existence. The existence of the man who lives without God is still on the subhuman level.

This view is, of course, widely challenged today. Many critics hold that religion is nothing more than an illusion, a projection outwards from man of something that is really a part of man himself. This was the view put forward by Feuerbach a century ago. It has been renewed in somewhat different form by Sigmund Freud, the general character of whose opinions is made clear by the title of one of his most famous books, *The Future of an Illusion*. Man is full of hopes and fears. He projects his own inner hopes and fears on to the clouds, divinises the projections, and worships them under the name of God.

If this account of the origin of religion is valid, it might seem that nothing better could befall the human race than to be definitively set free from this illusion and from the ills that have accompanied the acceptance of it as reality in the past. It is no longer necessary to treat this question as theoretical. At all times there have been atheists, but in all the centuries up to the twentieth, the vast majority of mankind lived in the belief that some kind of God or gods exist. Now for the first time in history vast masses of men live in the contrary belief. God has ceased to exist for them; and we are now in a position to estimate some of the consequences of disbelief.

Russia has been taught for forty years that religion is a relic of the prescientific age, to be abandoned by all those who have had the advantage of coming to understand the nature of scientific truth. The achievements of Communist Russia have been very remarkable* yet many in the West who are not Christians would hesitate to commit themselves to the view that the future of human-

*These lines were written before the launching of the first Sputnik.

ity is safe in Communist hands. Are those hard-faced men who control the destinies of Russia markedly more admirable than those for whom a religious faith has been a reality? Does the widespread disregard of human rights and human values in Communist countries suggest the possibility that those values cannot stand entirely by themselves, without reference to some transcendent source outside themselves?

It is not only in the Communist world that we meet men who have deliberately chosen to live without God. One of the most distinguished of the French Existentialists, Albert Camus, who in 1957 was awarded the Nobel Prize for literature, has written, in his book *L'Homme Révolté*, an account of those men of the nineteenth century who took as their basic conviction the view that "God is dead." It is impossible not to respect the courage and integrity of these men and the sincerity of their attempts to find a way for man to live in a world from which the religious dimension has been rigidly excluded. Typical among them is Friedrich Nietzsche, whose brilliant intellect moved forward fearlessly to the consequences of his convictions, including the pitiless rejection of Christianity as the gospel for the weak, and the development of the idea of the superman. Yet a careful reading of Camus's book may have on the mind of the reader the paradoxical effect of convincing him of the necessity of belief in God. If the removal of this little piece of mechanism called "faith in God" results in so much misery, so much violence, so much mental disturbance and suicide, may it not be that we should do well to replace the missing piece and see what happens? Is it possible that after all no genuinely human existence is possible, unless man enters into relationship with an unchanging God, that man cannot really be at home in time unless he is aware also of the dimension of eternity? The question is at least worthy of consideration.

We shall at once be prepared to make a number of concessions to the critics. It is certain that there will be an element of projection in every human experience of God. Even if we admit the possibility of a revelation of God by himself, that revelation will have to be received through human minds; a certain measure of distortion can hardly be avoided. But this need not mean that the whole experience is illusory. As we have seen, we can never

236

know one another perfectly because of the element of projection that is involved in all meeting between two human beings; but this does not mean that all knowledge of other human selves is impossible, or that our experiences of friendship and fellowship are the product of nothing but illusion. Similarly, the recognition that there is a very human element in what claims to be religious experience does not rule out the possibility that it may yet be an experience of a reality, which is not itself the product of human thought and imagination.

On the same grounds, we shall be ready at once to admit that there is bad religion as well as good. Some forms of religion degrade and imprison the human spirit, and from these it is most desirable that mankind should be delivered. But this is a case in which bad coin should not be allowed to drive out good. If we have identified certain forms of religion as harmful, what is needed is not the rejection of all forms of religion but discrimination between good and bad; and that involves the establishment of criteria in the light of which some content can be put into the words "good" and "bad" and the distinction between them can be rationally maintained.

Furthermore, we shall recognise that, if religious experience is to speak at all, it must speak in anthropomorphic terms, in expressions drawn from the world of human experience. The mystic claims to have experience beyond these limitations of thought and language; but such experience is by definition unutterable and incommunicable. If we want to talk to one another about religion, we have to use the words and the ideas that are at our disposal. This means that what we say will have only metaphorical or symbolic relevance. We can indicate what we mean, we cannot express it with mathematical precision. But this does not mean, of course, that we are not really talking about anything at all; the symbolic language of religion, like that of poetry, can be very highly charged with meaning. But it does imply that the words we use can never exactly correspond to the reality, and that we must always watch our metaphorical terms very carefully to ensure that ideas which we would repudiate are not smuggled in under them.

With so much of preface, we can begin to look at the terms in which Christian ideas about God are expressed.

The first term we encounter is "Father." At once it is evident that religion is drawing for its expression on familiar terms of human experience, and in particular on the well-known relationships of which we all have experience in the family.

It seems sometimes to be assumed that the "father figure" is present in all religions, and that the projection of the father-figure is the source and origin of the idea of God. The facts hardly bear this out. In the austere monism of classical Hinduism, there is no place for any personal God, and therefore terms which, like "father," are so closely associated with personal experiences are felt to be inappropriate. In the Koran there are ninety-nine names for God, but the name "father" is not among them. In certain systems of religion the mother figure is much more important than the father. Not all primitive religions recognise the father idea in God. Not long ago an African convert to Christianity was asked what new truth he had learned about God through becoming a Christian. His answer was interesting: "That God exists, that we knew. That God made the world, that we knew. But that God is Father, that we did not know at all." In point of fact, the idea of God as Father seems to be limited to certain types of religion, especially those in which the ethical emphasis is strongly marked.* Even in the Old Testament, though the term occurs, the picture of God as Creator, as Ruler, and as Judge, fills far more of the canvas than the picture of God as Father. In reality, it is only with Jesus that the fatherhood of God comes to be the central concept of religion.

It is important not to jump to conclusions as to what Jesus meant, and what Christians have continued to mean, by the use of the word in this connection. It may be useful to start by putting on one side certain misconceptions which have acquired a certain currency.

It seems sometimes to be taken for granted that the natural and inevitable relationship between father and son is that of rivalry

* Zeus, the father of gods and men in Greek mythology, is of course a familiar figure, but it is important not to overlook the difference between the god who is father in a *polytheistic* system, and the application of the same term in *monotheistic* systems of thought, in which God is the One beside whom there is no other.

and even hatred. The son fears the possibility of mutilation at his father's hands; the father fears the son as a possible supplanter. The rivalry takes on a sexual colouring; and there we have all the materials for the famous Oedipus complex. That this situation can arise is certain; it remains doubtful whether any conclusions as to the relations between fathers and sons in general can be drawn from what may prove to be the exceptional case. The Greeks were a very wise people, and their myths do express a profound understanding of the truth about human nature. If we look at the myth of Oedipus, the first thing that strikes us is that the story does not begin with Oedipus, but with his father Laius. Laius has been warned that he will lose his life at his son's hands; he therefore arranges for the new-born son to be exposed on the mountains. The Laian situation precedes the Oedipodean situation.* It is the anxious jealousy of the father that produces the violent reaction on the part of the son. Too little is known scientifically of the subject for confident statement to be made; but it seems likely that in modern times also it is only in such circumstances as these that the Oedipodean situation arises. It does sometimes happen that a married man does not want children; if they arrive, he regards them as a nuisance and as in some sense his rivals for the attention and affection of his wife. Happily this attitude is not common. Philoprogenitiveness, the desire to have children, is a marked characteristic of the human male. Its absence is generally a sign of adolescent immaturity in the married man. Freud did not invent the Oedipus complex, he found it; but perhaps he and his followers have tended to exaggerate its incidence. Probably most pastors engaged in deep pastoral work know more young men on whom an Oedipus complex has been foisted by a well-meaning psychiatrist than young men who have really been afflicted by this disturbing but happily rare abnormality.

Tensions can certainly develop within the family between fathers and sons; but it is unwise to make deductions from such phenomena alone to the exclusion of everything else. Almost everyone must have observed the intense delight with which a small boy welcomes

*This is the only correct form of the adjective. Unfortunately some psychologists have taken to using the form "Oedipal," but this involves treating a Greek word as though it were a Latin one.

his father back to the house after even a short absence, the total abandonment with which he throws himself into his father's arms. It is clear that he is delighted to have a father as well as a mother; the absolutely reliable strength of the father is the complement to the absolutely reliable tenderness of the mother. It is by no means always the case that this happy relationship changes with the years into one of embittered rivalry. In any case, since religion is potentially a universal experience, in our interpretation of the term "father" the relationship between fathers and daughters is as relevant as that between fathers and sons.

Some students of the subject see a certain ambivalence in the term, since the father can be both the provider of all good and pleasant things, if he is in a good temper, and at the same time the terrifying avenger, if his anger is aroused. From these two aspects are derived, so it is maintained, the two aspects under which God is apprehended—as the kind protector, who can be counted on to intervene in favour of his people, and as the pitiless God, who must, if possible, be propitiated and kept in a good temper.

By judicious quotation from the Old Testament, it would be possible to give the impression that this is what the Old Testament picture of God is like. In reality, the Old Testament is far better fitted to serve as a corrective of these views than as support for them, and this is still more true of the teaching of the Gospels. There is nothing capricious about this God. One of his most prominent characteristics is *Hesed*, the word which is often translated "lovingkindness" but includes within itself the faithfulness of One who can always be relied on to be true to the promises that he has made. The ethical demands made by this God are high. Nothing will be made easy for anyone. He calls his people to a high and bracing adventure, in which the rewards will be great, but will be available only for those who are prepared to pay the price in effort, in self-discipline, in the resolute overcoming of difficulties. If the people fail to play their part, and if their obstinate resistance goes beyond a certain limit, God cannot go on with them; but this is not capricious anger—it is simply recognition of the plain fact that two cannot walk together unless they be agreed. And when the people have sinned, so far from it being their business to propitiate an angry God, God himself has provided the propitiation, the means of reconciliation by which the sin can be covered. He always comes towards man as the gracious God, taking the intiative in creating and maintaining fellowship. Even in wrath he remembers mercy. What he offers as the highest reward is not gifts and privileges, but simply fellowship with himself. "Whom have I in heaven but thee, and there is none upon earth that I desire in comparison with thee?" All this is included in the Old Testament concept of fatherhood.

But is it not the case that even such a high and austere understanding of religion as this involves an element of regression to an infantile stage of development? However we use the word "father," does it not imply a desire for dependence, for protection, such as is appropriate in childhood, but must hinder growth in the direction of adult independence and self-sufficiency? If this were the whole truth, it might be necessary to regard religion as something that belongs to the infancy of the race and of the individual, and something therefore that needs to be cast away as the process of human development moves forward. We must recognise that, when this desire for dependence is present, religion is one of the many forms of which it can make use to express itself. But the resulting kind of religion is one that the Christian conscience must regard as debased and harmful, since it involves regression away from the realities of life, whereas the Christian is required to accept only those forms of religion which encourage the facing of reality in all its forms.

When we have made this admission, we must pass on at once to note that to identify the child-father relationship with dependence and nothing else involves an improper narrowing of the reference of the term. We are familiar with one pattern of the family and tend to generalise from it, forgetting that other patterns have existed in the past and still exist in many parts of the world. In many countries today it is the system of the joint family that has persisted. Marriage takes place at an early age, probably not later than sixteen for the boy and thirteen or fourteen for the girl. So far from the father trying to prevent the marriage of his son, it is the very thing that he is anxious to bring about; the sign that he has himself attained to full maturity is that he has seen the face of his grandson! The married son does not leave his father's home; a corner is found for him in some part of the large rambling house, and he combines private domestic felicity with the responsibility of playing an independent, though probably at this stage subordinate, role in the general affairs of the family and in the decisions that have to be made. We are used to the situation in which parents and children live together in a small house, with all the intensity of relationships, of affections, and perhaps of hatreds that that situation invites. In the joint family, a young man has to do with a far more complex situation—uncles and aunts, sisters-in-law, and cousins in all degrees of relationship. This is compatible with monogamy and with a very high standard of ethical conduct. We regard our system as normal; in point of fact it is of comparatively recent invention. The psychological pattern produced by the joint family is different from, and perhaps more healthy than, that to which we seem committed in the West. It is against this background that we have to understand the use of the term "father" by the biblical writers and by Jesus Christ. Here the question that naturally arises is as to the part played by a father in such a joint family and as to the nature of the relationship of a father with grown-up sons and daughters.

The last thing that a father would think of in such a situation would be to regard his sons as possible rivals. Sons are eagerly desired, the more the better. They are so extremely useful, whether it be for fighting or for farming. The principal desire of the father is that they should grow up as quickly as possible, and be able to play an adult part in the concerns of the family.

What he demands of them can be conveniently summed up under three headings—understanding, respect, when necessary taking the form of obedience, intelligent co-operation. The young man has first to learn the technique of the family business whatever that may be; it is his father's delight and pride to teach him. In any co-operative venture someone has to make the decisions; there should be opportunity for consultation, but often decisions have to be taken in a moment of time, and nothing can go right unless all the members are prepared to sink their individual ideas and to obey the directions of the one whose right to decide is recognised by all. Understanding and obedience are virtues, not in themselves, but in so far as they make possible the intelligent co-operation on which the prosperity of all alike depends. For each son there will be marked out a certain area of independence; but he will be required to throw his strength into the common concerns; and the profits go into a common purse instead of becoming, as they do in a more individualistic society, the personal property of the one who may be held to have earned them.

All this is familiar to anyone who has lived in a simple traditional society, and has been able to observe how fatherhood and sonship work, in a situation in which the same craft, the same trade, go on in one family generation after generation, and perhaps even century after century. It is not always easy to recognise the operation of the same principles in the very different situations produced by our Western way of living. But perhaps this means that we have become accustomed to operating with a reduced understanding of the idea of fatherhood, and that a recovery of the fulness of its meaning might greatly help us towards a better understanding both of the nature of society and of the meaning of religion.

The lack of understanding between the older and the younger generations can become a grave problem in any society. It is likely to be particularly grave in a rapidly changing society, and today is nowhere more acute than in West Africa, where the old patriarchal and tribal society of the past is yielding before more democractic ideals introduced from the West. It is not to be wondered at, if a society so constantly in movement as that of America also produces its grave problems in this area of life.

For this circumstances are in part to blame. Few serious students are likely to go the whole way with Mr. Geoffrey Gorer in his ingenious theory of the "excluded father" and his far-reaching deductions therefrom as to the reasons for the matriarchal character of American society.* But the development of the commuter society presents us with a new and hitherto unknown disturbance in the general balance of the family. The father is absent from home during almost the whole of every working day. He appears in the evening, as the strange, perhaps irritable, man who is almost

*On this a number of interesting and pungent comments are to be found in H. J. Eysenck's *The Uses and Abuses of Psychology* (Penguin Books, 1953), pp. 252–60.

unknown to his children, whereas the mother is always there as a kindly and beneficent influence. It is not surprising that in many cases family relationships become seriously distorted. Observation shows that in many cases fathers have played far too small a part in the inner and emotional development of their children.

But all the blame cannot be laid on circumstances. It is regrettable but undeniable that many fathers do not find themselves at home with their adolescent sons. The difficulty cannot be wholly accounted for simply by the difference in the outlook of the generations. All too often, the parents have not taken the trouble that has to be taken, if they are to know their own children. It is idle to expect children to grow in understanding of their father if the father has not taken the initiative in trying to understand his children. This demands time, patience, and humour. It is not enough that the law of the family should be laid down. It has to be explained, and reasons given for decisions. Ideals have to be brought out into the open and discussed, differences in viewpoint recognised and allowed for. Fathers who are prepared to take the necessary trouble are likely to find a rich reward in growing understanding and in the delightful companionship of developing minds. It is not to be expected that this will always take the form of the monotony of perfect agreement; but disagreement within the circle of confident trust and mutual affection adds variety to life without destroying its harmony.

It is good that children should respect their parents. But our society is no longer patriarchal, and it can no longer be taken for granted that this respect will be automatically accorded. It must be earned, as well as expected. A distressing situation arises when children no longer feel able to respect their parents; but it is not possible always to say that the fault is on the side of the children. We have no right to expect the veneration due to age, unless we manage to grow old gracefully. As we have already seen, part of the trouble is that so many men fail to grow beyond the stage of emotional adolescence. If increasing age is marked by dogmatism, the hardening of inveterate prejudices, irritation at disagreement, impatience with every manifestation of independence and the petulance which is often the mask for a sense of inability to cope with circumstances, home becomes a place in which no high-spirited adolescent can be expected to remain. If, however, we manage to retain the capacity to learn by experience, if we remain interested in the changing scene and in the viewpoints of those whom we cannot always expect to agree with us, age does lend authority, and the half-timid respect which a boy pays to his father can change with the passing of the years into a feeling for which veneration is the only appropriate term. The patriarch is not necessarily a jealous tyrant. He can be the sapient and honoured counsellor, to whom years have added the virtues of tolerance and patient understanding as well as the weight of rich and varied experience.

This is not an imaginary picture. Some readers like the writer may be able to draw on their own experience. If not, recent recorded history provides us with interesting examples of just such happy reaction between successive generations. In English history, it is natural to think of the family of the Gladstones, a useful example, because such exceptionally full information is available about them. It is evident that Gladstone's children adored their father, were quite capable of pulling his leg in spite of his immense eminence, got a great deal of fun out of being the Grand Old Man's children, and in their turn loved bringing their own children back to the old family home. This feeling only deepened with the passing of the years. It is possible that this adoration was carried a little too far, to the point at which it hindered the sons in the development of their own individual gifts and characters. Yet more than one of them rose to eminence in the careers which they had chosen, and the family continues to contribute to the national life men and women of integrity and distinction.

Intelligent co-operation in the fullest sense is possible only where, in the traditional pattern, children follow their parents in their profession or their business. But a family is not really a family unless it is a joint enterprise, to which all the members are honestly contributing. If the home is merely a place to which a number of people come to sleep, without any serious sense of responsibility for one another and without any sharing of common interests, the nature of the family is lost, and fatherhood and sonship become mere words without any profound significance.

It has been worth while to make this somewhat careful analysis of the nature of fatherhood and of the family in the human situation as an introduction to the understanding of the same terms when we meet them in the Bible, and particularly in the words of Jesus himself. We shall perhaps not be surprised to find that his favourite term for God is "Father," and that what he says about his own relationship to that Father falls exactly into the three divisions of understanding, obedience, and intelligent co-operation. "No man knoweth the Son but the Father; neither knoweth any man the Father save the Son." "I know him: and if I should say, I know him not, I shall be a liar like unto you; but I know him and keep his saying." "I came not to do mine own will, but the will of him that sent me. I do always those things that please him." "My Father worketh until now, and I work." "My meat is to do the will of him that sent me, and to finish his work." It would be tedious to multiply quotations; the evidence is to be found on almost every page of the Gospels.

We are dealing here not with an *idea* of God, but with a vividly experienced personal relationship. An idea is something that we make for ourselves, and that we have liberty to modify at our will. A relationship with a living person is quite different. That other exists in his own right. Our idea of him is constantly challenged by the reality of what he is. Those who discuss religion seem often to have difficulty in getting beyond the realm of ideas, and it is therefore hard for them to come to grips with what the Christian Gospel means. God for Jesus is not the Good, or the Absolute, or the driving motor of the universe, or the central concentration of ideals or the power that sanctions morality tinged with emotion. He is a living person, with whom he believes himself to live in the closest possible relationship. This relationship is more real, more exacting and more rewarding than that in which he lives with his closest friends. To that same relationship he calls those friends. To become a Christian is not to accept certain ideas or certain ideals. It is to make the supreme adventure of believing that a living personal relationship with God the Father is possible, and at his word it can become the supreme reality of our lives.

It is interesting to work out the effect of this belief in God on the life of Christ.

In the first place, he is evidently entirely free from self-concern, because his whole concern is directed to something immensely important outside himself. That something is what he calls the coming of the kingdom of God. This is not some airy ideal, some misty sentimental dream. It is an extremely practical concern, the first steps in the realisation of which must be taken by Jesus himself. Other men, as he sees them, have drifted from their anchor, and are living in the misery of that self-centredness which is idolatry. He alone is living in total and unconditional recognition of the sovereignty of God. That is the natural state to which men have to be recalled. The kingdom of God must be incorporated in a visible society, of which the first lineaments are to be discerned in the little group of friends whom he has gathered about himself.

So immensely important a task demands concentration. Priorities have to be established. Everything which is not relevant to the task that he has in hand must be abandoned, even the dearest ties of family and friendship when they threaten to stand between him and his work. And yet Jesus is no strained ascetic. He is the happy man. It is a psychologist's cliché that men are happy when they are "object-centred," and sick and restless when they are "self-centred." Jesus is the perfect type of the object-centred man. Most of us have at one time or another seen the look of intense and joyful concentration on the face of a craftsman when all his powers are engaged in the exercise of his craft. The demands made on him are exacting; everything else for the time being must be forgotten and cease to count. Yet in such moments what the craftsman is aware of is an almost fierce exhilaration of living. Men are happy when they are wholly committed to something outside themselves that they feel to be greater than themselves.

Just because he is concerned with an enterprise of such magnitude and such all-embracing significance, Jesus is free from the hesitations and vacillations that beset the paths of lesser men. He knows whence he comes and whither he goes; he moves with confidence towards an end which has been foreseen and accepted in advance. But this is not to be understood as though Jesus was a kind of superman, twisting circumstance to fit in with his will and thrusting all obstacles vigorously on one side. The picture of him given in the Gospels is of one who must always await the appointed time for everything that he does, who must not move ahead of the

247

will of his heavenly Father. At one moment, when his brethren urge him to go up to the feast at Jerusalem, he refuses to go, because his time has not yet come; yet later he does go up, though as in secret. This is not inconsistency or uncertainty; it is the mark of a sensitive spirit, alert to every changing situation, and in sympathetic contact with a heavenly wisdom, on which it is affectionately and not slavishly dependent.

In the end suffering is accepted by Jesus as the only means through which his mission can be fulfilled. Yet here too nothing could be less like the traditional picture of the superman. The Gospels indicate two different aspects of his experience. In the narrative in Mark, we can feel the human tension mounting as the crisis approaches. The story of Gethsemane makes clear the reality of the suffering and the intensity of the conflict through which it is accepted. And yet, this too is "the cup which my Father hath given me." In the midst of the suffering there is the certainty that it is not in vain. God is a thrifty workman, who will not let any of his materials be wasted. Suffering, death, and apparent defeat are also among the materials out of which he is building the everlasting City of God. In the Fourth Gospel, it is this side of the picture that is drawn. Jesus is at every point master of the situation; he moves forward confidently to what he knows to be his great victory.

All this is what it means to him to be the Son of the Father. It is into like sonship that he calls his friends with the promise of like results.

If they accept the call, they too will be required to know God and to understand his will. Nothing could be more unlike the faith into which Jesus calls his friends than the blind faith, involving the abandonment of the reasoning and critical faculties, which is all that some people can understand under the term, and which unfortunately has sometimes been commended by his Church. It is true that he does sometimes rebuke his disciples for their little faith; but the most characteristic of all his complaints is, "How is it that ye did not *understand?*" His appeal is always to men's intelligence and to their wills: "You know the answer, if you will only use the knowledge and the intelligence that you have"—so may we paraphrase his answers to many of those who asked him questions. It is only rarely that he gives a direct answer to a question. When a lawyer asks him, "Who is my neighbour?" his answer is to tell the story of the Good Samaritan—and to leave the lawyer to use his own wits to find the answer to his own question. One who would follow him today is required in the same way to bend his intelligence on the whole of life and all its problems, to consider what illumination falls upon them from the uncompromising realism of Jesus and his relating of all things to his understanding of the will of his Father.

The call of Jesus does, of course, demand also implicit and unconditional obedience. This term is one which is unpleasant to modern ears; it suggests an abandonment of independence and initiative such as seems inconsistent with the idea that we have been taught to hold of human dignity. And yet we do not need to look far, even in the modern world, to find situations in which total and implicit obedience leads not to the loss or annihilation of personality but to a new kind of freedom, to the expression of human liberty fuller than can be attained in any other way. At this point let the musician be our guide.

Nothing is more interesting than to watch an orchestra performing a symphony under the guidance of a great conductor. Without hours of individual effort and practice, nothing could happen. But now all individual idiosyncrasies and ideas as to how the music ought to be played must be abandoned. For the moment it is the conductor who is king, and it is his reading of the mind of the composer that is to be brought to expression through the co-operation of the many members of his team. At first this must seem like a suppression of liberty. But if the conductor really is a master, he will fire the whole team with his own sense of what the music means. He may bully them, insult them, harry them, treat them in a manner that in any other circumstances would certainly lead to legal reprisals, but they will play for him like demons, since they have found that through the surrender of their individual liberty they have been led out into a creative freedom such as they have never known before. It is perhaps unlikely that members of an orchestra playing under such a conductor would strike out so memorable a phrase; yet it is not inconceivable that one of them might be moved to say, "His service is perfect freedom." At the end of the performance of a great symphony, members of the orchestra are likely to find themselves exhausted and drained of all emotion; but they go home exalted and tranquillised by the feeling that they have for a brief spell greatly lived in the world of creative freedom.

The kingdom of God which Jesus came to call into being is a much greater enterprise than the greatest of all symphonies and makes far greater demands on its servants. But the parallel is reasonably close. Man becomes the servant of a great ideal. He finds to his surprise that that abandonment of self and of the trivialities of the second-rate, which might at first sight appear to be the bending of his neck to servitude, is in fact the beginning of true freedom.

The realist Jesus never for a moment suggested to his friends that they were in for an easy time. He tells them in the plainest terms that they will be as sheep in the midst of wolves and that they will have to suffer. In a world such as this, it could not be otherwise. He does not assure them that there will be compensation for suffering in another and better world. Everyone who has deeply suffered knows that there can be no compensation for suffering. He offers them something far better—the assurance that suffering itself is part of the creative process. The cross is not a defeat, which later by some kind of witchcraft is turned into a victory. It is the cross itself which is the victory. The resurrection comes to confirm the victory and to make it manifest to all the world as victory; it is the vindication of a principle that the world is inclined to repudiate as mere weakness and folly.

Any reader, by a brief reference to the Gospels, can verify the accuracy of this brief statement of the faith of Jesus, and of the faith that he required of his friends. What we cannot do is to offer demonstrative proof that there is a reality corresponding to his faith, that God really exists, and that he is Father in the sense in which Jesus used the word. It is always possible that he was the victim of illusion.

Perhaps we should not be too much disturbed by the impossibility of conclusive demonstration in the field of faith. There are in fact only two worlds in which conclusive demonstration is possible—the world of pure mathematics and the world of pure logic, and these are not relevant to the subject now under consideration. In any case, to demonstrate a negative is almost impossible. It may be hard to prove that God exists; it is considerably more difficult to prove that he does not exist.

Probably, as a matter of pure fact, no one ever came to the decision of faith on purely rational lines. We are far more influenced than we know by semiconscious impulses and by semirational feelings. One man has an inclination to believe, perhaps because he feels obscurely that it will be more comforting and reassuring to believe than to doubt; another man has an inclination not to believe, perhaps because he is alarmed at the demands that may be made upon him if he believes, or at the intellectual labour that is involved in any serious consideration of the evidence. All such semiconscious and semirational factors are as far as possible to be discounted. But we are not, in reality, abandoned to the mere irrationality of feeling: "You feel it that way, and perhaps that is true for you; and I feel it this way, and that has got to be true for me."

In areas where absolute certainty is unobtainable, we do reach a considerable measure of certainty along one or other of two lines, or better still by a combination of them both. One is the luminous assurance of the kind that comes to us when confronted by a thing of beauty—"This is beautiful." The other is the patient working out of probabilities in a situation in which action has to be taken, but in which the consequences of action cannot be foretold with precision. Both of these have their relevance in relation to the faith of Jesus, and to the faith which he asks of his friends.

A distinguished poetess had been brought up as a complete agnostic. As her children began to grow up and to ask questions about religion, she thought that it might be a good idea to look at the New Testament. Shortly after she said to a friend of mine, "I have been reading the Gospels, and I find that the things that Jesus says about God are true." Clearly this was a judgment akin to those aesthetic judgments which, with her highly developed artistic sensitiveness, she had been accustomed to make in the field of beauty. Such a conviction can come home to the one who arrives at it with the force of a revelation, and this explains why

reply to a quoter

so many people who have come to religious faith speak of it as a gift. But such assurance, however valuable to the experiencing subject, is of no direct evidential value to anyone else.

The other approach is that of weighing carefully and one by one the statements that the Gospel actually makes. If it seems that Jesus was right about so many things, that his understanding of human nature was profound, that his ideals were those which in our best moments most of us would wish to follow, there is at least a possibility that he may have been right in that central point which holds all the rest together—his conviction as to the reality and accessibility of God. If the initial probabilities seem to be reasonably strong, the only way to test them further is to act on them and to see what happens when action is taken on these lines. The process of verification in action may lead in the end to an assurance no less strong than that reached through the direct and intuitive conviction that "the things that Jesus said about God are true." But in faith of this kind there is always an element, perhaps a healthy element, of self-criticism, which is often though not always correctly called doubt—the recognition that after all the whole thing may in the end turn out to be illusion.

What in the end shows up illusions as illusions is that they do not match the phenomena, the things that actually happen. Illusion cannot stand up to the test of reality. If illusion is seen to be illusion, there is nothing to be done with it except to reject it. And if faith is illusion, paradoxically the one who more than any other should help us to get rid of it is Jesus, who on all the levels of purely human experience showed himself to be the greatest realist of all times.

It may be that Christians have all the time been feeding themselves on illusions. If so, they are not the only ones. It may not be out of place to cast a glance at a few other current illusions. For forty years our intellectuals have fed themselves on the illusions of Marxism and have believed the strange paradox that a system which starts by denying liberty for the individual can eventually lead on to a higher liberty for the human race. There has been the illusion of inevitable evolutionary progress, and its attendant myth of "religion without revelation." There has been the illusion that better planning and the spread of education would lead to the

252

elimination of social evils. There has been the illusion that the
United Nations could put an end to war. There has been the
illusion that the elimination of sexual restraints and taboos would
make for greater happiness. It does not need a prophet to tell
those who feed on illusions that the end of those things is dismay,
disillusionment, and despair. This is the point that we seem to
have reached; we live in a disillusioned world. Today it is not
the theologians who are passing judgment on our age. It is the
poets and the novelists. "Vanity of vanities," said the Preacher
long ago. Less euphoniously and less succinctly, Mr. T. S. Eliot
has told us in his too often quoted phrase:

> *This is the way the world ends*
> *This is the way the world ends*
> *This is the way the world ends*
> *Not with a bang, but a whimper.*

It appears that what is common to all forms of illusion is that
each is vividly aware of certain aspects of reality to the exclusion
of some others. When the disregarded aspect reasserts itself, illusion is likely to be turned into disillusionment. The only safeguard against disillusionment is to have faced the whole of reality,
including the very worst that is or that can be. Two systems of
thought at the present time claim for themselves the distinction
of disillusioned realism. The first is the Existentialism that is so
influential in France and seems to exercise so strong an attraction
upon young people in many lands. The Existentialist has surveyed
the whole of reality with calm and disillusioned eyes and has come
to the conclusion that there is no meaning in anything. Life is
just absurd, and yet we must go on living it. There is something
dignified and admirable, though perhaps a little melancholy, in
this stoical resignation. The alternative system is that of Christian
faith. In the cross, that faith has faced the worst that could possibly be and has survived. The adventure of the kingdom of God
is so wide and all-embracing that nothing need be excluded from
it. Failure and frustration, disappointment and disaster can all
find their appropriate place. Even evil itself is not wholly negative,
since it provides the opportunity for the exercise of that good will

by which it is to be overcome. With the question of abstract and objective truth we are not at the moment concerned. If the choice lies between these two systems, there can hardly be a doubt as to which of the two holds out the better prospect for a full and genuinely human existence.

XI Towards a Human Family

THE FAMILY and the immediate community are the places in which we begin to learn to be human. But that is not the end of our education. Modern man has to learn to live in larger units, the nation or the commonwealth, which make heavy demands on his services or at least on his income. He may not be personally interested in international affairs; but in time of war the international situation may descend upon him and carry him to places that he would never have imagined it possible that he would one day visit. Like the family, each of these larger groupings can be a means to a new intensity and range of human experience. Like the family, each of them can become a threat to genuinely human existence. As in the family, the true and creative character of each can be preserved only by constant watchfulness, and constant rediscovery of the principles on which it is possible for human beings freely to live together.

Men in large numbers do not act in the same way as men in small groups or as individuals. A whole department of psychological study is directed to the investigation of the psychology of the crowd and of the mass.

Most people have had experience in some degree of the way in which a crowd can be carried away by a sudden storm of emotion. All the usual restraints—of reason, of the fear of the disapproval of others, of the fear of consequences—are swept away. The emotion of each acts on the emotions of all the rest. Enthusiasm is directed unanimously in a single direction, and carries with it the assurance of approval for all those who move in the same direction as the rest of the crowd. Men find themselves doing things of which at times when reason is in control they would be completely incapable. Such upsurges of emotion can be harmless and even beneficent, as for example the unbridled enthusiasm of the spectators at a football game. It is good that we should sometimes be enthusiastic and set free for a brief space from the ordered and inhibited existence to which most men in modern society seem to be condemned. But equally they can be dangerous and horrifying when it is impulses of hate and anger that are released and ordinarily sober citizens find themselves swept on to participation in deeds of violence and blood. In either case, the reaction in the opposite direction is likely to follow very quickly. The middle-aged business man wonders what it was that made him stamp on his new hat. The crowd that has tasted blood, when its passions have cooled, is likely to slink away and disperse with sick feelings of emptiness and dismay.

This manifestation of human nature, like so many others, finds striking illustration in the Gospels. The members of the crowd that surged round Pilate's judgment seat shouting "Crucify him" were doubtless at ordinary times respectable, law-abiding people. But the enemies of Jesus had managed to work on their feelings. The sullen resentment of a proud people suffering under the detested authority of a colonising power was a standing element in the situation in Palestine. At that particular moment, there was in the air a strong feeling of frustration, since the people had been disappointed in their expectation that the deliverance was about to appear and that Jesus would declare himself the liberator. In such circumstances it is not difficult to provoke angry passions, and such passions look around for a victim on whom the anger can be vented. Luke's account suggests that no sooner was the victim dead than the reaction set in: "And all the people that came together to that sight, beholding the things that were done, smote their breasts and returned" (Luke 23:48). They had already begun to realise something of the significance of what they had done.*

No man can assert confidently that it is impossible for him to

*There is an astonishingly close parallel in modern times in the case of Captain Green, recorded by G. M. Trevelyan in *Ramillies* (1932), pp. 249–57.

lose his head in this way. The primitive passions remain in all of us, and it is possible that at a certain point of tension they may take control and sweep away all normal restraints. Clearly, however, this is much less likely to happen in the case of the man who has come to know himself on all levels, and is accustomed to engage in that dialogue between impulse and reason which we have described earlier in this book. It is much more likely to occur, if the strength of the irrational impulses has never been clearly recognised, if they have been merely suppressed and kept in place by artificial and rather brittle checks. Our subject in this chapter is, under one aspect, the contribution of the adult and balanced individual to the life of nation and society.

Serious as momentary outbreaks of something like a collective neurosis may be, they are less serious than that collective neurosis which it seems possible for a modern government to maintain over considerable periods and throughout the greater part of a large population, by a judicious use of the propaganda methods at its disposal. Fear, hate, and jealousy are powerful motives. By playing on them continuously, by feeding them with partial truth and fabricated error, a government seems to be able to do very much as it wills with even a highly educated and traditionally civilised people. The fear and suspicion may be directed against a supposed enemy in the midst—the unassimilable minority, racial, religious, or political—the Jews, the Protestants, the Communists—which just because it is different from the rest can so easily be picked on as the scapegoat. It may be the enemy beyond the frontiers whose dark designs are unmasked and whose secret enmity is denounced. The neurosis can be kept in a state of moderate fermentation; or it can at moments be whipped up to the kind of frenzy that results in violent and unrestrained action on the part of the crowd. If a government is uncertain of its own position, one of the simplest methods of drawing attention away from itself and its own defects is that of focussing ill-will upon the alleged external foe and inventing the occasion for frenzy if none exists. All this is too familiar in recent history to need detailed illustration. We are more aware of it as part of the policy of the totalitarian powers than among the nations which claim to be democratic in the Western sense of the term; but it is doubtful

257

whether any government can establish a claim to a perfectly clear record in the matter.

Such phenomena as these, whether momentary and explosive or more calculated and continuous, alike represent a travesty of the true existence of men in the fellowship of society. The point that they have in common is that each represents a regression from the adult to the infantile level, that level of spontaneous, unexamined, and uncontrolled impulse which it is the aim of all education to relate to the demands of reason and of principle. If all societies lived and moved on this level, human existence would hardly be distinguishable from that of the wild beasts that live by instinct without discourse of reason. The subject with which we are here specially concerned is the nature of the adult society and of the responsibility that rests on the individual to work towards the development of a society in which he and his fellowmen can live together in harmony, without prejudice to the adult freedom and individuality of each.

One of the factors in human history of which account must be taken is the tendency for the units in which men live and in which they seem to feel at home to increase in size. This is not an unvarying process. The Roman Empire brought more people under one single rule than any empire before it; when it collapsed under its own weight, the tendency was reversed, and the Roman peace was succeeded by the endless wars of a number of larger and smaller barbarian kingdoms. Yet the movement towards coalescence in the end reasserted itself. A good many centuries have passed since England ceased to be made up of seven diminutive kingdoms; the unity which replaced fragmentation was a necessary precondition for the part that England was later to play in human history. The unity of Germany and of Italy was much more recently brought about. There are men and women still living who were born when neither of these nations existed as a nation. In each case certain features of the unification may be regarded as deplorable; but hardly anyone would wish to put the clock back and reintroduce the principle of division. Both halves of divided Germany still maintain the principle that Germany is a single nation and regard the division as only a passing phenomenon. We are seeing the same process at work in Africa today. Here it is colonialism that has proved the unifying factor. The recession of colonialism has brought new nations into existence. The clan and the tribe are losing their primary importance, and a larger loyalty, as in Ghana and Nigeria, is winning the enthusiasm of peoples to whom it is entirely new.

But already there are signs that the nation is proving inadequate as a framework for the life of modern man in society. New federations are in process of formation. Some of the age-long divisions of language and tradition no longer seem to have the power to divide that once they had. The moving factor is in the main economic; and this is a factor that is likely to increase in significance as greater rapidity of travel and growing mutual interdependence draws all nations together in bonds of unity which they can neither avoid nor repudiate. Some thinkers are already looking forward to a world government, in which all the nations will become politically as well as economically one. This may be regarded as something that can be relegated to a still very distant future, but it cannot be treated as purely visionary. The possibility has come a great deal nearer than would have been deemed possible even fifty years ago; and it may be argued that the fulness of human existence can be attained only in a society which includes all the peoples of the earth.

The prospect of such a unification of all the peoples of the world in one great society is one towards which the Christian cannot but feel sympathetic. Believing, as he does, in one God who is the creator of all men, he cannot admit that any divisions of race, of colour, of political organisation, or economic theory can be ultimate. From the start the Church has been convinced that the Gospel was to be preached to all nations, and that the men of all nations had the capacity to hear and to understand it. From the Christian point of view the most important fact about every man now born into the world is that he has been born into a world which has been redeemed by Christ, and that therefore he is potentially a member of a world-wide unity which is already beginning to take shape in a world-wide Church. The Christian might further remark that in the past all political unities have seemed to need a religious or quasi-religious "myth" as well as a political organisation to hold them together; that there is no reason to suppose that this would be less true of a world-organisation than of the smaller units that have

259

preceded it; and that "the Christian myth,"* to adopt for the moment the language of some sociologists, is well qualified by its essentially universal character to serve as the religious factor in a world-wide unity.

But whether we view the matter simply from the political angle or admit also religious considerations, we must recognise that progress towards unity will be difficult and will have to make its way in the face of contrary tendencies of immense strength and persistence. That which is commended by reason will not always find ready and whole-hearted acceptance. We must guard against certain current illusions which take no account of some elementary facts of human psychology.

Three such illusions are widely current at the present time.

The first is the view that there is an ultimate harmony between the interests of all nations and all men and that, given time and freedom of action, this will make itself manifest. A good case may be made out for this in theory, but the arguments fall far short of demonstrative proof. History warns us against too ready an acceptance of the idea. The principle of the harmony of interests was used rather more than a century ago by the Utilitarians to defend the horrible inequalities produced by the Industrial Revolution, or at least to treat them as no more than temporary results of certain unfortunate maladjustments. In any case, most men are incapable of looking far ahead to a possible identity of interests; they are much more aware of the very real clash of interests in the immediate present. The principle announced by the Duchess in *Alice in Wonderland* that "The moral of that is—'the more there is of mine, the less there is of yours'" is still true over wide areas of economic life. It may have been to the interest of certain sections of the American economy and of American plans for defence that the import duty on Swiss watches should be doubled. It certainly was not to the interest of Switzerland, a small country, poor in natural resources, and almost wholly dependent for its prosperity on its export trade. We all tend to identify our own interests with the interests of the whole world; the validity of the identification may be less apparent to others than it is to ourselves.

*For a criticism of such use of language, see chapter II, pp. 44–46.

The second illusion is that the principle of self-determination will bring peace to the nations and will enable them to live in that harmony which should be the preliminary to world-wide fellowship. The question at once arises as to the size of the unit or the percentage of a population which may demand the right of self-determination. Very few populations are homogeneous; and the decision of a majority to claim political independence may spell nothing but bitter oppression for the minority to which the right of self-determination has been denied. May force be used to impose the will of a majority on a minority? At what point has the minority the right to establish, by rebellion if necessary, its own right to self-determination? A clear illustration of the force and difficulty of these questions may be drawn from the history of Ireland in the early part of this century. When the question of home rule for Ireland was being debated, more than a million Irishmen made it clear that they would never submit to a form of Irish independence which they believed (and as history has shown, rightly believed) would separate them from the United Kingdom and the British Crown, to which they were and are fanatically devoted. Is it right, in the name of liberty, to use force to subject more than a million human beings to a government which they have repudiated in advance? The Ulstermen made it clear that they would fight rather than submit. The only alternatives were civil war, or the irrational division into two of a small country—a division which seems to have become irrevocable and permanent. Much the same story has repeated itself in India; and, with further complications, in Korea and Vietnam. Even peaceful Switzerland is not without its problems in the presence of a French-speaking population in the mainly German-speaking canton of Berne.

The third illusion is that unity can be created through a fellowship of nations, in which all nations are treated as equals, and each is provided with a single vote. To treat great nations and small as though they were in every way equal is to introduce an element of unreality into the proceedings. Among the many services rendered by Professor Reinhold Niebuhr to contemporary thought, none has been greater than his insistence, at a time when most people were very unwilling to recognise it, on the truth that power always remains power and is a factor the workings of which in politics political realism cannot afford to discount. It was on this lack of realism that the old League of Nations foundered. It is already evident that the present United Nations organisation is in danger of going the same way. The joyful recognition of so many nations, including the newest among them, as equal partners in the enterprise has not produced unanimity. It has, on the contrary, resulted in the formation of more or less stable and permanent blocs—the West, the Communist-controlled countries, the Afro-Asian nations —the complex relationships of alliance and tension between which are not infrequently of such a kind as to paralyse the Assembly and to exclude the possibility of any decisive action.

Clearly, if world unity is to come about, it will not come about through any adolescent optimisms, but only through a sternly adult realism, and through conviction and devotion on the part of a very large number of people to consciously thought-out and rationally defended ideals.

But even if a world government were achieved, it does not necessarily follow that peace would be for ever established throughout the world. The nation as a unit exists for the maintenance of peace and fellowship among all citizens. But tension is a permanent factor in the life of even the most peaceful nations. There are different groups, classes, parties, factions, within the nation, each of which is liable at any moment to make claims which the others are unwilling to accept as valid. Generally the unity can be maintained in spite of the tension, but not always. The underlying principle of democracy is that government should be by free discussion and by the appeal to reason. The basic fallacy of a good deal of democratic thought is the naive belief that reason will always prevail. This is not true, though it would be much pleasanter for the world if it were true. Conflicts within the nation cannot always be solved by reason, and the tensions may mount to the point at which reason is overwhelmed by the appeal to force. The most dramatic period in American history is that of the war of 1861 to 1865. Americans, like Spaniards, have good reason to know that civil wars tend to be even more bitter and savage than wars between independent nations and that their results are even more deeply and more permanently scored into the life of a people than those of international conflicts. If a world government were established, tensions would not thereby be abolished. If it came to the point where the voice of reason could no longer be heard, every war would be of the nature of civil war; no one could remain exempt from participation in the struggle, and the consequences might be even more terrible than those of the two world wars through which we have lived, or than of the third by which we are now threatened.

We are driven back from politics and international ideals to a more fundamental question. What is it that makes it so difficult for nations, for groups, and for individuals to live at peace with one another? There is one constant factor in the life of nations, as of individuals, of which realism has to take account. That is aggressiveness. This is certainly an infantile trait. To say that it cannot be cured or eliminated would be unduly pessimistic. To refuse to take account of it would make serious political thought impossible and would prejudice through a naive optimism all reasonable and realistic calculation of the possibilities that lie before the world. It may be deplorable that the nations have made so little progress towards adult handling of their affairs; but, if that is the way they are, that is the situation with which they have to deal. If nations tend to behave as children, we may perhaps conveniently reverse the process by considering the sicknesses of the nations in the light of the problems of childhood.

Aggressiveness in children is a phenomenon with which almost all parents have to deal. In extreme cases the help of the skilled psychiatrist is almost indispensable. The problem is complex, even in those children whom the observer would be most inclined to class as normal.

Just because the aggressive factor produces so many acute and vexing problems, there is a tendency to concentrate on it and to forget that in most children it is to a large extent balanced by other and contrary tendencies. Observation shows that the altruistic instincts in children develop very early. They like being given responsibility for children smaller than themselves, and will take a great deal of trouble to help them, provided that the demands on time and patience are not from their point of view unreasonably heavy. They like giving presents, often to the extreme embarrassment of older people, who have great difficulty in unloading elsewhere a highly unsuitable gift without hurting the tender feelings of the giver. In many cases the problem of aggressiveness can be solved gradually and without crisis by the kind of education which encourages the altruistic at the expense of the aggressive instincts.

Sometimes what passes as aggressiveness is no more than the individual's assertion of the right to be. In order to exit as real human individuals, we do need a certain amount of living space, and in our crowded world that space is not always easy to find. The child is the centre of its own world and is inclined to insist with passion on its own rights. It takes time for it to realise that others too have a right to living space, and that the claims of the individual may have to be modified in view of the rights of others. In one sense this lesson can never be finally learned. The conflict between my own need to exist and consideration for the rights of others is one of the elements of tension in any normal adult existence. The claim to *Lebensraum* is one clue to the complexities of recent world history.

This impossibility of a perfect adjustment of rights and claims perhaps constitutes the element of truth in the view sometimes held that each of us has in him a certain amount of aggressivity, that this must somehow be worked out of the system, and that it is important to find harmless ways in which this can be done. Hence the importance, for those engaged in a competitive existence, of playing golf. This may be one reason for playing golf, but it can hardly be the only reason for encouraging a pursuit which certainly is a useful part of civilised existence for those who can afford it. Apart from the relaxation it affords, it has a further and by no means negligible value, in that it gives the middle-aged business man an opportunity to acquire in a limited sphere that skill and satisfaction of the craftsman, from which he is otherwise almost completely debarred by the way in which he earns his daily bread. The man who tries to work off his ill-temper of vindictiveness on a golf ball is, as a matter of fact, not likely to hit it very far. He is also revealing himself as an immature person, who has never been liberated from childish aggressiveness by the normal processes of growth.

If all this is true, is it possible to define more precisely the nature of harmful aggressiveness and to indicate the causes that appear to bring it into existence? It would seem that in the vast majority of cases, if it goes beyond the limits of an as yet undisciplined self-assertion, aggressiveness is the counterpart of fear—fear of losing some precious possession; fear of losing the love of someone whose love is very precious; fear of losing that personal significance without which a human being is no longer human. In many cases such fears may be imaginary. On the other hand, they may have all too serious a basis in fact. Where children of different ages play together, the rights of the weaker can be roughly overridden by the stronger; the smaller child may find his precious toys taken from him and broken before he has had time to play with them himself. Parents may unconsciously neglect a first child in favour of the needs of a second. A single child thrown too much into the society of grown-ups may come to feel that he counts for nothing and that he has no rights. In such cases the child's aggressivity is likely to be a compound of resentment, despair, and the fierce resolve to assert his claims as a human being, even if the result be to bring annihilation on himself.

Can anything be done about such aggressivity? Is any cure possible, or is it to be regarded as a permanently undesirable element in character with which no more can be done than to keep it rather precariously under control? Happily the answer is not theoretical; there is abundance of evidence from the experience of good homes for maladjusted children, and from well-conducted child-guidance clinics. In a great many cases aggressivity can be reduced to the point at which it is no more than a robust, and occasionally excessive, affirmation of the fact that I am I and not you. And there can be no doubt as to the primary factor in this transformation; it is the restoration of the sense of being loved and valued. Only thus can a measure of self-confidence, and with it a measure of confidence in the world in general, be recreated. Care has to be taken however not to replace illusions of despair in the child's mind by illusions of importance or of security. To be loved and respected is not the same as, in that sense, to be important. And it is idle to pretend that there are no causes for fear in the world. Fear can be reduced to its proper proportions, and the real distinguished from the imaginary; yet there are many things in the world of which it is only reasonable to be afraid. As the aggressive instincts yield place to the co-operative, the child has to learn to exercise the voluntary surrender of some of its rights in favour of others, and not to insist always to the limit on what may be judged to be its rights.

It has to learn the sad fact that there is always a measure of injustice in the world, and that a necessary part of growing up into adult manhood is learning the art of putting up with such injustice without repining and without resentment, without prejudice, however, to the individual's right to self-defence, if the aggressions of others are carried to such a point as to threaten the integrity of his personal existence.

It would be an error to carry too far the parallel between the child and the nation; though evidently humanity in the mass is nearer to the childish level than it is in the individual and in the smaller groups.

The parallel is seen at its closest in the part which fear plays in the relationships between the nations. As the tangled history of the origins of the first world war are worked out, it seems to become clear that the Germans were genuinely afraid (though there was no foundation whatever in fact for their fears) that an attack on them was being prepared by Britain; the German government would not have been able to carry almost the whole of its people enthusiastically into war unless this fear had been shared by a large part of the population. It is equally clear that the major factor in the continuing tension between East and West is mutual fear. Nor can this fear be classed as belonging simply to the world of imagination. Each side sees itself threatened with the loss of what it judges to be real values. Such tensions cannot be eased by conventional oratory on the subject of the restoration of confidence; when confidence has been undermined, it cannot be so easily restored.

But this restoration of confidence, desirable as it is in itself, would not eliminate the possible causes of conflict. If the nations also are to reach the level of adult and rational conduct, they must be prepared at certain points to waive what they regard as their established rights in favour of others, even possibly at considerable cost to themselves. And they must be willing not to regard every real or fancied act of injustice by others as an immediate cause for retaliation. One of the errors of Karl Marx was the supposition that men are actuated almost exclusively by attention to their economic interests. In point of fact the actions of men and nations alike are often determined by considerations of prestige, by unwillingness to yield an inch on the point of honour. Nations have allowed themselves to be gov-

266

erned for generations directly contrary to all their real interests, or to be plunged in suicidal wars, because prestige forbade them to take the obviously reasonable decisions or to yield where yielding would have been on every ground the course most compatible with their true interests. The days have gone by in which in civilised society grown men were permitted to engage in duels, sometimes with fatal results, on microscopic grounds of honour. We have not yet reached a time when nations find it possible to let reason play an equal share with pride in the management of their affairs.

Clearly the education of the nations is going to be a long and gradual process, with many setbacks and few assured gains. And one consequence of the growth in size of the units in which mankind lives is that the individual cannot hope today, except in very unusual circumstances, to exercise such influence as was within his reach when societies were smaller. Yet the influence of the individual is not to be disregarded. It is not true that societies represent simply the sum of the qualities of the individuals of whom they are made up; there is a reciprocal influence. Certainly one particular family would not be what it is unless it was made up of these particular members and of no others; yet the qualities of each react on those of all the rest, and this individual would not be what he is if he had not happened to be a member of this family and subject to the influences which have played upon him within it. The action and reaction of forces within the field of society is so complicated that the most careful analysis yields only approximate generalisations as to their operation; yet it still remains the fact that even the largest society is made up of individuals, and that no individual is entirely without influence on the mass. If a society is to behave with the restraint and judgment which are expected of adult and reasonable human beings, that happy result can be attained only through the development of the adult qualities of intelligence, self-restraint, and tolerance in the majority of its citizens. By educating himself, the individual citizen is helping to determine the destinies of his nation and so of the world.

The destinies of all the nations are now so inextricably interwoven that any generous-minded man of the present day is likely to feel that the strongest of all claims to loyalty is exercised upon him by the human race as a whole. Yet it must be noted as a matter of practical conduct that we cannot contract out of the limited and local societies in which we are placed. In certain circumstances a man can and should seek citizenship in a nation other than that in which he was born. But this is merely to transfer himself from one local society to another. It is desirable that we should feel a strong sense of loyalty towards the world community that is painfully coming into existence; but this loyalty cannot be exercised by disregarding responsibility to and within the smaller society to which we are attached. Attempts on the part of well-meaning individuals to declare themselves citizens of the world and of no particular nation have resulted in most cases only in their becoming citizens of nothing at all, stateless persons, and therefore disqualified from exercising any responsibility or any influence whatever.

Exactly the same is true in relation to the world-wide Church which is an embryo reality, and which is the profound concern of those who have become interested in what is now called the ecumenical movement. Once the vision of a single, united, and world-wide church has been descried, membership in a single separated denomination may come to appear as a nuisance, an embarrassment, or even as an act of treachery to the cause of the Universal Church. But, in reality, membership in "the Church" is impossible; to be a member of the Church involves becoming a member in one part of it, and therefore by definition not a member of other parts in it. This is as true of Roman Catholics as of anyone else, though their exclusive identification of their part of the Church with "the Church" and their refusal of the name of Church to any other body, makes the difficulty sometimes less obvious in their case than in that of other Christians. The only way to work for the world-wide unity of the Church is to recognise the reality of its divisions, honestly to accept the responsibilities of membership in one denomination, and through loyalty to that single part to work for the well-being of the whole and for the manifestation of its unity.

Naturally, whether we look at the political or at the religious sphere, the combination in one person of more local and more extended loyalties is bound to produce tension. The reconciliation of the two may be attended by difficulties, and at many moments it may not be at all obvious to which of the two loyalties the priority is to be accorded. But such tensions are a necessary part of any adult life which refuses such unreal simplifications as may appeal to the adolescent or undeveloped mind. It was so in the days of Jesus; it is equally so today. From the beginning of his work, he was conscious that he had been called to a universal mission; yet he was willing to live as a Jew, to accept as real the authority exercised by the rulers of that people, while criticising the manner in which they exercised that authority. From the start the Gospel which he proclaimed was of universal significance, and he himself affirmed that it must be preached to all nations. Yet during the time of his personal ministry, he limited himself to his own people, though recognising the exceptional faith through which Gentiles might qualify themselves to be treated on the same terms as Jews. From time to time the idea of turning from the unresponsive Jews to the wide and open fields of the Gentile world seems to have presented itself to him, but he recognised it as a temptation to be quietly but firmly rejected. It was only from the less that he could proceed to the more. Only through his steady and open-eyed acceptance of the limitations of a single nation could the universal quality of the Gospel be gradually disclosed. And yet the acceptance of the limited loyalty was possible for him, only because it was related at every point to the larger loyalty which was the basis and the foundation for all that he did.

Any individual who wishes to live a genuinely adult life in the modern world is almost certain to be faced both by such limitations and such tensions; and if we are not to be cramped by the limitations or torn asunder by the tensions, we must all be prepared for the task of a good deal of self-education and self-criticism. We must set ourselves to the task of emerging out of the chrysalis in which inheritance and education have enclosed us.

We all tend to think in what the psychologists conveniently call stereotypes. It is impossible to think at all without a certain amount of generalisation. The multiplicity of individual sensations and individual events has to be concentrated in a simplifying system of concepts if it is to be handled effectively by the mind. There is no danger in this if it is recognised that every generalisation involves a certain amount of distortion, and if the generalisation is constantly checked by reference back to the individual occurrences or existences of which it is a generalised formulation. Danger begins when the concept is itself taken as a form of reality and as it were endowed with a life of its own. The danger is specially great in the field of political, social, and religious thinking. It is natural, for instance, to speak of "the Jews" as a single entity. The Jews are a remarkable people, with a history and a special character of their own. But among them, as among other peoples, there is an almost infinite variety of characters and points of view. If "the Jews" are taken as a concrete entity, which may become the object of suspicion or dislike, as in the case of the young man who was heard to say, "The Jews killed Jesus Christ; I would like to kill ten Jews," rational thought is easily displaced by mere prejudice, and prejudice may easily transform itself into unthinking animosity. Then the situation can become really dangerous.

We all start with a certain number of stereotypes. They are imposed on us in early childhood, by the conversations between adults which we overhear, by the general traditions of our society, by the standards presupposed in the books that we read. We cannot escape them; we accept them unthinkingly as unchanging parts of our mental universe. A vital part of self-criticism and self-education, a necessary part of progress from the childish to the adult reaction, is the honest recognition of the stereotypes in terms of which we tend to think and feel, an attempt to trace them back to their origins, and a serious effort to see how far they correspond to any reality. Anyone who makes this effort is likely to encounter some highly disturbing surprises.

A great many good Protestants, perhaps more in past times than in the present, were brought up on Bunyan's *Pilgrim's Progress*. Their mental picture of the Roman Catholic Church was perhaps determined for them by the vivid picture of Giant Pope shaking his fist at the pilgrims, and saying, "Ye will not mend, until more of you be burned." It is quite possible to maintain an attitude of considerable aloofness towards the Church of Rome and yet at the same time to recognise that such a stereotype is based on something less than a complete understanding of the nature and character of that Church. But a genuinely independent attitude becomes possible

270

only if the element of inherited prejudice in the stereotype is frankly recognised and discounted.

Races and nations tend to think of themselves and of one another in fixed and traditional ways. In view of the tendency of nations to personify themselves, as John Bull or Uncle Sam, and of the justification for this in the quasi-personal character that societies do assume, this is quite natural. It can become dangerous when the stereotype bears little relation to reality; but it has also its amusing side. The Asian tends to think in terms of the spiritual East as contrasted with the material West, a view in which the West, with its abounding traditions of spiritual achievement, finds it hard completely to acquiesce. The British regard themselves as an honest, humorous, kindly, and rather simple people. They find it difficult to recognise themselves either in the Russian stereotype of the bloodthirsty imperialist; in the American picture of the dangerously cunning diplomat, always at work to circumvent the simple and honest American; or in the French view, summarised by Salvador de Madariaga, as "a hypocrite endowed with commonsense." On the other hand, the British traditionally regard the French as a light-hearted and even frivolous nation, "the giddy and godless French"; they are likely to be profoundly disturbed if confronted either with the almost passionate devotion to rationality of the French intellectual or with the hard unyielding realism of the French peasant. There is hardly any limit to the list of traditional stereotypes that could be compiled.

A useful experiment, which can be carried out by anyone who is prepared to take a little trouble, is to make a list on a large sheet of paper of perhaps a dozen groups or peoples, the names of which recur fairly often in conversation in the circles in which the experimenter moves—the Jews, the socialists, Negroes, "Britishers"—a word unknown in Britain—the Japanese, Latin Americans, and so forth. The next step is to write down honestly the thoughts and ideas that come into the mind as each name is recalled. The third stage is to analyse, as accurately as possible, the sources from which these ideas come. How far are they simply traditions inherited from an ancestral past, such as the traditional Irish hatred of England, which is certainly still widespread among Irish Americans of all generations? How far are they the result of mere prejudice or dislike, based on a small number of personally unpleasant experiences? How far are they related to any reliable source of information? How far are they obviously contrary to fact and to reason? It is certain that the analysis will never be complete or wholly accurate—the complexity of our minds and of the way in which our thought patterns are formed excludes the possibility of completeness. But the exercise is not without its value.

The converse of this is the attempt to consider seriously other people's stereotypes, especially as they relate to groups or interests with which we ourselves are intimately concerned. One of the advantages of living in a foreign country and reading the local newspapers is that one is regularly confronted with a picture of one's own country and its policies as seen through the eyes of another people. Considerable irritation is likely to be generated from time to time—so hard is it for even sympathetic observers to understand from within the life of a nation other than their own. But much can be learned even from the misunderstandings. Unless a report is based on pure malevolence, in which case it will probably bear no relation to the facts at all, it is likely to pick out some weakness in national character of which we may be ourselves unaware and which deserves our careful attention. For the past century and a half Christians have taken it for granted that they have a right to send out missionaries into all the countries of the world; they have not always paused to consider what these missionary efforts look like from the other side. Not long ago an official commission in India produced a document which has come to be known as the Niyogi Report. In this, a random collection of criticisms of the methods of missionaries and of objections to "proselytisation" has been somewhat uncritically brought together. It has not proved difficult for the Christian forces in India to refute the report in general and in detail. But there is something more important than refutation; it is the willingness to learn, the serious attempt to understand why the sincere efforts of Christians to do good according to their lights have resulted in such uncritical resentment in the minds of intelligent Hindus.

What is true on the level of the nation and the group is true also on the level of the individual. Our best friends are our critics. As we have seen, morbid anxiety as to what other people may be saying or thinking of us is one of those forms of childish subjection to the wills of others, deliverance from which is a part of the process of growing up. A real willingness to see ourselves as others see us, without anxiety and without resentment, is an indispensable ingredient in the balanced adult character. Every writer of books knows that his best friends are the reviewers. This is true even if the review is harsh and the reviewer is unfriendly, provided that he is honest and sincere. We can never know ourselves fully, however hard we try. Nor can anyone else ever fully understand us. What we shall see in their minds will always be to some extent a distorted image of ourselves; but even from the distorted image there is very much to be learned.

All that has been said so far is of universal application. But the Christian as such has a special interest in this kind of knowledge and criticism, both of himself, and of the nation and Church to which he belongs. He is pledged to a thoroughgoing realism in all the relationships of life. This lays upon him the obligation to reach, as far as is within his power, a balanced and objective judgment on all matters that come before him as a citizen and as a member of a nation which has its part to play in international affairs. The sad truth that achievement is likely always to lag a long way behind the ideal provides no excuse for failure to recognise the demands that the profession of the Christian faith lays upon its adherents. In personal life the Christian is called to be ruthlessly honest in his knowledge of and judgment upon himself. He is pledged to seek the realisation in himself of a character from which pride, self-seeking, and self-interest have been eliminated, though he is well aware that the ideal of such a character has been attained only once in history. He is pledged to the service of a world-wide community, in which the differences between the nations are to be the ground for mutual respect and service, and not for prejudice or jealousy.

It is clear that this is going to be literally an endless process. If one set of prejudices has been eliminated, it is likely that another set will within a short time form themselves. Human nature is so deep and so intricate in its convolutions that there is no end to the increase of self-knowledge. But to say that it is endless is not the same as to say that it is useless. The hyperbole will never touch its asymptote, but it can approach ever nearer to it. The tragedy is that so many physically adult people, including Christians, fail to realise their own condition of adolescent retardation and fail to make the patient and persistent effort without which progress towards maturity is impossible. This makes it all the more important that we should if possible discover the means, and practise the methods, through which personal growth can be stimulated and maintained through all the years of life.

There is no clearer sign of personal growth, and no greater help towards it than a sense of humour. This is by no means the same thing as the faculty of wit. Wit can be superficial, or merely brilliant, or in certain cases bitter and savage. The accusation that we lack a sense of humour is an insult which we all find it hard to forgive—we are all convinced that we have it. Unhappily, however, in many people the sense of humour does not seem to have progressed very much beyond a sense of the ridiculous, which is perhaps valuable but is certainly not more than humour in its most rudimentary form. The grand, genial, compassionate humour of the great writers—Shakespeare, Cervantes, Molière—is closely allied to a sense of proportion, which is itself one of the most important aspects of the apprehension of the truth. It is prepared to take tragically those elements in life which are really tragic. It refuses to take too seriously anything else. It is endlessly patient with the follies, the foibles, the weaknesses of the human race. It is generous in forgiving and always appreciative of sincerity. Above all, it is prepared to laugh at itself and at its own class and race, and refuses to be wounded by the laughter of others. Nothing is perhaps a more certain sign of adult growth in man (or nation) than this capacity to direct the shafts of laughter at oneself. Nothing serves better to keep in due proportion the rational and the unruly elements in the human make up. Nothing perhaps has greater survival value in a competitive and troubled world.

But willingness to laugh at oneself implies also a right to laugh—albeit kindly—at other people; and laughter, even the kindliest, is a form of criticism. To refrain from criticism may be a refusal of the truth, and so a regression to a less than adult level of experience.

It is on the liberty of criticism accorded to the subject that the regimes traditionally called democratic rest. All human institutions and organisations are so imperfect that they must be regarded as being at all times the legitimate targets of criticism. Every regime tends of course to regard itself as the final and permanent revelation of human, and even of divine, wisdom. The critic renders the valuable service of making more difficult this process of self-deification. In a democratic state the opposition is almost as important as the government. In Britain this strange state of affairs finds expression in the fact that the leader of the opposition is "leader of Her Majesty's opposition," and is paid a considerable salary by the state instead of being sent to the Tower of London as a traitor. The law may impose limits on criticism and on the free expression of opinion; it is a basic principle of democracy that those limits must be as wide as is consistent with the safety of the state.

What is true of the state is true also of the Church. The Church has its divine aspect. But it is always also in all its manifestations a sadly human body, with all the weaknesses of human organisations. The Churches have tended to identify themselves with particular regimes and outworn forms of human society, and to suppose that what is inevitably transitory is somehow eternal. They have been narrow in their outlook; they have been strangely insensitive to the changing needs of men and to the injustices by which they have been surrounded. The rebel in the Church may be as important as the defender of the orthodox faith and the traditional positions. Not all Churches are alike in the liberty they accord to their children to criticise and to suggest. In this sphere, however, if in no other, the Protestant principle of the right of private judgment may be held to be of unshakeable validity. Harsh and even violent criticism is fully compatible with loyalty to the Church in its true nature and to the eternal truths for which it stands.

In general, a totalitarian regime cannot and does not permit criticism. This is because such a regime claims for itself an absolute and lasting validity, in contrast to the provisional validity which is claimed for themselves by the forms of human society that take a more modest view of their own status. Self-criticism is welcomed and encouraged in Communist China; but it is self-criticism in relation to the standards and demands of a regime, or of a form of human thinking, which claims to be absolutely and permanently valid. No criticism of the basic principles can be permitted; and any criticism of the regime in which these principles have found their incorporation is likely to be regarded as treason.

It seems that we are driven to ask whether at this point we do not come up against two fundamentally different understandings of human society and of the nature of a genuinely human existence.

For a generation the West has been living through a period of violent self-examination, of gnawing at its own vitals, even of denying the validity of its own existence. The defects of our Western societies and their failures are so gigantic and so evident that the violence of the reaction can be easily accounted for. But most of the leaders in this campaign of self-criticism are men who have never lived under any other kind of regime, and who therefore perhaps find it a little difficult to stand far enough back from the West to be quite objective in their attitude and in their evaluation of its achievements. For after all, though we have learned slowly and fitfully, certain things have been learned. It is generally accepted among us as right that men should take a share, the fullest share possible, of responsibility for the shape of the society in which they live. It is believed that, through debate and dispute, through the clash of opinions, truth will slowly emerge, and that that which has no survival value will disappear. It is believed that a man has a right to his own thoughts, and a right to express them, and that only if this condition is fulfilled is any progress towards maturity possible. Under a totalitarian regime there is no place for independence. The greatest virtue is the virtue of the child—unquestioning obedience. The ordinary man has no share at all of responsibility for society; his business is simply to accept the higher wisdom of those in power. Every attempt is made to ensure that his thoughts follow the accepted pattern; if by any chance he should be thinking dangerous thoughts, it will be only at his own personal peril that he will express them.

Faced by two such contrasting systems, we are bound to choose between them. By what criterion is our choice to be determined? And what grounds can we allege for supposing our choice to be the right one? The basic presupposition of this book is that human existence has value. This may not be self-evident; but we cannot start without any presupposition at all. It has been further assumed that a "genuinely human existence," one in which human nature develops to the full range of its capacities in accordance with the inherent laws of its own being, is "better" than one less genuinely human in that there man's existence has been checked in its growth, thwarted or distorted by inner or outer circumstance. Are we right in thinking that liberty is as much a necessity of human existence as oxygen; that societies which, however imperfectly, promote liberty and therefore make possible growth into genuinely adult manhood are in that degree good; and that societies which inhibit liberty and thereby make progress towards adult manhood difficult are in that degree bad?

This raises a new range of problems, as to the status of "good" and "bad" in the universe. To the further exploration of these problems our next chapter must be devoted.

XII The Eternal Dimension

THE AFFIRMATION of the right to criticise is part of the heritage of the free man. This involves taking up an attitude of detachment from, in certain cases even of opposition to, a society to which in general he is attached by sincere and devoted loyalty. But how far may criticism be carried? It is certain that society will react against the critic. If he goes beyond a certain point, society is likely to demand his life as the price of his rashness. Is it ever justifiable for a man to carry opposition to the point at which he will have to die for his convictions? *Jesus – critic & his society*

Precisely this problem arose in the life of Jesus. At a fairly early stage of his public ministry, the existing authorities of his people recognised that, if Jesus were allowed to continue, the effect of his teaching would be permanently to undermine their position and their power. Various means were within his reach to limit or to mitigate the conflict. He might have modified his teaching in such a way that his essential disagreements with the traditions of the scribes and Pharisees could be concealed. If he had limited the field of his ministry to Galilee, he might well have been left undisturbed. But it seemed to him that the conflict could not be avoided without surrender of essential principle. For the sake of truth and of the real well-being of his people, the challenge must be presented, and it must be presented where it would hurt most, in Jerusalem. He was well aware that the result of open conflict could hardly be anything but his own death. The Gospels give plain evidence of the tension under which his decision was made; they equally make it plain that to him, with his sense of special vocation, this presented itself as the only course that he could follow.

At all times men and women have been found willing to die for causes in which they have believed.

It is impossible not to pity the dumb, sheeplike obedience with which in the past masses of men have allowed themselves to be led to the slaughter by their rulers. It is hard not to be indignant at the methods of propaganda by which in modern times governments have inflamed patriotic passion to the point at which countless young men have come to feel it a far more glorious thing to die for one's country than to live for it. It is possible to judge dispassionately that many of the causes, many of the slogans, for which men have died were trivial, mistaken, or infamous. But this leaves still unanswered the question as to whether there are circumstances in which it is desirable to choose death rather than life.

In the eyes of those who hold that all is relative and that there are no absolutes such throwing away of life as is involved in martyrdom for the sake of a cause must necessarily seem a wasteful folly. If the words "right" and "wrong" have no absolute significance and are related only to social utility, if the major aim of human beings is no more than successful adaptation to that form of society in which they live, no circumstances can arise in which death is to be preferred to life. Life is, after all, the most precious thing that a man has. Has he any right to barter it away before his natural time has come, on the ground of what he is pleased to call his convictions? If all is relative and nothing is absolute, there can be only one logical answer. The Preacher of the Old Testament was right; a live dog is better than a dead lion. Yet the unvarnished statement of this position is likely to cause disquiet to a good many people. We are not governed only by logic. Most of us feel deep down in our hearts that the world, bad as it is, is a better place than it would otherwise be precisely because there have always been among its inhabitants a certain number who have judged life well lost for the sake of, or in the affirmation of, principles beyond and above themselves in which they believed.

Fifty years ago, throughout the greater part of the Western world, such a discussion as this might have seemed highly theoretical. In

279

times of calm and prosperity we get along very satisfactorily with our relative and conventional convictions. But times of crisis alter the picture, and we may find ourselves compelled by circumstances to face questions of absolute choice which we would very much have preferred to keep out of our minds.

For a large number of our contemporaries these have not been theoretical questions. Any totalitarian situation at once raises in sharp form the ultimate questions of right or wrong. A totalitarian regime is usually inclined to adopt what has been called the "positive" view of justice—justice is not some abstract quality inherent in the nature of things; it is simply that which, as Nazis would have said, tends to the strengthening, the prosperity, or the glory of the German people; or as the Communists say today, that which promotes or forwards the revolution. Any attempt to find a sanction for justice outside and beyond the immediate and the actual is mere speculation, lacking any solid foundation. But is this true? Has any human organisation of society the right to claim an absolute and total loyalty, without reference to anything beyond itself? Or are there standards by which even that society is to be judged? If so, what are they, and on what does their validity depend?

It was in circumstances such as these, not so many years ago, that many citizens of Western countries, faced by the challenge of total war, found that their own feelings were being precisely expressed by a Greek play written more than two thousand years ago, the *Antigone* of Sophocles. The situation represented in that play is not likely to be exactly reproduced in any modern society. Polynices, Antigone's brother and the invader of his country, had been declared a public enemy and refused those rites of burial which according to Greek ideas were necessary to secure the entry of the angry and outraged spirit into the home of the dead in the other world. Antigone had gone out by night and scattered on the body those few handfuls of dust which were considered sufficient as an emergency fulfilment of the burial rites. When challenged for her disobedience to the commands of the ruler, Antigone appeals to that other and higher law, by which states and rulers are to be judged, and which no state or ruler may set aside. In the course of her defence, she lets fall the memorable words, *Aei zè tauta* [these things live for ever]; they stand above the relative, above the moving changing life of men, unchanging and inexorable. For her failure to obey the rulers of her country Antigone is condemned to death. It seems such a trivial affair, to give or to withhold a few handfuls of dust. Perhaps a foolish waste of a young and promising life. But, if the dramatist is right—and part of the value of this example is that it is drawn from the pre-Christian era and is wholly independent of any Christian concern—the spectator is compelled to recognise that what he is watching is the conflict between two different worlds, and that he must make up his mind to which of the two he himself belongs.

Equally from the pre-Christian world, and equally dramatic, is the scene in the book of Daniel, in which three young men are offered the choice between bowing down to the golden image which Nebuchadnezzar the king had set up, or being cast alive into the burning fiery furnace. This story brings us one step nearer to the directly religious issue. But the answer of the young men is as memorable as that of Antigone: "O king, we are not careful to answer thee in this matter. If it be so, our God whom we serve is able to deliver us from the burning fiery furnace and he will deliver us out of thy hand, O king. But if not, be it known unto thee, O king, that we will not serve thy gods, nor worship the golden image which thou hast set up".

Most of us feel a lifting of the heart when we read such words, or when we read the records of those who made similar answers to Hitler and his minions and perished at Buchenwald or Dachau. Some would go so far as to say that no genuinely human existence is possible without the capacity and the willingness to recognise values that transcend the human scene and if necessary to die in order that these values may be asserted and maintained. But is all this merely illusion, a vain and pompous heroism, signifying nothing; or is there some human and more than human reality to which it is, in fact, a response?

In this field, as in all others which deal with ultimates, no logical demonstration is possible in either direction. It is impossible either to prove or to disprove the existence of the eternal values. Certain considerations may be adduced on either side; but in the end we are left face to face with what it is now fashionable to call an existential decision, but in earlier times would have been called a willingness to experiment and to consider dispassionately the results which follow. It may not be out of place to consider briefly the parallel situations which arise in every form of man's approach to and contact with reality.

The physical scientist deals with nature under its three-dimensional aspect, as that which can be measured, numbered and weighed. Evidently to a large extent the picture of physical reality is the product of the human mind; but the physicist repudiates emphatically the idea that he is dealing only with the products of the fertile human imagination. He is in contact with something outside himself, something mysterious and only in part intelligible. He is a discoverer. He has observed real correspondences and regularities; and though his formulae and equations can never give more than approximate and imperfect representations of that reality, they are related to external existences and not merely to human mental processes. At times the nature of that external existence strikes on him with the force of a revelation.

A similar affirmation will be made by the artist, who is concerned with the universe under its aspect of beauty. Most artists would declare that, before putting pencil to paper or brush to canvas, they had encountered beauty, order, and proportion in the world around them. Sometimes to them too this beauty has come with the shock of a revelation. Dazed and dazzled with the splendour of this revelation, they have set to work as best they could to interpret, knowing full well that the interpretation will always fall short of the vision, but being assured that what was conveyed in the vision was a reality external to themselves.

The moralist, who is concerned with reality under the aspect of right and wrong, good and evil, also regards himself as a discoverer. It is not his aim to impose artificial rules or classifications on human society; still less to interpret human phenomena in the light of his own personal beliefs and prejudices. His aim is to see whether there are permanent factors in human relationships, some of which always tend to produce a richer, more natural, more effective human existence, and others of which always tend to the weakening or the impoverishment of that existence. His experience, too, is one of encounter, of a human reality which is only dimly discernible

282

and which it is most difficult to express in the formulations which are the tools of his trade, but which nevertheless is not the creation of his fancy.

The religious man goes beyond these other three to ask the ultimate questions about reality. His concern is with absolute truth, absolute goodness, absolute existence. But once again, he will affirm that his experience is of encounter, of something which is really there, which exists outside of himself, and which comes to meet him in the experience of a genuine meeting of person with Person. He too is sadly aware that what he can express of this encounter will fall far short of the reality; the most eloquent human words are inadequate to it. But he is sure that what he is trying to express is a transcendent reality, and not simply the elucubrations of his own brain.

It is at once clear that no one of these students of reality can prove demonstratively the truth of that which he affirms. Idealists have denied the independent existence of the physical world outside us. Many thinkers have maintained that beauty is simply one aspect of man's response to his world—it is in the eye of the beholder and is not a characteristic of that world itself. Human life in societies may, after all, be a purely fortuitous affair, a constant movement of uncontrollable and unpredictable human impulses, beneath which no permanently solid principles are to be discerned. God may be no more than a projection of human thoughts and desires upon the clouds. These are possibilities which must always be kept in mind and which cannot be logically or demonstratively disproved.

The man who concerns himself seriously with any of these four approaches to "reality" has in point of fact made what may be called an existential decision in favour of the validity of the approach with which he is concerned; in favour of the view that it makes possible encounter with a reality outside himself, a reality the value of which justifies the effort involved in becoming acquainted with it. The decision may lie far below the level of consciousness and may never emerge into consciousness, but may be none the less real for that. The physicist takes his stand on the belief that there is a physical reality outside himself which has its own order and splendour. The artist, or the man who is concerned to appreciate art, affirms that beauty is a quality of things and persons apart from any apprehension of it by his own mind. The moralist affirms that there is a moral structure of human life and relationships, imperfectly as this may be visible in any existing society or community. The religious man is convinced that behind the visible universe, behind all human life and striving, there is an ultimate and eternal reality, with which it is possible for man to enter into relationship.

Once the existential decision has been made, thought and action along certain lines become possible. The verification of the underlying affirmation can be made only experimentally. In one way or another, this verification seems generally to include two things— the capacity to bring a complicated mass of phenomena together under a small number of simple principles, and ability to predict with a measure of accuracy what results will follow from certain experiments or actions. It is clear that the phenomena to be dealt with become increasingly complex as we move forward from one approach to reality to the next, and that the verification will be less tangible, though not necessarily less effective, at each stage than at that which went before it.

Jesus lived in an intense awareness of an eternal reality in the world. As he understands it, the most important things in the universe are truth, justice, compassion, and love. These, according to him, are far more powerful and far more lasting than any human power or force. Eternity is not something that belongs to the future; it is not to be understood in terms simply of an endless continuation of time. It is already present, a dimension of reality different from those accessible to the five senses with which the human frame has been provided. This is the significance of the distinction between flesh and spirit, on which the fourth Gospel so often insists: "That which is born of the flesh is flesh, and that which is born of the spirit is spirit." "Flesh" means ordinary human life, limited by space and time and by everyday experience; "spirit" is that same life enlarged to include the dimension of eternity. All men, it is affirmed, are related to that eternal world whether they know it or not. They may deny or ignore that dimension of reality; it remains none the less real for that. Jesus calls men to an existential decision of faith. This decision involves the conscious and deliberate affirmation of the reality of the eternal order, and the adoption of a conscious and deliberate attitude towards it. But in the thought of Jesus, this eternal world is not a world of abstractions; it is a world of personal relationships with God. He does use abstract terms, but these cannot be understood outside the personal reference. "Love" is not some impersonal quality in things; it is simply a convenient abbreviation for a loving God, a God whose love is always manifest in redeeming action. The call to decision is also a call to faith in such a God as this. Moreover, Jesus is aware that in himself this eternal world has become visible in the fulness of its reality; he is the way and the truth and the life. The call to faith in God is, therefore, also a call to faith in Jesus, in what he is—human nature undistorted by imperfection; in what he accomplishes—the restoration of human nature to what it was always intended to be; in what he represents—the ultimate reality of the universe revealed as love, justice, and compassion. This and this alone is reality; this, according to Jesus, is the true life of man.

It should be noted that in this existential demand there are three elements, which are always held together in the Gospels, but which for the sake of our argument can and should be separated. There is first the affirmation of the eternal "values." There is, secondly, the affirmation that these "values" have value only because they are the expression in abstract terms, which are useful for the purposes of communication, of the nature of a living and personal God. Thirdly, there is the belief that through conscious and deliberate faith in this living and eternal God, man can himself become eternal through the gift of everlasting life.

There are many men of good will who are glad to accept the "values" represented in the life and teaching of Jesus, yet do not find it possible to go forward either to belief in God or to a belief in everlasting life. Such men raise the question, and rightly, whether the belief in immortality should have an effect on the way we behave in daily life. If we see certain things to be "right" and "good," should we not attempt to put them into action, quite regardless of any question of possible rewards or punishments in another world? The answer to this question must be an emphatic Yes. Even if it were to be finally and conclusively demonstrated

285

that there is no afterlife either for the human individual or for the human race, the Gospel would still be the best news in the world. It supremely shows the way in which the life of men ought to be lived. The demand it makes for total self-forgetfulness and self-denial is hard for human nature to accept. But the Gospel makes plain that this is the only way of true happiness. These are the only principles on which life can be made tolerable for the weak and the unfortunate. Indeed, it might be maintained that, if this is in fact the only life we have, if there is no hope of any compensation in another world for misfortune in the world, the application of the Gospel principles becomes even more important than it would be, if belief in the existence of another world could be maintained. Only then, the critic might say, can the Gospel principles of compassion and service to the weak be seen in their full value.

Those who believe in God but not in immortality would frame the question in a rather different way. Is not the desire for personal immortality an evidence of selfishness, or at least of an overestimation of our own individual value? Is it not enough to believe that what is real lives on, even though we ourselves shall not be there to see it? Once again, while holding over for the moment the problem of whether the idea of eternal life for the individual is credible or not, we shall be inclined to meet this question also with a qualified affirmative. This was the faith of the saints of the Old Testament. They had little or no belief in any life worthy the name after death; yet they held passionately to their faith in God, hoping to live on in their children and in the fulfilment of the purposes of God for his people.

Not dissimilar has been the faith of many mystics:

> With wide-embracing love
> Thy Spirit animates eternal years,
>   Pervades and broods above,
> Changes, sustains, dissolves, creates and rears.
>   Though earth and man were gone,
> And suns and universes cease to be,
>   And Thou wert left alone,
> Every existence would exist in Thee.

(Emily Brontë)

Splendid expression has recently been given to this point of view by a distinguished Italian writer, not as the confession of his own faith, but as a point of view which he can understand and with which he can sympathise:

> To have believed in the kingdom of God before its full manifestation has come, to have staked our whole existence on this faith, to have served it in this epoch of expectancy, of decision, of conflict, may be, when all is said and done, as desirable a destiny as that of living in the joy and peace of the perfection of the lower creation, realised within the limits of its purely temporal existence. No one is robbed of his share in the kingdom of God who has lived believing in that kingdom and working for its coming. It is possible to accept the destiny of having lived as one of the pioneers of the kingdom, in the thought that others will rejoice in the fulness of its manifestation; it is possible to lay down our tools at the end of the day and to enter into the rest of our Lord without thought of any other reward. Do we really need to desire any other reward? What honour could be higher than that of having lived for the kingdom and in the service of the kingdom? What is there for us to regret except that we have served it so ill, with so little faith and with so many cowardly compromises? What more could we desire than to enter into silence, with the hope, yea, more, with the assurance that our failures and our faults will be forgiven?*

And yet, when all this has been said, we have to reckon with the remark of Paul that, if in this life only we have faith in Christ, we are of all men most miserable. Why so? With all that has been given us in this life in Christ, why should the thought of death without anything beyond in any way add to our misery?

The answer to this question can be given, in my opinion, only by attempting to define the special quality that is added to human life by faith in Christ. I would identify that quality by the single word "delight."

It is hardly necessary to insist at this point yet once again that

*Giovanni Miegge: *Per Una Fede* (1950), pp. 211-2. I have now completed a translation of this fine book, which is shortly to be published under the title (American edition) *Christian Affirmations in a Secular Age.*

the realism of Jesus and of the Gospels involves a full awareness of the tragic dimension in human life, and a steadfast refusal to insulate ourselves against whatever is painful, sordid, distressing, or frustrating in our human situation. And yet the recurring emphasis of the New Testament is joy. I have chosen the word "delight" rather than "joy," partly because the word "joy" has grown a little worndown by too constant use and partly because "delight" serves better to express that element of surprise (rightly stressed by Mr. C. S. Lewis in the title of his recent autobiography *Surprised by Joy*) which is a constant element in the experience of the Christian.

The Christian goes through life in a constant state of astonished wonder.

He looks out with perpetually renewed amazement on the beauty and varied richness of the created world. This is, of course, an experience which he shares with all souls that are sensitive to natural beauty; but perhaps the belief that all this is the creation of the hands of a loving God, and that this beauty is an overflow from the infinite and invisible beauty, adds depth and dimension to the experience.

The Christian goes through the world perpetually astonished at the delightfulness of ordinary people (and undismayed by their less delightful qualities). He is awed by the astonishing experience of Christian friendship, which can grow to maturity in a couple of hours, can remain untouched by time or distance, and can be taken up again twenty years later not merely at the point at which it was left off but with an added sense of intimacy or nearness. For this mysterious but incontrovertible fact the Christian can find no other explanation than that, when friendship is "in Christ," amid all the changes of human life and circumstance Christ remains the unchanging and perpetually creative factor in a relationship between two human beings. It is evident that the most intimate of our encounters with other human beings can be no more than beginnings and that sooner or later their fair promise will be interrupted by death. But the Christian is not unduly disturbed by the reality of physical extinction; believing as he does in eternal life and in the fellowship of all God's people in the heavenly kingdom, beneath the end of each instalment of fellowship here he can write, "To be continued in our next." But if it were to be shown conclusively that his hope is an illusion, he would feel a profound sense of deprivation and loss. It is precisely the heightened sense of living that has come to him in Christ by which the measure of this loss is to be gauged. If this glorious spring is to be followed by a yet more glorious summer, reason is satisfied. But if no summer follows on this spring, we might be tempted to feel that we have been deluded by promises that will not be fulfilled.

There is more than this. The Christian believes himself to have become personally acquainted with Jesus Christ, and this is the most precious thing that life affords. However far he has gone in the life of faith, he knows that he is still only a child playing in the shallows and that there is far more to be discovered of the riches of the friendship of Christ. Here more than anywhere else he desires to be able to write at the bottom of the page, "To be continued in our next." He has been assured by Paul, whose views in other contexts he has found to be worthy of respectful consideration, that a time will come when we shall know even as we are known, when the promise of the earthly seedtime shall be fulfilled in a heavenly reaping, and when our limited and imperfect knowledge of Christ shall be raised to the height of perfection in so far as it is ever possible for the finite to apprehend the infinite. If this were proved to be untrue, the believer could not but be overwhelmed by a desolate sense of deprivation and loss. If this glorious promise is never to reach fulfilment, the measure of that great new thing that Christ has brought into his life would be also the measure of his disappointment.

The critic may return to the assault with the old accusation that this is simply another example of wish-fulfilment; the Christian dislikes the idea of death and therefore calls into existence an imaginary world through which the painful reality of death is annulled. We must always allow for the fact that our desires do influence and distort our thinking. But it would be merely superficial to dismiss the whole of human interest in the question of immortality as no more than another instance of wish-fulfilment. The ultimate question is as to the nature of the universe. The whole universe, in Paul's phrase, seems to be subject to frustration; it has produced creatures which are capable of entertaining hopes, visions, and ideals; and yet none of these seems to reach its perfect realisation in this world of space and time. Is this the end of the story? Is there nothing beyond? If that is so, then the whole of life might be regarded as a rather cruel practical joke, and the best way to face it would be a dour and perhaps slightly bitter resignation.

It is important at this point to distinguish between the Christian answer to this question, and other answers that have been given. The Christian is not very much interested in the ideas of immortality and of human survival after death as such, apart from his belief in the reality of a living God. This problem has been debated by philosophers for many centuries, and on the whole they have not been able to give us more than a dusty answer. Later thought has not been able to add much to the arguments adduced by Plato in the *Phaedo* more than two thousand years ago. Nothing can be asserted with great confidence on the basis of purely philosophic arguments; perhaps the best that philosophy can offer is a possibility and a faint hope. And whether the answer given is optimistic or the reverse, it is difficult not to think sometimes that the conclusion reached by the philosopher depends, not so much on the arguments actually adduced, as on some existential decision previously taken on personal and intimate grounds that do not emerge clearly in the arguments. This comes out plainly in the remarkable exchange on the subject of immortality between two of the most intelligent men of this century, William Temple and Bertrand Russell. "I remember," wrote Temple, "once saying to Bertie Russell: I believe in it far more than the evidence warrants. He said: And I *dis*believe far more."* It is not always that eminent thinkers are so honest about their prepossessions.

The Christian need not be in the least embarrassed by an admission as to the existential character of the decision on which his hope of a future life depends. It rests, not on any philosophical arguments, but on a certain view of God, and of human relationships with God, which has been set before him by Jesus Christ. In a notable passage Jesus affirmed that the relationship between God and those who trust in him is determined by the changeless

*F. A. Iremonger: *William Temple, Archbishop of Canterbury* (Oxford, 1948), p. 626.

290

eternity of God and not by the transitoriness of human existence: "Now that the dead are raised, even Moses showeth at the bush, when he calleth the Lord the God of Abraham and the God of Isaac and the God of Jacob. For he is not a God of the dead but of the living; for all live unto him." The argument is of course quite unconvincing, unless the premise is accepted. But if Jesus was right about this, as he was right about so many other things, the conclusion does seem to follow from the premise. If God is the living God, and if he does call men into a personal relationship with himself, and if a relationship of that specifically personal character has been established, then that relationship cannot possibly be interrupted by so trivial an event as the death of the body.

It is for this reason that the resurrection of Jesus is treated in so many contexts in the New Testament as literally the most natural thing in the world. That is the way the world is made. Perfect fellowship between God and man, as exemplified in Jesus and in his perfect acceptance of the will of his Father, is naturally followed by perfect victory over death. The resurrection came upon the disciples as a surprise only because they had not understood either the Scriptures or the power of God. Immortality to the Christian is not some uncertain and undefined survival; it is the unbroken continuance of that fellowship with God into which he has been introduced by taking seriously the words of Jesus. Belief in the resurrection of Jesus is the principal ground for his belief that he himself will live again after death; but behind that conviction stands faith in the God in whom Jesus believed, the perfection of faithfulness, justice, power, and love.

The question of eternal life is not marginal to an enquiry into human nature. It is the very heart of the whole matter. If man is, as a matter of fact, a being capable of personal fellowship with a living God, and if he may hope for the continuation of that fellowship in a sphere of being in which the imperfect strivings and ideals of this life find their fulfilment (and fulfilment is an entirely different idea from that of compensation), then the whole of his existence must be considered in the light of this central reality. The first thing that must be known about icebergs is that there is seven to ten times as much iceberg below the water as shows above it. The navigator ignores this elementary

291

fact at his peril. If it is the case that man upon earth can live in an eternal dimension as well as a temporal one, and if this fact is denied, disregarded, or ignored, the resulting estimate of human nature will be at every point distorted and unsure. Immediate practical consequences follow, as is evident if we return to the problem with which this chapter opened. In what circumstances, and for what causes may I rightly throw away my life? If death closes all and there is nothing beyond the temporal and the relative, the sacrifice of life cannot be at best more than a heroic gesture, and at worst may be a foolish squandering of what has a certain though limited value. If, however, the eternal is the real, in any situation in which a conflict arises between the eternal value and a temporal advantage, it is always the eternal which must be chosen even at the cost of life itself. If the eternal means not only impersonal values but the living God whose eternity is the guarantee of human immortality, the willingness to die rises above the level of Stoic endurance to a glad acceptance of what at that moment is seen to be the will of God.

But the significance of the Christian doctrine of everlasting life cannot be grasped in any single illustration. It involves a change of perspective, through which the understanding of human nature under every aspect and in every part is changed. The opinion may be hazarded that what our sick society needs more than anything else is a recovery of the eternal dimension in both the senses of the term—in the belief that there are transcendent values that must at all costs be preserved, and in the conviction that man himself can here and now be a sharer in an eternal world which is beyond the reach of the cruel grasp of death.

The present climate of thought is unquestionably unfavourable to this conviction. Mass observation and polls of public opinion show that modern man in the West is on the whole doubtful, indifferent, incredulous, or hostile to the idea of immortality. This is what so clearly distinguishes him from the man of the Middle Ages, who lived his whole life in an ever present sense of an eternal world always hanging over him and to whom the issues of heaven and hell were a very present concern. Now, if the belief in eternal values and eternal life were mere imagination or superstition, the disappearance of them ought to be followed by a great liberation of the human spirit, comparable to the liberation that followed on the disappearance of the belief in astrology and magic from the minds of rational men. It may be doubted whether this consequence has followed. If such a liberation had followed, there should be a good deal less work in modern society for the psychiatrist than there is. And perhaps the recrudescence of the belief in astrology and magic is in itself a sinister symptom of the sickness of a society that to so great an extent lives in a purely temporal and relative world.

We know a great deal more about man than was known to medieval man. We know immensely more about our bodies and the way in which they work. Modern psychology has revealed whole worlds within us that were previously almost unknown and has shown the extent to which the unconscious controls our apparently rational choices and decisions. The study of man in society has given us almost unlimited new information about the problems, economic, social, and ethical, that arise when men live together in society. But have we really come to understand ourselves better than the men of earlier ages? Why do we still turn back to Dostoevsky, to Shakespeare, to Augustine, to Aeschylus, to Isaiah? Is the reading of the great writers of the past no more than an archaeological interest? Or have they still a direct relevance to ourselves because human problems are perennial, and the understanding of these great prophets of the past is at many points deeper than that which we can ourselves reach unaided or with the help of modern scientific equipment?

To one accustomed to range widely over the great literature of the past, the study of a good deal of contemporary writing feels rather like coming in from life under the wide spaces of the open heaven to an ill-lighted and ill-ventilated cellar. Many of the writers of the present day who are most widely read have deliberately or unconsciously rejected the dimension of the eternal. They are concerned with the immediate and the contemporary. The depths they plumb are those of the human consciousness turned inwards upon itself and not those of man's relationship to eternity. Much of this writing is marked by brilliant and accurate observation, by clear though limited psychological understanding. What it often seems to lack is the element of compassion which is present in all the greatest writers of the past. To read some of these works is rather like watching an ant's nest under glass. The creatures are not allowed any privacy. Their habits are relentlessly observed and described. They go hurrying this way and that without apparent purpose, and in the end they die.

It is not fair to judge an epoch by one book. But by way of illustration, mention may be made of one highly distinguished novel, which appeared while this book was being written, and was honoured by the award of the Goncourt prize—*Les Mandarins* by Simone de Beauvoir. This is a brilliant study of the life of Paris intellectuals in the troubled days after the war. In that world of confusion and disarray, all the elements of tragedy and heroism are there; but the result is neither tragic nor heroic. If that is all there is to human life—this mixture of vague idealism and astonishing naiveté, of quite amoral sexual irregularity, of vanity, intrigue, malice, and an almost cynical tolerance—there seems to be no particular reason why anyone should wish to have been born or why anyone should wish to continue to live.

It is not the business of a writer to preach. The moralising author is merely a nuisance. But the impression left by an author on the mind of the reader depends in the last resort on the total picture of the universe that is present to his own mind; and the reader has a right to ask how much of the wide spectrum of human life is within the range of the writer with whom he is for the moment concerned. It can hardly escape notice that many of the writers of the present day either make no attempt to depict genuine, simple goodness or are singularly unsuccessful in doing so. Admittedly, the representation of goodness in its infinite diversity and interest is far more difficult than the depiction of evil in its limited varieties and its endless monotony. It is at this point that really great writers of the past, such as Dickens, have failed; their supposedly good characters are all too often intolerably smug and unreal. But simple devotion to duty and quiet self-sacrifice do exist and are part of everyday human life. If our writers have failed to observe them, or have abandoned the attempt to represent them, it may be that their spectrum needs to be extended, and that a missing dimension needs to be restored before really great art can be produced.

Writers are in a measure representative of their age. What we have suggested as being true of the writers may turn out to be true also of the age which they depict in their writings.

For the last two generations the greater part of Western society has chosen to live its life entirely within the categories of time and space, without reference to the possible existence of an eternal and transcendent dimension. This is a new situation. Every previously existing society has believed itself to be related to something outside itself and more durable than itself. These ideas of the transcendent have frequently been confused, uncertain and even self-contradictory, but they have existed. The results of the rejection of this other dimension do not seem to have been entirely satisfactory. Is it possible that we encounter here the explanation of the sickness of modern society?

We have noted several times that a great part of mental sickness results from the rejection of one or other aspect of the reality by which the human self is confronted. Mental sickness is, in this way, curiously parallel to the deficiency diseases from which the body can suffer. Until recent times a certain type of goitre was endemic in a number of the Swiss valleys. When it was discovered that this condition was due to iodine deficiency, it was possible almost completely to eliminate this disfiguring ailment by the addition of a minute quantity of iodine to all the salt sold in the affected areas. If full and healthy human existence depends upon a right and natural relationship to all the aspects of reality by which man is confronted, the cutting off of relationship to any one of those aspects is bound to result in disturbance, malaise, and unhappiness. The recovery of health depends on the restoration of the missing relationship and on nothing else. Now if the transcendent is one of those elements in reality, a right relationship to which is one of the essentials for the fulness of human existence, the cutting off of that relationship would almost certainly produce just the effects of malaise and discomfort that are observable in much of modern society. If this diagnosis of the malaise is correct, restoration of a direct relationship to the missing dimension of reality and a rediscovery of the true nature of the lost reality will be the only means by which recovery can be brought within the reach of our sick society.

This is not a pragmatic argument—belief in transcendence is good for society, therefore the belief in transcendence should be restored. Our concern is not with immediate results; it is with the nature of the reality with which man has to do, and with the realism that is required of him if he is to accept and to face that reality.

If the transcendent dimension is real, and in particular if it is such as is indicated to us in the Gospels, it serves in at least four directions as a ground for the recovery of that confidence in life, without which a healthy and balanced human existence is hardly possible.

In the first place, it restores confidence in the rationality of the world. Some of our contemporaries make no attempt to find any reason or pattern in things; life is absurd, and that is all that can be said about it. The materialist holds that "matter," to use the old term for what we now know to be essentially energy, is the principle of all things, and that matter has evolved from within itself all the various forms of reality that we know. I admire the sincerity of those who hold this belief. But of course to hold that matter has produced out of itself life and beauty and mind and conscience requires a far greater effort of sheer faith than acceptance of all the clauses of the Athanasian creed. The Christian view, in comparison, commends itself by its simplicity. If it is true, as Jesus maintained, that the origin of all things is in spirit, and that the creator Spirit in the beginning impressed on the energy that we call matter an impulse to strive upwards and to return to its Creator, then, though much may still remain mysterious to us, the grand drama of the ascent from the non-living to the living, from the living to the self-conscious, from the self-conscious to man in fellowship with God begins to take on a shape and a pattern that are intelligible to beings that have discourse of reason.

Secondly, it is this view of reality which alone makes possible an unshakable defence of the democratic doctrine of the equality of man. What is immediately obvious is the inequality of men. They are unequal in stature, in intelligence, in the contribution that they can make to the common well-being of mankind in general. Why, then, should equal rights and privileges be granted to all? The view that democracy is "acknowledged folly" was put forward powerfully by the Athenian Alcibiades in the fifth century B.C.—

296

democracy means putting power into the hands of the stupidest and most incompetent elements in society. The case against equality was put forward with crushing force by Thrasymachus in the first book of Plato's *Republic*—so-called justice is merely a device of the weak to guard themselves against the justified self-assertion of the strong. It is extremely difficult to find any logical refutation of these arguments. Every totalitarian form of government is based on the fundamental conviction of the inequality of men. Belief in the innate superiority of the white races to all others is very far from having disappeared. A merely sentimental defence of the principle of equality cannot stand up against the arguments that can be adduced against it.

Everything is altered if the transcendent dimension is admitted. Then the equality of men is seen to be not intrinsic, but an equality of relationship to a reality outside the world of men. If it is the case that all men are equally dependent on the Creator of all, that God of his goodness bestows on every man an equal share of his interest and concern, that all men equally though diversely are called to an eternal destiny, the doctrine of equality needs no further defence. The changing inequalities of existence sink into insignificance in the light of an unchanging relationship. A rational ground has been discovered for a view which is held by most men of goodwill today, but which they might well find it difficult to defend if the idea of God and of man's relationship to him is excluded.

Thirdly, a valid basis can be found for the maintenance of such values as justice, kindness, honesty, truthfulness, modesty, and mercy. The exercise of these virtues obviously puts the individual, and even the nation, at a disadvantage in contacts with those who have no regard for them. Why then should they be regarded as desirable? It is natural to the cynic to regard all such values as mere moonshine. And there have not been lacking thinkers of great power who have maintained the view that all such virtues represent a slave mentality and are positively harmful to the progress of mankind. Friedrich Nietzsche in the closing years of the nineteenth century wrote with prophetic energy and power. A great part of his work is directed to the exposition of the view that the Christian tradition of humility and meekness is a betrayal

297

of mankind, and that what is needed is a transvaluation of all values in favour of the self-assertion and the dominance of the strong. Only so can the superman appear; and on the appearance of the superman depends the future of the race.

It is interesting that in recent years at least two attempts have been made to affirm the moral values previously associated with religion without calling in any dimension of transcendence.

Dr. Julian Huxley has maintained that we now have such a knowledge of the process of evolution as to be able to see the emerging pattern of it. We no longer think of nature as "red in tooth and claw." We see the values of co-operation and social existence emerging at a far more elementary level than that of the emergence of self-conscious man. Perhaps Dr. Huxley would not be in disagreement with Dr. Albert Schweitzer in his maintenance of the view that the basic principle of existence is that of "reverence for life."

Dr. Arnold Toynbee, similarly, on the basis of his vast acquaintance with history, has maintained that we can see an emerging pattern of history, and that this is favourable to the values for which the Christian tradition, however imperfectly, has always stood.

Such attempts are interesting and suggestive. It is to be noted, however, that by no means all scientists or all historians are in agreement with these distinguished writers. And the reader is left in some uncertainty as to whether these conclusions can be derived with any certainty from the material under consideration. It is clear that the writers genuinely believe in the principles that they maintain. Is it possible that these principles are a survival from the Christian tradition in which they have grown up, and which they have rather read into their material than deduced from it?

The Christian has no hesitation about calling in the dimension of transcendence. On his view, if these things are true and valid upon earth, it is because they are true and valid "in heaven." If we have come to believe that truth, justice, and mercy are the pillars of the universe, this is not because we are subject to some illusion; it is simply recognition of the fact that God is like that. God has made the world. Inevitably he has impressed his own character upon it. Truth, justice, and love are abstract terms; they derive their meaning simply from the fact that they are convenient terms by which to describe the character of a faithful, just, and loving God. If we discern these things as desirable, as the only possible basis on which a satisfactory form of human society can rest, we are not inventing; we are discovering something that is really there. We are entering on a genuine encounter with reality. Behind the phenomena is the unchanging reality; and that reality is neither abstract nor impersonal—it is a living and active God, the God of whom the clearest account yet available to us is that provided in the words and acts of Jesus Christ.

So far in this book we have tried as far as possible to avoid the use of the equivocal words "good" and "bad," and have usually been content to speak of "better" and "worse." But we have perhaps at last come to the point at which the use of these words is natural and inevitable. The eternal reality which underlies phenomena is of one kind and not of another kind. God is a God whose nature is known; he is this kind of God and not another kind of God. He has made the world in one way and not in any other way, on one pattern and not on any other pattern. That which is in accordance with the nature of God and of the world which he has made is good; and that which is discordant is bad. To be good, in terms of our human existence, is to live in the true relationship to God and to the world as God has made it, and that of course includes the other human beings whom he has made. To be bad is to have missed that true relationship, and to have substituted another for it.

That which is "bad" is that which is maladjusted to the true order of the world. The pastor and the psychiatrist are dealing with the same phenomenon, though their approach to it is different, and the terms that they use will not be the same. The theologian will probably speak of sin. The psychiatrist will probably speak of sickness. But each recognises that what is needed in human life is the recovery of contact with reality, of a right adaptation to the order of the world. Of course this does not mean simply adjustment to the imperfections and distortions of human society as we know them—that is merely another form of maladjustment. What man needs is to be genuinely adjusted to the nature of the universe as it really is.

Fourthly, if "that which is good" is part of the structure of reality, to die on behalf of "that which is good" need no longer appear ridiculous. If a genuinely human existence depends on the maintenance of the Christian and human values against everything that threatens them, if through every act of sacrifice by which they are maintained something is permanently gained for the universe, it may well seem worth while to die on their behalf. Men are generally better than their creeds; and in all ages men have been found willing to die on behalf of that which they believed to be right, even when they were not sustained by a belief in the transcendence of those values for which they were prepared to die. Yet such a man perhaps dies a little ruefully, not being entirely sure whether any consequence will follow commensurate with his sacrifice. The believer at least knows what he is doing. If his premise is false, of course he is the fool of all the world. But he knows that if his premise is sound his sacrifice will not be in vain.

These four principles have been stated in somewhat general terms in order not to tie them at once too closely to one particular religious scheme. But it must be evident to a reader familiar with the Gospels that these four principles are threads that run through every part of the Gospels, and form as it were the warp on which their varied patterns are woven.

For the first principle, that all things have their origin in God and return to him, it is not necessary to cite more than the profound word of Jesus that God is spirit. This is the creator Spirit, that was present at the beginning, that is the inner life of all things, that enters into the spirit of man, and finally is revealed as the Spirit of the risen Jesus.

In defence of the equality of all men an imposing list of passages could be chosen. There is, for example, the affirmation of Jesus that the very hairs of our head are all numbered, an oriental form of expression for the minute and loving care that God directs to all men without distinction or difference. There are the words of Jesus himself uttered in warning against offending one of these little ones—for the man who does so, it were better that a millstone were hanged about his neck and that he were drowned in the depths of the sea—and the words of commendation to those who had showed compassion to the least of these my brethren. This is human equality in practice and without argument.

The whole of the Gospel is an expansion of the definition of the nature of God given in the tremendous scene of the vision of Moses in Exodus: "The Lord, the Lord God, merciful and gracious, longsuffering and abundant in goodness and truth." He is the king who forgives the debt of his servant and is angry when that servant fails to forgive his fellow servant. He is the loving father who welcomes back the son who has got into trouble.

On the acceptance of suffering and death, when necessary, in the defence of right and truth, we need quote only the saying about the corn of wheat: "Except a corn of wheat fall into the ground and die, it abideth alone; but, if it die, it bringeth forth much fruit. He that loveth his life shall lose it; and he that hateth his life in this world shall keep it unto life eternal."

A man's character is to a large extent determined by his basic convictions about life and about the nature of existence. What kind of a character is likely to result from an acceptance of these four main strands of the Gospel as corresponding to the reality of the universe in which we live? An answer may be readily found by considering once again the character of Jesus. If one word is to be chosen to sum up that character, the right word would be perhaps "serenity." It must already be clear that this serenity is wholly different from the "apathy" of the Stoic, who treated all the slings and arrows of fortune as though they did not exist. It is also entirely free from the taint of that escapism which tries to create for itself a rose-coloured world in a world which is very far from rose-coloured. It faces reality. It takes account of all the suffering and heartbreak in the world, and is not unduly dismayed. In the phrase made famous by Professor Reinhold Niebuhr, it is beyond tragedy. Such an attitude is not easily reached and is not easily maintained. It can exist only in a state of tension; but tension, as we have already noted, is one aspect of every form of adult life.

This serenity can exist, in the first place, because it has an ordered and rational world in which to move. Much remains mysterious, but in so far as the plan can be apprehended it is seen to be good. Life is seen as related to a purpose far wider than any which the individual can fully grasp, or with the totality of which

301

he can co-operate; but in which all the purposes of the individual in so far as they are directly or indirectly related to this whole can find their meaning. This is akin to that liberation of spirit which is one of the gifts of patriotism at its best, but it is free from the limitations of patriotism and the distortions to which it is subject. Apprehension of such a purpose at once makes life worth living; it ceases to be pointless and has meaning and significance. The worthwhileness of life sets free the instinct for creative activity, which is present in all men, but which tends to be inhibited by doubt as to the value of life and activity. Men are happiest when they are nearest to pure creation; creative activity brings a sense of quiet satisfaction. It is this satisfaction that makes it possible to put up with frustration and even with suffering and death, in the assurance that nothing is lost, and that suffering itself may be accepted, as Jesus accepted it, as one among the forms of creative activity that are offered to man upon the earth.

It is likely that many psychiatrists would accept as valid this description of serenity and would recognise in it something very close to the aim of their own form of service to distressed humanity. Their purpose, too, is to bring men back into relationship with reality; to help them to recover that confidence in life without which mastery of the problems of living is impossible; to set free those creative instincts, which are present in all, but which in many are terribly frustrated. Serenity is the mark of the integrated personality. It is a quality of the man who is well adjusted to himself and to the world of men in which he has to live. Serene people are easy to live with, and help to make life easy for others.

The psychiatrist, like everyone else, has his own basic convictions as to the nature of reality and the purpose of life. He can, however, carry out his professional task without ever bringing these fundamental questions and his own answers to them into the picture. Nevertheless, these questions will be asked. What is the nature of reality? Is life really worth living, and, if so, why? To refuse to give an answer to this question is in fact to have given a negative answer. The Christian is the man who, having looked honestly at the world and its problems, is prepared to experiment with life on the basis of the conviction that the final answer is given in the affirmation that God is, and that God is love.

302

Conclusion

Natura simplex est. Nature is simple. Such was the affirmation of one singularly well qualified to judge, Sir Isaac Newton. False simplification, either through ignorance of phenomena or through refusal to face them in all their multiplicity, is the enemy of truth. But no one was less likely to fall into this error than the endlessly patient researcher into the realities of the physical universe. Fifteen years were to pass between Newton's first apprehension of the nature of gravitation, and the publication of the *Principia Mathematica,* in which he set forth with full proofs his new understanding of one vital part of the mechanism of the universe. Many and complex phenomena were to pass before his inspection; but in the end the nature and purport of his discovery can be set out in a few simple words: Bodies attract one another inversely as the squares of the distance that separate them.

The phenomena of the universe are complex. But again and again it has happened in the history of human discovery that the identification of the right clue has produced order and simplicity where previously chaos seemed to reign supreme.

It was so with the solar system when Copernicus lighted on the idea that the earth moves and that in relation to it the sun stands still. The old Ptolemaic astronomy had wrestled faithfully and earnestly with the phenomena; but, as observation increased, everything became increasingly complex, and endless cycles and epicycles had to be called into account for the strangely unaccountable movements of the heavenly bodies. And indeed the phenomena are complex. The ancients believed that the heavenly spheres revolved in perfect circles, and regarded this as the perfection of motion. Most annoyingly none of the heavenly bodies moves, or even appears to move, in a perfect circle. This supposedly orderly system suffers from the incursion of such odd bodies as comets and meteorites. Just to make things really difficult, whereas all the other members of the solar system move in orderly fashion clockwise, one of the satellites of Mars defies all order and moves with extreme rapidity in the opposite direction. And yet, once the basic principles of the Copernican astronomy are grasped, everything does fall into place, everything can be accounted for, and the heavenly bodies will appear in the places and at the times calculated for them by the astronomers.

Of late physicists have been much perplexed to know how we should think of light. Is it to be thought of in terms of waves or of particles—or should we make the best of both worlds by speaking of wavicles? Not long ago the outstanding physicist Professor Heisenberg was maintaining that, in order to express accurately the phenomena under observation, it is necessary to make use of no less than four different kinds of mathematics. Quite lately Heisenberg revealed his conviction that the difficulty had been overcome and that the nature of the physical universe can now be mathematically set forth in quite a small number of basic equations. It is too soon to say whether his convictions will commend themselves to all his colleagues in the world of physical science; if they do, we shall be entitled once again to say, *Natura simplex est*.

One of the most widespread of human maladies is malaria. It has been known and observed from ancient times. It has played no inconsiderable part in human history through the wasting away of armies exposed to its ravages. The harm it does to the human frame is manifold and grievous. The almost fortuitous discovery that quinine is a specific remedy for it made it possible to set a limit to its ravages. But this was purely empirical, and the cause of the disease remained unknown. Then at last light dawned; the anopheles mosquito was identified as the criminal. With knowledge came power. Cyprus, for centuries malaria-ridden, is now entirely free of the disease. A single cause had been found for a wide range of phenomena; much research still remained to be done, but one central clue had been found to serve as guide through the labyrinth of problems.

Once we come to the human level, the phenomena become more complex still, and we are tempted to use the overworked adjective "infinite" of their variety. In this book, we have recognised the validity in their own sphere of many and diverse approaches to the human problem. Art and history, the social sciences, religion, and psychology all have their rich contribution to make. But we have asked whether, in this sphere too, it is possible to find one central clue, one central principle, which will serve as a guide amid the tangle, a principle of true simplification without evasion or distortion of the realities. Is it possible to say here, as in other fields of observation, that nature is simple? *Summary*

We have accepted, hypothetically, the view that the life and teaching of Jesus of Nazareth may serve as such a clue and such a principle. We have considered the possibility that in him for the first time the full stature and reality of human nature was made manifest, and that therefore he can serve as a criterion for the measurement of the normal and the abnormal, the sound and the unsound in human nature as we see it and as we experience it in ourselves.

Starting from this hypothesis, we have tried to survey the human scene as it actually exists, not inventing problems where none exist, but not evading anything that presented itself as a genuine problem. We have taken account of human nature in its splendour, in its shame, and in its mediocrity. We have given full recognition to the element of tragedy in the human experience. We have looked at man in relation to himself, in relation to his immediate surroundings in the family, in relation to the larger society in which he lives; man as caught up in the international tensions of a world at strife, in relation to the universe of which he is a part, in relation to the eternal dimension, which if it exists at all is the limit and boundary of man's existence in time and space.

At every point we have become aware of tension. This is not necessarily and in all circumstances a bad thing; in fact, we have been led to affirm that a measure of tension is a part of all adult life in the world of men as it is now constituted. The action and reaction of a living thing with its environment is the sign of life; when such action and reaction ceases, life is no longer there. But when tension goes beyond a certain point, it produces mental sickness; it results in strain, inefficiency, and in the too rapid wearing out of the machine.

At every point, we have found that the Gospels have something to say relevant to our problems, either in the words that Jesus actually uttered, in the way that he behaved, or in what he essentially was. Since we are here dealing with the rich variety of a life that was actually lived, and with words spoken in actual situations, nothing is handed to us ready-made on a plate; there are no easy solutions for casual acceptance by the careless. Yet at point after point the mistakes that we daily make, the weaknesses of which we are conscious in ourselves, are shown up in sharp contrast to that which is represented in the Gospels. The life and words of Jesus prove themselves effective as pointers to the accurate diagnosis of the ills from which man suffers. They serve also as indications of the way in which fulness of life may be recovered. Nor is any of this theoretical; it has been worked out in the light of the experience of those who have tried to take the Gospels seriously, and have found empirically that they are the one fully satisfactory manual of mental health that has ever been written. They are, of course, far more than that; if the general argument of this book is sound, they can hardly be less.

But this statement leads on to the indication of two questions on which this book has had little, if anything, to say.

In the main the method here followed has been that of enquiry, of discovery. The Gospels are available to everyone; every reader has a certain experience of life, in the light of which he can judge and criticise what has been written. But there are certain other possibilities that cannot be altogether excluded, and have in fact at certain points obtruded themselves on the exposition in the preceding pages.

What has God been doing about all this? That is the first question. We have spoken of man's relation to the eternal dimension as that of encounter with a living person. We must reckon with the possibility, to use the modern phrase, that God himself is active in the knowledge that we have of him. The initiative is on his side. If that is true, it is not so much man's business to discover God, as to allow himself to be discovered by him. What has been written in terms of man's search for God could be turned round and rewritten in the opposite sense, in terms of God's revelation of himself to man. If this is true, the Gospels are not simply the history of a good man who lived many years ago. They are the record of God's decisive act in the history of man. The life and death and resurrection of Jesus of Nazareth are not simply events among other events—they are the Event, the central happening of

306

human history, from which all other events can be measured forwards and backwards in unending series to the end and the beginning of time.

The second major question concerns each man's personal attitude to this Jesus Christ. We have seen that in the Gospels Jesus bade man stand and deliver; they must make up their minds about him. And the impact of his personality was such that men were divided as by a sword. Some rejected him and found themselves driven on into an almost crazy hatred that could be satisfied with nothing less than his destruction. Others accepted him and found themselves led on to illimitable love and devotion and willingness to suffer for his sake. But the point of the Christian message is that Jesus still presents to men the same demand that they should make up their minds about him. It is possible for a man to be interested in the Gospels as a piece of history, to be touched by their pathos, to accept many of the ideas of Jesus as good and sound—and to miss the point of the whole affair. It is you who are being judged, and by your choice you will be saved or lost.

Throughout this book, we have not stressed these two questions, and as far as possible have kept them in the background. But sooner or later they must be asked; and the answer that, each man gives to them is bound to have the most far-reaching effects on his understanding of himself, and of the whole of life as he experiences it.

If a man comes to the conclusion that Jesus was in fact the act of God in human history, and that he was able to do what he did only because he came forth from God and went to God, what effects will this have on his judgment as to the nature of human life and of the needs of men? The word sometimes translated "save" in the Gospels can often just as well be translated "heal." But is this the whole story? Are we called to think in a dimension of salvation such as has only occasionally been hinted at in this book?

If a man has found himself confronted by Jesus Christ, in a situation in which he has had to say "Yes" or "No" with the whole of his being, and has in fact said "Yes," how will this affect his attitude towards other men? If he has been led to an attitude of whole-hearted love towards Jesus Christ, obedience to him, and serviceableness to him, how does he translate these fine words into acts and deeds? How does he set to work to be *alter Christus,* a second Christ? In particular, if he is called to serve as pastor or healer, candid friend, or critic of his fellowmen, how does he bring to bear on this work the insights of the new world into which he has been introduced by his faith in Jesus Christ?

These are large questions, and they cannot be answered here. They must be the theme of a further book or books, which may in course of time come to be written.

INDEX

Accessibility, 55
Acquiescence, 155
Adler, Alfred, 31
Adolescence, 178; problems of, 181
Afterlife, 285
Agape, 15
Aggressivity, 139, 263–66
Ahab, 13, 14
Akhnaton, 13
Aquinas, Thomas, 25
Aristotle, 21, 25, 26
Artists, 79–80, 200–1
Authority, 54

"Bad," 299
Behaviourism, 27–28
Blake, William, 79–80
Buddhism, 48
Byzantine art, 16

Cabanis, Pierre, 26
Casuistry, 146
Catholicism, 57
Character, 301
Chastity, 179–80
Christ. *See* Jesus Christ
Christocentricity, 57
Churchill, Winston S., 132
Commonwealths, growth of, 258–59
Community, influences of, 160
Compassion, 284, 286, 293
Conduct, 125, 126–27

Confessions, 25, 101
Confessions, 16
Conflict, 72–74, 133
Conformism, 96, 155
Confucius, 23
Consciousness, 98
Co-operation, 133–34
Courage, 53–54, 137, 195, 197
Criticism, 274–75, 278–79
Crucifixion, 45
Cynicism, 25–26

Dante, 81–82
Dark Ages, 24
David, 13, 14
Democracy, 297
Discipline, 139, 156, 187–88
Dostoevsky, Fedor M., 19
Drama, 17–18
Dreams, 106

Elijah, 13
Entelechy, 35. *See also* Soul
Equality, 261–62, 296–97, 300–1
Escapism, 171, 301
Eternity, 284
Ethics, 126
Everyman, 17
Evolution, 133–34, 181, 298
Existentialism, 253

Family, 142–43, 150–53, 255; joint type, 241–43; role of

309

father, 241–45
Fear, 189, 190–200, 266
Flaubert, Gustave, 18–19
Flesh, 284
Forgiveness, 116, 209–13
Form, 78, 84
Freedom, 153, 214–16, 233
Freud, Sigmund, 31, 72, 76, 106, 235
Frustration, 189, 200–7

God, faith in, 236; as Father, 237–46, 250; kingdom of, 59, 74, 247, 250, 287
Gogh, Vincent van, 81
Golden Mean, 22–23
"Good," 299
Grace, 116–18
Greece, 14–15
Guilt complex, 113–16

Habits, 145
Hamlet, 18, 36, 75
Happiness, 286
Heraclitus, 21
Hippocrates, 26
Hitler, Adolf, 48, 132, 139
Holy Communion, 44, 45–46
Homosexuality, 177, 205
Hope, 117, 121
Human nature, aberrations of, 25, 171–72; approaches to, 27–32; in harmony, 83–85; in imbalance, 85; inner multiplicity, 75–76; intuitive approach, 30; laws of, 29–30; normal, 34–35; virtues of, 20–21
Humility, 54
Humour, 274

Idolatry, 170, 247
Iliad, 14
Illusions, 252–53, 260–62
Immortality, 285, 286, 290, 292
Impatience, 226–27
Inferiority, 218–22; compensations for, 222–25
Inferiority complex, 218, 230
Inner self, 77
Insignificance, 221–22
Intelligence tests, 28–29
Interests, 260
Inward voice, 105
Islam, 43
Israel, 11–14

Jesus Christ, 22–23, 36–37; as an artist, 82–83; the Event of, 305–6; and fear, 197–200; and forgiveness, 211–13; and friends, 120; and frustration, 206–7; historical evidence, 46–50; human character of, 50–56; as lawgiver, 65–69; and Mary, 143; purpose of, 59, 269; as a rebel, 146–47; role in history, 39, 56; and society, 134–50
Jezebel, 13
Judaism, 43
Jung, C. C., 31
Justice, 131–32, 137–39, 284, 297, 298

Kingdom of God. See under God

Lawrence, D. H., 77, 105
Leadership, 47–48, 60–62
Legalism, 146
Libido, 175
Life, fulness of, 84–85

Literature, contemporary, 293–94
Love, 15, 230–33, 284, 285, 298

Macbeth, 13
Madame Bovary, 18–19
Mariology, 57
Marriage, 173–75, 182–84
Martyrdom, 65, 167, 279
Marxism, 252
Mary, 57, 144
Masochism, 65
Mass disobedience, 147
Mass neurosis, 255–58
Mass society, 227–29
Masturbation, 177
Matter, 78, 84
Maturity, 143, 160, 173; definition of, 163; and fear, 192
Mental operation, 76–78
Mercy, 139, 298
Middle Ages, 16, 25, 57, 292–93
Miracles, 59–61
Monastery, 24
Monotheism, 14
Moralistic judgement, 129–30
Morals, 124–25, 126
Mores, 128
Movements, 47–48
Muhammad, 136
Myers, F. W. H., 31
Mysticism, 24
Myth, 44–45

Napoleon Bonaparte, 58–59, 67
National Socialism, 48
Nations, equality of, 261; internal tensions, 262–63
Newton, Isaac, 40, 78, 303
Nicomachean Ethics, 22
Nonconformism, 96
Novels, 18–20

Objectivity, 32–33
Odyssey, 14, 170
Oedipodean situation, 239–40
Oedipus, 15

Panic, 190–92. *See also* Fear
Patience, 203
Personality, 23, 26
Personality tests, 28–29
Perugino, 81
Pessimism, 25–26
Plato, 20–21, 26, 125
Pope, Alexander, 80
Portraiture, 16–17
Power, 50–51
Prestige, 266–67
Protestantism, 57–58
Psychoanalysis, 100
Psychometry, 28
Psychotherapy, 30–32

Ramanujan, Srinivasa, 78
Reality, 133, 134, 139, 146, 253, 269, 283–85, 295, 296, 301
Rebellion, 161–62, 164–68
Redemption, 25
Reformation, 57
Relationships, 122, 134; in family, 156–59; principles for, 135–37; types, 216; in society, 142, 164–68
Relativism, sources of, 127–31
Religion, 32–34
Rembrandt, 16
Renaissance, 16, 26
Renunciation, 203
Resentment, 190, 207–9
Rieu, E. V., 14
Russia, 235–36; literature of, 19

St. Augustine, 16, 24

St. Benedict, 24
St. Bernard, 24
Scepticism, 25–26
Scholasticism, 24
Self-confidence, 233
Self-determination, 261
Self-renunciation, 62–64
Serenity, 301–2
Severity, 54–55
Sex, 172–80, 185–89; in Old Testament, 173
Shakespeare, William, 17–18; 19, 36, 110–13, 207–8
Sincerity, 53, 137
Sixth sense, 234–35
Society, 215; role of, 255; sickness of, 295
Socrates, 20
Solitude, 55–56
Soul, 25. *See also* Entelechy
Southern, R. W., quoted, 24
Speech, 51–52, 86
Spirit, 284, 300
Status quo, 162
Stereotypes, 170, 269–72
Stoicism, 214

Sublimation, 176
Suffering, 65–66, 139, 165, 199, 248

Taboos, 154
Tension, 305
Theology, 16
Traditions, 145–48, 160
Transcendence, 296, 298
Truth, 137, 284, 298

Unbelief, 34
Universe, nature of, 289–90; simplicity of, 303–4

Values, 297; eternal, 280–82, 285, 292
Violence, 147

Watson, J. B., quoted, 27
Weakness, 139
Welfare state, 229, 234
Western world, 20; character of, 85–86
World unity, 262

lacuna

246 bull 302

61 sermon on Luke 4. 'liberty to captives' 279-84
61° quote for Lent sermon. 'take up cross 249,250 62f deny self' *
62 sermon on Jn. 6 'will you also go away?'
74 Tempt. of Jesus sermon 206   ethics
                                  83 He that looses his life -- sermon p24 on self interest 297-
87 Serm' 'the stones would cry out' Triumphal Entry 255-6 crowd
116¹¹⁵ let the dead bury the dead   137 Sermon-Lent - on 'Hope anyway' 178
143-4 Jesus' family; whoever does will of God sermon
238 sermon on "our Father"
276 gain by giving sermon 286